REVISIONS AND DI

REVISIONS
–and–
DISSENTS

Essays

PAUL E. GOTTFRIED

NIU Press, DeKalb, IL

Northern Illinois University Press, DeKalb 60115
© 2017 by Northern Illinois University Press
Printed in the United States of America
26 25 24 23 22 21 20 19 18 17   1 2 3 4 5
978-0-87580-762-1 (paper)
978-1-60909-217-7 (e-book)
Cover design by Yuni Dorr
Composed by BookComp, Inc.

Library of Congress Cataloging-in-Publication Data
Names: Gottfried, Paul, author.
Title: Revisions and dissents : essays / Paul E. Gottfried.
Description: DeKalb, IL : Northern Illinois University Press, 2017.
Identifiers: LCCN 2016020062 (print) | LCCN 2016032635 (ebook) | ISBN
    9780875807621 (print : alk. paper) | ISBN 9781609092177 (ebook)
Subjects: LCSH: Conservatism. | Liberalism. | Right and left (Political science) |
    Political science—Philosophy
Classification: LCC JC573 .G67 2017 (print) | LCC JC573 (ebook) | DDC 320.5—dc23
LC record available at https://lccn.loc.gov/2016020062

Contents

Acknowledgments

A MONG THOSE I WOULD LIKE to thank for reading and commenting on parts or all of this anthology are Professors Lee Congdon, Robert Weissberg, Jeff Taylor, David Brown, David Gordon, Boyd Cathey, and W. B. Newsome, as well as Mr. Duncan Clark. Mention should also be made of the staff of the Elizabethtown College Library, who tracked down hard-to-find references, and of an Elizabethtown College student, Vincent James McGonigle, who put my text into a technically acceptable form. To Daniel McCarthy and his monthly *American Conservative* go special thanks for allowing me to republish parts of my essay on Herbert Butterfield and my comparative study of Edmund Burke and Charles Maurras.

I am also grateful to Amy Farranto of the Northern Illinois University Press, with whom I discussed this project extensively through correspondence and later through a meeting at Borders on Erie Boulevard in Syracuse, New York. During our Syracuse meeting, Amy seemed so interested in my anthology that she convinced me that I was engaged in a worthwhile enterprise. My wife Mary also kept me focused throughout the grim period when I was laboring on this anthology. To her credit, Mary listened, albeit with growing impatience, to the summaries that burst out of my mouth while I was conceptualizing the longer essays.

Finally, I am grateful to my older son, Dr. Joseph D. Gottfried, who may recoil from most of what he finds in this book. Joey may even scold my wayward thinking in a phone conversation that has not yet taken place. Indeed, it is hard to think of any significant historical issue about which the two of us would agree, beyond the acceptance of certain empirically verifiable data about the issues in question. But that disagreement matters less than the fact that my son ably defended positions that I argue against in this book. Would that prominent historians who held his views did the same!

Paul E. Gottfried
Elizabethtown College, Pennsylvania

Foreword

THE ESSAYS AND COMMENTARIES that follow are of differing length and deal with miscellaneous subjects. Autobiographical sketches can be found at the beginning and end of this anthology, where I present material that was not included in my *Encounters*.[1] Since that earlier work centered on famous political and intellectual figures, I could not weave into it the personal reminiscences that grace this volume. Besides including previously unpublished autobiographical material, this anthology addresses a variety of historical and topical themes. Here, as well as in my earlier writings, I approach these themes in an unorthodox fashion, from beyond the parameters of discussion that prevail in universities and the national press. My critical engagement with political correctness is already well-known and has made me *persona non grata* in many circles.

Early in life, that is, already during my graduate school years at Yale, I was struck by the dogmatic way in which certain interpretations of modern history were presented. This anthology offers alternative views to ideas that never seemed quite right. The "revisions and dissents" mentioned in the title are directed against positions that I would argue need to be reexamined, and both the longer and shorter essays target such positions. The "revisions" that appear in the title therefore apply less to my work than to certain contemporary interpreters of the past.

Originally I was tempted to borrow my title from one of my favorite thinkers and stylists, Arthur Schopenhauer. His gallimaufry of occasional pieces, *Parerga und Paralipomena*, which may be translated from Greek as "Addenda and Fragments," was published in the 1850s, when its author had already attained some degree of eminence as a philosophic gadfly.[2] Contrary to the implication of the title, however, Schopenhauer was not serving his readers with mere addenda or fragments. Like me, he was offering detailed discussions of various topics that were intended to arouse controversy. A chief inspiration for my anthology came from Schopenhauer's withering analysis of sham "academic philosophy" and the "salvation-bringing" confidence with which honored academics trot out their hobbyhorses.[3] Almost everything Schopenhauer attributed to pompous philosophy professors in Germany during the late 1840s applies equally well to what I have witnessed in today's historical profession.

My oft-stated attraction to the Frankfurt School Marxist Herbert Marcuse as a teacher did not flow from sharing Marcuse's admiration for Lenin or his shotgun marriage between Freud and Marx.[4] I respected this professor for his willingness to consider historical questions from more than one angle. As a student I never hesitated to put forth in his presence an "illiberal" view of past events, such as the revolutions of 1848 or the Spanish Civil War. Unlike other professors I encountered, Marcuse never berated me for being morally wrong in my historical judgments.

This was not true of my exposure to German history, where my "liberal democratic" instructors were caricatures of the authoritarian German personality that they railed against. Their views on any aspect of their field of study were easily guessed, even before they and their students looked at an original source. It has never ceased to amaze me how closely their historical interpretations followed certain ideological guidelines. I have often wondered whether, borrowing the phrase of Antonio Gramsci, historians help to frame the "hegemonic ideology" in their societies as members of the master class, or whether they reflect and convey the political belief system that has originated elsewhere, for example, in the media.

In any case it is clear to me that many leading historians are not engaging in balanced inquiry when they purport to be saying the last word on a topic. Their settled views usually embody what are "acceptable" ideas, particularly when historians write about race, gender, fairness, human rights, and other political concerns. Contemporary historians also generally display a bias against certain groups and their histories, namely against those human aggregations that do not enjoy "liberal" respectability.

A list of these unpopular groups that stopped with the Germans, the French peasantry after 1789, southern whites, and medieval Christians would be woefully incomplete. This enumeration would leave out other groups that respectable academic and popular historians now scorn and even diabolize. Those who take the arbiters of moral and professional respectability more seriously than I do have often complained about my quarrelsomeness. If a historian is featured in such publications as the *New York Review of Books*, *the Economist*, or *Weekly Standard*, then it behooves me to accord that person the appropriate honor.

My own perspective is far less deferential and more open to the idea that networking cliques of opinion create and perpetuate lines of interpretation. These often interlocking cliques are aligned with journalists and publishers and convey those ideas that are ideologically dominant in a particular period. New research ceases to be critical for what become the prevalent interpretations. What does becomes decisive is whether the favored view fits the political and emotional needs of verbalizing elites. Once an opinion becomes enshrined, then new "data" can be conveniently unearthed or certain facts cherry-picked to make the acceptable view appear to be impregnable.

One such case of skewed scholarship that has attracted my interest for decades is the degree of culpability attached to the Central Powers for World War I. Those who hold the good professional cards have often browbeaten the other side for want of a convincing case. They take their position at least partly by reading the events of World War II back into those of World War I and by understating what the eventually victorious side did to provoke the conflict in 1914. A formidable body of scholarship and documentation about the background and origins of the war already existed in the 1920s. The now triumphant school of interpretation, however, addresses this inconvenience by dismissing as biased or out of date anything from an earlier age that does not confirm their slant.

Such widely esteemed research scholars dealing with the background of the Great War as George Kennan, Sidney Fay, and Harry Elmer Barnes have undergone the fate of being ignored for not having stressed the wickedness of the Central Powers sufficiently. My own views, which have been influenced by these historians, have also been misrepresented. Although sometimes pilloried as a "German propagandist" for my interpretation of World War I, I have never absolved the defeated side for its mistakes. Least of all have I excused the Central Powers for having contributed to a disastrous struggle. Although the Germans and Austrians had been encircled, and quite deliberately, by the Entente powers, they plunged into a general European war in the worst conceivable way. I freely admit that my family's fate in having been on the losing side of that prolonged bloodbath sparked my interest in the topic, but this familial involvement has never caused me to deny that Austria-Hungary had a hand in starting the conflict.

Above all, it seems necessary in the present circumstances to argue against historical positions that enjoy consensus among the media and "respectable" scholars. One should be willing to offer counterpositions, particularly when the endorsed positions seem to have been removed from the table for reasons other than irresistible, overwhelming evidence. For example, in the case of the Franco-Prussian War of 1870, there is staggering evidence to suggest that the empire of Napoleon III not only declared war against Prussia; the French government jumped into the conflict on a pretext after seeking to humiliate Prussia's ruler, Wilhelm I.

These facts became increasingly obvious to me as the result of reading about the Franco-Prussian War as a middle-aged historian. Contrary to what I was taught in graduate school, the Ems telegram that Prussian minister president Otto von Bismarck released to French and German newspapers in the wake of a dispute between the two countries, and which fanned the already existing strife, was not a "fudged" document.[5] Bismarck's account of the set-to between Wilhelm and the French ambassador to Berlin, Vincent Count Bénédetti, was in its major points accurate.[6] The French ambassador had tried to bully the Prussian king, in an amazing display of tactlessness. He appeared before him uninvited during the king's walk and tried to push Wilhelm into pressuring his Catholic cousin into renouncing the vacant throne of Spain. Wilhelm had already accommodated the French once before, and the attempt to drive him and his cousin into eating crow a second time was planned by the French court as a way of humiliating its Prussian rivals.

At Yale in the mid-1960s I was taught that Bismarck and the Prussian state bore sole responsibility for the conflict that erupted in 1870, just as the Germans were solely responsible for all later struggle in which they became embroiled. Supposedly a straight line could be drawn from the Iron Chancellor in 1870 to the Nazi chancellor in 1933. Although that line never struck me as a particularly straight one, noticing how it zigs and zags wouldn't help the career of a young assistant professor in German history here or in Germany.

Although I don't wish to sound monomaniacal on these subjects, they do bring up my first disconcerting encounter with history turned into dogma. A long-range consequence of the atrocities committed under the Nazi regime is the tendency to blame the German past for tensions and mishaps that other European powers also caused. The extent of the blame that Germans seem delighted to embrace is sometimes truly mystifying. I'm still trying to figure out how the German Imperial Army was actively complicit in the massacre of Armenians during World War I. This is the newest collective disgrace being laid by German federal president Joachim Gauck on his people, or on his imperial predecessor who ruled a hundred years ago.[7] German journalists rejoiced at Gauck's use of the incriminating term *Mitschuld*, shared guilt, in indicating the major role assigned to their country for the killing of Armenians in the Ottoman Empire. Unfortunately for Germans who revel in national guilt, the evidence of collective guilt in this case is not particularly convincing.[8]

The German commanders and the Turkish government—neither of whom, it is being claimed, were angels—were so divided in 1915 that it is difficult to imagine how any German leader could have stopped most of the atrocities in Anatolia that Turkish units were carrying out against Armenians, whom they claimed to be "relocating."[9] Concerned reports about the massacres came predominantly from German consuls and officers in Turkey, and given the situation that the Armenians had taken up arms against the Turks and Germans on the side of tsarist Russia, it is remarkable that German officials exhibited such outrage. Clearly some of the superiors of those who were passionately protesting the massacres—for example, German military adviser Wilhelm Leopold Colmar Baron von der Goltz—regarded the Armenians as an enemy population and were indifferent to their fate. Other German officers, like von der Golz's major rival and fellow adviser to the Turkish forces, Lieutenant-General Otto Liman von Sanders, managed to save the Armenian populations in Izmir and Edime. Von Sanders also tried to call attention among government officials to the massacres in Eastern Anatolia. Still, it is hard to see how these mixed reactions among German officers constituted active participation in the atrocities inflicted on Armenian civilians.

Perhaps if the Nazis had not come along, few people, if any, would now be exaggerating the previous misdeeds of the country that they ruled. But there are other reasons for the attitudes being criticized. A historiography abounding in incrimination may have become popular because of a general shift in the political climate. If the United States had not moved in the ideological direction that it has since the 1960s, we would not be awash in studies exposing the sexism and ethnic prejudices of early American heroes, nor would we have revisionist works on Reconstruction turning the Radical Republicans into forerunners of the 1960s civil rights movement[10] or sympathetic portraits of John Brown and other leaders of slave revolts. There is definitely a market for such partisan historiography and generally for publications that enjoy media approval. But can anyone who questions a doctrinally embedded interpretation in the historical profession make headway professionally? And will anyone with academic ambitions dare to attack in our ideologically charged culture what we are urged to accept as proper opinion?[11]

An axiom once heard that the further one moves chronologically from the events described the more detached the historian becomes is now open to question. A more accurate statement would be that in a highly politicized age, any past can be made to serve an obligatory ideological consciousness. Publicized discussions and exhibits about the American Civil War have been turned into occasions for meditating on our onetime bigotry, conducted by moralists who have no ancestral attachment to either side in that conflict. I have also seen to my astonishment the Peloponnesian War treated as a tragic struggle between a linear predecessor of our present American democracy and a Spartan totalitarian society. This long-ago war, if memory serves, took place between two slaveholding societies, in neither of which did more than a low percentage of residents enjoy citizenship. From the historian Thucydides, who participated in the war as an Athenian naval commander, we may infer that Athenian expansion in the fifth century BC set off a chain of effects, and that Athenian overreach led the Spartan military aristocracy into taking up arms against its northern neighbor.

A less prescribed view of the past came from a classmate of mine in graduate school, who was writing a dissertation on the English Parliament held by King James I in 1621. Although I expected this graduate student, who idolized Third World Communist revolutionaries, to declare for the antimonarchist Puritans against the would-be autocrat King James, his research produced markedly different conclusions. After careful research, my classmate became convinced that King James had been cornered by his Protestant opposition, who denied him financial support unless he made himself entirely subject to their will. James was dealing with adversaries who were trying to take over his state.

These interpretive views did not flow out of my classmate's political commitment. A long tradition on the Marxist left going back to Marx and Engels and forward to such Marxist historians as Christopher Hill had treated the Puritan Revolution as a social breakthrough culminating in a capitalist order and eventually in the victory of revolutionary socialism. My self-professed radical leftist acquaintance took a position that flew in the face of an already fixed Marxist understanding of early modern European history.[12]

Such professional independence can be found even more clearly in my longtime friend Eugene Genovese, who wrote as a Marxist about the social history of the southern planter aristocracy. In Genovese's gracefully constructed writings, I noticed how well his Marxist focus on class consciousness was balanced by transparent sympathy for the "master class." Genovese understood the sense of honor felt by his subjects in terms of their social position and respected as well as contextualized their moral standards. He tried to understand the status of the slave class in relation to a society that was suspended between a premodern, seigniorial economy and a fully capitalist one.

Unlike our present generation of historians writing in the prescribed manner, Genovese did not rage against racism and sexism in his analysis of an earlier socioeconomic system. One should not therefore have been surprised that his closest disciple, Robert Paquette, faced sharp criticism when he dared to present his teacher's "Marxist" interpretation of social history in a "conservative" journal.[13] Readers expressed shock at Paquette's racial insensitivity.[14] His true sin was to have summed up what was still an orthodox Marxist interpretation during Genovese's career. A conclusion that may be drawn is that real Marxist historians are no longer politically correct and therefore no longer welcome in their profession.

Since I have not risen high enough in my profession to have to worry about my career and am now too old to have one, I have been busy developing counterarguments to zealously defended conventional views about the historical past. My counterpoints are presented in this anthology, and if I occasionally display annoyance in going after the dogma of the academic magisterium, I offer no apology. The self-important figures that are in my crosshairs remind me of the Communist bureaucrats I encountered at the Hungarian Academy of Historical Science on a visit to Budapest in the mid-1960s. These stuffy dignitaries came in chauffeur-driven cars to propagate their *történelmi tudomány*—historical science—and any subordinate who disagreed with their "scientific" interpretation could be dismissed from his post as a "counterrevolutionary." Schopenhauer would have recognized the type immediately.

Although things have changed for the better in Hungary since the Communist Party was disempowered, the once established mind-set of the Hungarian "historical scientists" who claimed to be teaching "Marxist science" may have traveled across the Atlantic. I am now seeing their entrenched American counterparts in action and am not impressed by their cliquishness and obliviousness to alternative interpretations of the past. Basking in the glow of acceptability, these publishing celebrities may have forgotten the maxim that history is supposed to be a contentious discipline. Unfortunately at this point neither these luminaries nor their subordinates have any reason to remember it.

1

Reminiscences

A FEW YEARS AGO my cousin, who from time to time visits Bridgeport, Connecticut, a city that lies twenty-five miles east of her present home in Greenwich, sent me a picture book showing her birthplace as it looked in the late 1940s. Both of us immediately recognized the faded pictures of Bridgeport in an earlier era and such onetime landmarks as the amusement park at Pleasure Beach—which partially burned down and ceased to operate in the 1950s—and the stately Wheeler mansion at the conflux of Golden Hill, Congress, and several other streets that may no longer be where they once were. As I looked at this out-of-print picture book, it became obvious that its presence did not depend on any tangible object. The places were irremovably embedded in my consciousness and in that of other family members of my generation; alas, our numbers may now be dwindling.

Equally significant, this internalized past has to be understood as occupying a particular space. Groups that have traditionally highlighted a time dimension rather than a spatial one have sometimes shifted this emphasis in light of certain historical events. The Jews—who mourned the loss of their temple and second commonwealth—became more centered on spatial identity once a Jewish state was reestablished. Their spatial dimension never disappeared entirely; it simply grew less important than the sense of time in sustaining a national consciousness.

I can only trace back my family roots about 120 years. As fate would have it, I have already devoted a long chapter to my known ancestors in the introductory chapters of my memoir *Encounters*.[1] I learned that Nazi bullies dragged off cousins of mine living in Budapest to a labor camp, where one or more of them died of typhus. I also learned that a half uncle and his son died during Nazi German occupation of the Hungarian capital of Budapest, but don't know in what circumstances or who killed my unfortunate relatives. Uncles on my father's side served in the Austro-Hungarian army during World War I, so we lost the only war that, as far as I know, my family ever fought in.

Although I confess to being partial toward the Hapsburg Empire that fell in 1918, I would not defend every cause that my ancestors embraced. I have relatives who were ranking Communist officials in the regime that took over Hungary in 1919, yet I see no reason to rush to defend the honor of these relatives or that of the brutal regime they served. But I'm also not inclined to condemn these people whom I have never met. I know next to nothing about the half brothers of my father, except that they rallied to a short-lived Communist government and then came to the aid of other family members. To their credit, these Communist officials generously assisted my grandparents, whose sewing machine equipment they managed to have returned to them. Despite the grinding poverty to which my family was reduced after the "war to end all wars," we were declared to be *Polgarsag*: certified bourgeois who were oppressing the working class. I'm not sure how my grandparents—who were then scrounging for food—qualified as such, but they did get back their equipment, thanks to nepotistic Communist relatives. Familialism does have its moral merits, as my father strongly hinted while telling me this story.

The paucity of generations that I can discuss knowledgeably may be one reason that I think about my early youth spatially. I grew up in a delimited space—a specific neighborhood in a specific city—and it contributed to both the formation of my thinking and how I viewed the world in the 1950s and later. We lived in the North End of Bridgeport, which when I was very young had a certain cachet. In a sense, it was postethnic American, since all the other "ends" were characterized by ethnic concentrations. The West End was "Hunkieland," as the Hungarians themselves proudly referred to it; the South End embraced Greeks, the University of Bridgeport, Seaside Park, and—together with the East End—what there was of a black population. Most of the East End—to my memory—was Slavic. Eastern European Jews lived with the Poles and Czechs in the East End. Hungarian Jews were found mostly in the West End; that is, until they collected enough money to move into the North End and learned to think of themselves as American, Jewish, or anything but Magyar. Finally, there was a section of the city—just beyond the West End and the railroad tracks—called Black Rock, which seemed to encompass everyone—including my cousin and her parents—who still hadn't moved to the North End. Well-heeled professionals resided in a part of Black Rock, which abutted Long Island Sound, and they were rumored—or so my mother told us— to have built "fabulous places." Since I never had the opportunity to visit their homes, I have to take the word of those who did.

Lest I forget, the Italians and Irish were scattered throughout the city, but the Italians also had a claim to their own part of town. I recall an unmistakably Southern Italian neighborhood from my preteen years, which was about a mile and a half from our house and in which all the clustered two-family dwellings flaunted grape arbors and bottles of homemade wine. The wine was kept on outdoor tables in what looked like courtyards, but which may have been decorated driveways. These reconstructed scenes from a Sicilian or Calabrese village abounded everywhere along Pequonnock Street—a thoroughfare that led from North Park Avenue—at the edge of the North End, into downtown Bridgeport. I managed to visit one of these houses when my first-grade teacher, Miss Milano, took us on a "field trip" to her parents' residence on Jones Street, just off Pequonnock. The heavily shaded courtyard and Miss Milano's mustached father sitting at a table under grape vines—only a few feet away from pecking chickens—was like the setting in *Cavalleria Rusticana*, an opera that I attended at the Met many years later. The opera's composer, Pietro Mascagni, must have visited this home on Jones Avenue before he began his great work.

There was also a sprawling region just west of our neighborhood in the North End called Stratfield. It belonged to Fairfield Township and represented a desired destination for Bridgeport's status-conscious inhabitants. Those who moved to Stratfield and then continued to accumulate money sometimes went on to the actor-saturated community of Westport, just west of Fairfield. By then they had abjured their identification with our rustbelt city. A few years ago my brother offended someone's wife at a cocktail party by reminding her that (horror of horrors!) he and her husband had both been born in Bridgeport. The lady was obviously trying to associate her husband with a more chic place of origin than where he grew up.

This migration would have occurred, albeit more slowly, even if certain demographic changes had not taken place. In the 1950s Bridgeport absorbed, somewhat fitfully, a growing Puerto Rican population, and in the 1960s it began experiencing racial issues that had not been encountered there before. Before the 1960s we did have some black residents, but their presence was not felt as any kind of disruptive force. The blacks in Bridgeport lived peacefully in mostly two-parent families, had a low crime rate, and went to public schools with most everyone else, with the exception of those attending Catholic parochial schools. In the 1960s all that changed as the black population seemed to explode and then became associated with escalating violence. Meanwhile, white flight came to the suburbs, and what had once been the farm regions of Trumbull and Easton began to swell in population. It is by no means difficult to find a correlation between these temporally connected situations. In my view, however, the migration would have occurred independently of the increased crime. Bridgeport was on its way down after World War II, during which the population had soared to nearly 300,000 and the city had been a major source of arms production.

In the postwar years the number of residents slipped back down to about 150,000, and many of the local industries began relocating to regions of the country where labor costs were low. When I was a teenager it was common to hear contrasts drawn between the affluence of Fairfield County—of which Bridgeport was the county seat—and our already rapidly declining industrial center. Although racial tensions added to the reasons that people moved out, the migration had begun earlier. The war years were for us a boom time, and although many suffered as a result of the foreign conflict, Bridgeporters referred to it nostalgically. My father and uncle—who both owned fur stores—always spoke of those "good times when everyone did business," which meant of course, during the war. By the late 1950s my father's once-thriving business was declining. This trend was clearly connected to the economic shrinkage that started at war's end, and it grew worse in the succeeding decades. One can understand why our politicians argued for national pay guidelines and national mandatory wages. We were losing our industrial base to regions of the country that had weaker unions and lower pay scales.

The area in Bridgeport that I knew best was the North End, or more precisely that grid of streets that ran northward to Capitol Avenue, eastward to North Park, and even farther east, to the cluster of grocery stores on Madison Avenue, westward to Brooklawn Avenue, and southward to North Avenue. Most readers who have never been to Bridgeport—or who have never consulted the appropriate municipal map—would have no idea about what I'm describing, but since the space delineated may no longer exist in the way it once did, my reference points may now be disembodied memories.

I did venture beyond familiar streets even as a preadolescent, to attend a Hungarian synagogue in the West End. Later I went to junior high and then high school, well to the west of where our house was located. By then I had begun to move beyond my established neighborhood parameters. In my teens I extended my reference points further to include Maplewood Avenue, which is three blocks west of North Avenue, where my closest friend lived. My consciousness moved simultaneously northward, in the direction of the store where my aunt worked, which was about a quarter of a mile beyond Capitol Avenue.

Despite these extensions of my living space, there were limits to how far my sense of place could then be stretched. The area I knew best was like the sacred precinct that ancient Greek poets exalted, the *Hieron Temenos,* even if my precinct was far less entwined with myth than the legendary abode of Pallas Athene on the acropolis. I recall that each time I traveled—usually by bus—to my father's business in downtown Bridgeport, I felt that I was leaving my sacred ground. I initially had the same feeling when I crossed a certain line on the way to junior high, but as a teenager I was able to incorporate these peripheral areas into my sense of home.

As a preteen I was a bit unsettled each time I visited my father's store downtown, on Congress Avenue, after a bus trip of about fifteen minutes that began a block and a half from our house. Eventually this outer region became attached to the inner precinct, as my consciousness of place continued to expand. But this extended range of association was never enough to entirely erase the distinction between the spot where I felt most at home and the rest of Bridgeport. I continued to feel this difference many years later, when I had already entered my late forties, especially at the time when my brother and I jogged from our parents' house—my mother was by then widowed—all the way downtown and then—by way of the Wheeler mansion on Golden Hill—back home to the North End.

Once we crossed the outer boundary of our precinct, I knew that we were no longer fully at home, even though we were still physically in the same city. The houses may have looked more or less the same as our parents' dwelling, but they seemed different from the wooden frame buildings on Pierce Avenue, where our home had stood for ninety years. By then I was married and had lived in different parts of the country, yet Pierce Avenue and the surrounding streets meant something to me that none of those other places where I had lived and raised a family did. It was not just the house of my parents that had this meaning, but also the two or three square miles that surrounded our homestead.

After my parents' death the sacred precinct lost most of its importance in my life, particularly after we had sold the family house. Thereafter we rarely returned to Bridgeport, although my brother lived no more than fifty miles away in northwestern Connecticut, where he practiced medicine. Although living by then in southeastern Pennsylvania—less than five hours away by car—I returned to Bridgeport only twice in the next twenty years. Only once in all that time did I visit Pierce Avenue; when I did, I could barely bring myself to look at the house where I grew up. I did, however, visit my widowed aunt, who lived a few blocks away. After her funeral, however—she died soon afterward—I never bothered to test Thomas Wolfe's aphorism about going back home again. I just never tried.

I was very much of a loner, particularly as an adolescent. I read a great deal, avoided unnecessary social entanglements, and walked around the sacred precinct as a form of exercise and occasion for reflection. Years later my brother would joke that unwinding for me as a teenager meant reading Plato in Greek with the aid of a tattered German-Greek dictionary. Although I only engaged in this activity later in life, my brother was right that I had been a painfully serious, solitary adolescent. Many of the characteristics I eventually came to value—such as a social sense and a passion for physical fitness—were developed in later years. They were totally missing from my youth.

If someone had asked me at age fifteen what I would like to do, I would have answered like many of my peers: move out of Bridgeport. That was then becoming the standard reply to such a query, and for many of my contemporaries nearby cities such as New York and Boston exerted a magnetic attraction. I remember my mother saying quite matter-of-factly each time someone left town that "there

was nothing in Bridgeport" to hold that person back. As an isolated adolescent—
with an immigrant father and relatives jabbering in Hungarian, and for my sake,
occasionally in German—it was hard for me to see my city as the ideal residence.

Yet I remained bonded to it in a strange way. We had relatives in the area, and
we were used to hearing some of the older generation chatter in Hungarian on
the streets. Later my father became a fire commissioner and held other municipal
honors. I have been told that his name graces the cornerstone of the rebuilt main
firehouse, near the bridge that spans the muddy Pequonnock River. Perhaps one
of these days I'll go see whether the cornerstone and building are still there. I may
even bestir myself to cycle by the firehouse that bears my father's name. In a rare
example of touristic enterprise, Bridgeport is now clearing a Pequonnock Trail for
bicyclists in a once ramshackle part of the city.

Bridgeport, and particularly our neighborhood, had long been for me a source
of creative energy. Living there and afterward visiting my family allowed me to
develop my ideas for books and essays. Being in a large city would not have had the
same effect; I would have been too distracted by the excitements and noises of big-
city life. It's not that I don't enjoy the amenities of world cities and—particularly in
the case of European cities—their architectural magnificence. It's just that I don't
find them conducive to work. In any case, I relish the compactness of small towns,
the human size of these settlements, and the possibility of not being disturbed by
world-class problems. My children—who prefer to live in urban concentrations—
are exactly the opposite. They assume my taste in habitations—as well as that of
my younger brother—betokens a narrow view of life's possibilities.

Indeed, my late father-in-law—with whom I got along in every other way—
was always shocked by my *Kleinstädterei*; that is, my preference for small towns.
He used the German term—perhaps for emphasis—to characterize my inordinate
fondness for the provincial, a quality that he feverishly contrasted to his predilection for living in the heart of urban areas. We used to visit my father-in-law—who
lived and practiced medicine in downtown Toronto—for about two weeks every
year: once at Christmas and once during the summer. After having to listen to
buses and trolleys rattle by his house, I didn't mind returning to our home in
Rockford, Illinois.

Nor have I ever wanted to live in the suburb of a sprawling metropolis, the
streets of which are usually clogged with commuting traffic. The least agreeable
space I've been forced to inhabit was a Maryland suburb of Washington, D.C.,
from whence I commuted to the east side of the District to work as an editor.
By the time I arrived at my office, I was drenched in sweat and far too exhausted
to look at unedited texts. Although at least some of my coinhabitants on this
planet may not mind such an experience, for me it was a foretaste of hell. I left the
nation's capital with the sense that anyone who could stand such a life—there are

many who can—must be either a political junkie or someone who is being paid huge wads of money for stress-laden time. Significantly, I had taken this position after having lived and raised my children in Rockford, Illinois, a factory town about ninety miles west of Chicago that has fallen—or so I've been told—into even worse repair than Bridgeport. Yet as soon as I turned my back on Rockford to take what seemed a conveyor belt to better things, I regretted what I had done. I pined for what Karl Marx called "the idiocy of rural life" or, in this case, the blue-collar residential uniformity to which I had long been accustomed.

There are cities that continue to impress me—for example, Vienna, Budapest, Zürich, Florence, London, Istanbul, and Paris—but I doubt that I could stand the pressure or distraction of living in any of them. I prefer tasting such places at reasonable intervals and then returning to my small-town existence, away from the crush of humanity. It is possible to trace this attitude to the existentially delimited neighborhood in a declining factory town where I spent my youth. Unlike others, I felt no compelling desire—even if I once claimed that I did—to flee these familiar surroundings. Although the circumstances of my life required me to move away, I didn't think negatively about what I was leaving behind. In this sense, my brother and I were different from many of our acquaintances, who as onetime Bridgeporters tried to sever any connection to their birthplace.

Some of my young friends assure me that those who live in small towns suffer from a more restricted consciousness than those who have the good fortune of residing within a ten-minute walk of Times Square or Piccadilly. They may be right, if what they're saying is that young people who want to get ahead can find more opportunity in metropolitan regions than in what my critics characterize as "Dullsville." I suppose this all depends on what one considers to be an opportunity and how much excitement one needs for serious thinking.

I went to college in New York City but—to the consternation of those around me—fled home on the train on weekends. The noises of the city and my urban classmates were simply too much for me. When I was at Yale in the mid-1960s as a graduate student, I was attending an institution that was only eighteen miles from Bridgeport. My classmates and teachers viewed me as a nonaristocratic native of the region. Indeed, I was deemed to be an unteachable local who didn't even have the decency to hide his unhappy, telluric connection. To make matters even worse, I held views on every subject that ran counter to those of my peers. The friends I made were rarely—let me be honest, never—New Yorkers, but much more typically fellow students who came from small towns in the South and Midwest.

I received a particularly dim or stark view of nonurban life from graduate school professors at Yale. These instructors insisted that fascism, religious fanaticism, and other undesirable developments flourished in countrified surroundings; the more readily one could embrace or be embraced by urban life, the less receptive one became to what offended intellectuals. As a graduate student I recognized the foibles of my professors, who trotted out their hobbyhorses as informed judgments about our cultural and social choices. Later on, as an academic, I recalled the pretentious put-downs of ordinary Americans that came from my colleagues. These (not surprisingly) were from people who viewed themselves as being in the vanguard of a social-cultural upheaval that would be carried out in the name of the downtrodden and marginalized. But these social critics had fastidious sensibilities and, other than designated victim groups, showed little interest in anyone outside their circle.

The essays in this anthology were produced in an area that numbers no more than about fifteen thousand residents, more precisely in a borough in southeastern Pennsylvania that teems with German Anabaptist farmers. The more unreconstructed of these Anabaptists—some of whom live in the surrounding area—still travel in buggies. Occasionally I watch these farmers trot by in their horse-drawn vehicles and am relieved when their horses don't leave droppings in front of my house. A more common sight in my neighborhood is college students scurrying along on the way to class. My wife and I live in a brick house, shaded by trees, across from the college where the students are headed. It is the last place where I taught before I retired. It amazes me to think that I worked there, in what seemed the twilight of my career, for more than twenty years.

This is my fifth or sixth place of residence, not counting the time that I spent in college dorms or sojourning in European cities. The earlier inspiration for my work came from living in a demographically declining city with a shrinking working class. This was my original home, or at least the outer belt that enveloped my sacred precinct. Memories of that place still flood my consciousness and are now superimposed on the daily sights of my current living space. This is no longer the Bridgeport, Connecticut, of my youth. That place no longer exists, so home for me may just as well be Elizabethtown, Pennsylvania.

About a year ago I tried to read for the first time the abstruse lectures on the German poet Friedrich Hölderlin by Martin Heidegger, a philosopher who has always impressed me by his widely ranging thought.[2] Although Heidegger's discourses are painfully dense, I did resonate to his theme of "*Heimkehr* (Returning Home)." This is the core theme of "*Der Ister*," the rambling, sonorous poem to which Heidegger devoted lectures that he gave during World War II, which were subsequently published in book form.[3] The poet Hölderlin (1770–1843) was a Swabian German who visited France in 1802. While in this neighboring country he repeatedly returned in his mind's eye to his home near the source of the Danube. *Nostein*, the ancient Greek word for returning home, dominated the poet's mind, together with the awareness of the spiritual powers emanating from the river that defined his physical surroundings. Hölderlin knew that the ancient

Greeks venerated the Danube, which they named the Ister, as a sacred landmark, and in his poetry he played on the Danube's association with divine energies, more specifically with the Greek god Heracles and the German goddess of fertility, Hertha.[4]

I took away from this poem and Heidegger's lectures a renewed sense of my own rootedness. I too was tied to a place, although I would be the last to identify Bridgeport with the sacral, as Hölderlin does his birthplace. Bridgeport was simply where I grew up, yet it became integral to my personality in a way that made me think of it when I came across Heidegger's interpretation of Hölderlin as someone who was spiritually tied to the Ister.

Despite my lifelong rootedness in a particular region, I extended my sacred precinct little by little over the years. This process of extension is continuing even now. About three years ago I stopped at Yale University with my grandson, on the way back from visiting his aunt in Boston. Although the adjoining neighborhood in New Haven had gone down considerably since I lived there as a graduate student, the college buildings appeared very much the same. Many years earlier I had felt like a stranger while attending classes there, but all this had changed with the passage of time. Local sights like Maury's, the neo-Gothic Sterling Library, and Connecticut Hall—where American revolutionary Nathan Hale once resided—metamorphosed into my version of Hölderlin's Ister. These places became unexpectedly the site of a homecoming, and when my grandson told me that he liked the buildings on the Yale campus more than those he had seen the day before at Harvard, his words sounded like an affirmation of my very being. I can't say that I recognized a single face as I walked around the university that Sunday, and perhaps my only continued connection to Yale may be the copies of my books that are stacked somewhere in the Sterling. All the same, it was for me a homecoming, and one that I had not been prepared for.

2

Robert Nisbet: Conservative Sociologist

A GERMAN ENCYCLOPEDIA OF CONSERVATISM begins its entry for Robert Alexander Nisbet by noting that he was a "conservative sociologist."[1] For American academics, such a characterization may seem strange and even oxymoronic, since in the United States and almost everywhere else in the Western world today, the Left dominates sociology as a discipline. This ideological association applies not only to the vast majority of academic sociologists, but also to famous sociologists who were Nisbet's contemporaries. Talcott Parsons, Gordon Allport, Thomas Merton, C. Wright Mills, Paul Lazarsfeld, and Thomas Bottomore are only a few of the illustrious sociologists who were active fifty years ago and who belonged to the American Left. Indeed, even a social thinker who was beloved by the Right and who excoriated the therapeutic society, Philip Rieff, was never a self-described conservative.[2]

Some interpreters may identify Nisbet as a historian of social theory, as someone who brought forth such distinguished surveys of social theory as *The Sociological Tradition*[3] and *The Social Philosophers*.[4] I believe, however, that Nisbet would not have settled for this honor. His work *The Social Bond* is a detailed study of the sociological method; even his widely read defense of the "sociological tradition" as the creation of nineteenth-century opponents of the French Revolution and the modern "unitary state" is intended as a vindication of Nisbet's approach to social analysis. In any case, Nisbet would not have accepted the title of being a mere chronicler of ideas, as opposed to being a social scientist who appreciated the legacy of conservative social thinkers. Significantly, non-rightist social thinkers whom Nisbet admired, such as Karl Marx and Émile Durkheim, were transformed in his alembic into exponents of "conservative insights."

It is also relevant to distinguish between Nisbet's identification as a conservative and the now conventional use of the term to refer to Republicans as opposed to Democrats, or fans of FOX News as opposed to viewers of other news networks. Nisbet never sang the glories of "American exceptionalism," nor did he

call for the spread of the American democratic model to distant climes and peoples. From *The Quest for Community* onward, he targeted American crusades for
democracy and American popular culture. In the epilogue to *The Present Age*, he
depicts the United States as a "giant in military resources but not in the exercise
of military power and responsibility. Befuddled by belief that God intended it to
be the moral teacher to the world, our giant stumbles from people to people, ever
demonstrating that what American touches, it makes holy."[5]

America is "a giant too in domestic bureaucracy" that generates an "awful
total of indebtedness" and the growing dependence of the population on public
administration; moreover, "in structure our giant is a horde of loose individuals,
of homunculi serving as atoms of the giant's body as in the famous illustration
of Leviathan in Hobbes's classic." Nisbet finds a diminishing organic connection
among the tissues and organs of the American body social:

> Economically our giant is bemused by cash in hand rather than property and wealth.
> Growth is for weeds and idiots, not for the illuminati and literati. Culturally reign-
> ing symbols are two in number: deconstructionism and minimalism, each resting
> securely on the conviction that self-exploration is the mightiest truth of them all.[6]

Nisbet can be viewed as a true product of the New World. He was born and
raised in Southern California, and—except for wartime service in Saipan—spent
most of his life in Southern California and Arizona. But Nisbet saw in America's
postwar hegemony intimations of decline. He was relentlessly critical of twentieth-
century American life, and although emphatically on the right, he inveighed
against a moralistic foreign policy, consumer capitalism, and American public
administration. Dominant themes in his social criticism—such as "progress and
anarchy in modern America"[7] and the "twilight of authority"[8]—are unmistakably
linked to the United States in the present age.

Nisbet's prolonged inspection of American politics and culture made him
extremely unhappy with what he observed, albeit not in the same way as another
despiser of mass democracy, the satirist H. L. Mencken, who aimed his shafts at
the "boobocracy." Nisbet had no Menckenesque flair for satire. Unlike the exu-
berant journalist and "Baltimore Sage," he never satirized his targets in order
to amuse others. Although a reluctant agnostic like one of his heroes, the Swiss
German historian Jacob Burckhardt, Nisbet was a Protestant moralist who hated
American triumphalism.

He was also no friend of another mainstay of the current American "conservative movement," the religious Right. Nisbet regarded it as a competitor for influence
in the "new absolutism" that was runaway modern government. Like public sector
unions and the steadily expanding list of designated victims of "discrimination,"

evangelicals were eager to increase their political influence. They discovered that "if politics is the name of the game and it is in our age, then let born-againness become a political as well as religious rite."[9]

Nisbet deplored the nakedly political approach of the evangelicals to such matters of morals and faith as abortion and prayer in school and other public places. He concludes his negative judgment in *The Present Age* by predicting: "There will be a great deal more of this in the decades ahead." Least of all did Nisbet consider the religious Right to be an exalted spiritual project that went astray. It was first and foremost in his mind a secular movement, as he explains in detail in *The Present Age*: "The agenda of the group that began under the label of the Moral Majority was as political as concerned with strictly political ends, political techniques, and political power plays, as anything witnessed back in the 1930s with the labor unions."[10]

For someone who was opposed, as Nisbet clearly was, to the administrative state and its incorporation of traditional family functions, his savaging of the religious Right is difficult to explain. Arguably the evangelicals and others who joined this group were rightly concerned about the government's role in subverting traditional family morality by supporting abortion rights, gay lifestyles, feminist programs, and a strongly secularist public educational agenda. The state is not being neutral by protecting the right to abortion and by punishing discrimination against nontraditional social behavior. It is arguably taking sides in a social-cultural war. Christian traditionalists therefore should have the same right as their adversaries to push the government in their direction.

Nisbet's refusal to take this position and his intense hostility toward evangelicals may both be mysteries. This lack of a full explanation persists, despite the attempts by his biographer, Brad Lowell Stone, to find more coherence in this stand than may exist there. Stone presents Nisbet as sharing the putative religious doubts of nineteenth-century conservatives, who viewed churches as only one among other socially useful arrangements.[11]

There may be two more plausible explanations for Nisbet's opposition to the religious Right and its work. One is that he viewed that movement as an excrescence of the unitary state and the "new absolutism," competing with other groups to wield the sword of power. Evangelical leaders were not babes in the woods, but rather like Pat Robertson, who was the son of Senator Absalom Willis Robertson (D-VA), or Jerry Falwell, who devoted most of his life to political activism, were political players with a nationwide profile. They were in no sense humble Christians whose chief interest was "preserving spiritual and moral autonomy under existing political power."[12] Rather, they represented an "apparently fast-growing minority of Americans whose zeal for Christ and overwhelming confidence in their righteousness made politics an irresistible beacon."[13] The other explanation is that

Nisbet placed the religious Right into a democratic, populist camp and identified the democratic will with easily manipulated aggregates of uprooted or desocialized beings. This group was seen as being especially susceptible to demagogues. Those whom Nisbet respected were not given to "enthusiasms," a condition that encouraged excess in politics and religion. Although Nisbet loathed the consolidated managerial state, he was equally unhappy with those enthusiasts who were trying to take away the state's power in order to empower themselves.[14]

Nisbet's appeal to conservative thought, particularly to nineteenth-century classical conservative sources, must be understood in terms of his critical view of the United States and the present age. These were not abstract interests but related directly to how Nisbet analyzed American modernity. The conservative model of social organization that he explored in *The Sociological Tradition*,[15] *The Making of Modern Society*,[16] *The Social Bond*,[17] and *The Social Philosophers*[18] was not an arbitrary reference point. It was placed in stark contrast to the rootlessness, bureaucratic manipulation, and egalitarianism run riot that Nisbet associated with the United States in the last third of the twentieth century. Contemporary America was abandoning any relation to his preferred social vision, and Nisbet believed this falling away would spell disaster.

A quintessentially conservative vision of how society should function blends with other inspirations in Nisbet's critical commentaries about the present age. Whether referring to Alexis de Tocqueville's warning against the descent of democracy into totalitarianism and the removal of "intermediate institutions" by overbearing democratic administration[19] or Hannah Arendt's nightmarish picture of modern tyranny in *The Origins of Totalitarianism*, Nisbet drew on writers who were in no way classical conservatives. But they were made to serve a single overarching purpose, which was a sustained, critical analysis of where the United States as the West's premier power and wealthiest country was headed.

Most views about Nisbet as a professional loner are clearly overstated. Although someone of his persuasion would not likely prosper in today's more leftist academic world, in the middle of the twentieth-century—when Nisbet was teaching at Berkeley—he was anything but a lone wolf. He was passionately involved in trying to organize a sociology department at Berkeley. When his plan failed to develop, he went on to Riverside, where he managed to create the department he hoped for; not as a peripheral figure, but as a rising star in his profession. His book *The Quest for Community*[20] was one of several widely sold works in the postwar years dealing with the socially uprooted individual in modern society. Like David Riesman[21] and others who examined the same themes in readable prose, Nisbet had a popular following as well as professional cachet.[22]

The fact that Nisbet is far less widely read today than during his lifetime can be ascribed to changing ideological and political concerns. Much of what he found

to be troubling and even frightening—for example, the political war on traditional communities—is far less upsetting to educated Americans today than it was
fifty years ago. Although the inroads of government-backed social engineering
bothered Nisbet deeply, they are less disagreeable to those who now inhabit his
profession and who are concerned with enlisting government in the war against
prejudice. Nisbet's complaints about "egalitarianism" as socially destructive are no
longer commonly shared. Many contemporary Americans, and perhaps a majority of those under thirty, feel there is too much inequality, and most women and
visible minorities express no objections to having public administrators address
social issues for the rest of us.

This can help explain why Nisbet's work may no longer resonate as it once did.
It is, after all, exceedingly difficult to appreciate a social theorist and social critic
if one does not share *his* worldview and sensibilities. It is also doubtful that an
American conservative movement that once celebrated Nisbet would feel affinity
for him now. Nisbet, who was not of their world, would seem out of place to those
who are allowed to participate in today's media-guided political discussion. These
discussants assume and usually affirm many of the political developments and
social change that were anathema to Nisbet.

My comments about blurred "conservative visions" go beyond any discussion
of Nisbet. They apply equally to most attempts to draw on older conservative
sources to provide an understanding of contemporary society that would be per-
suasive to contemporary readers. Nisbet's critical lenses were twice removed from
the current scene. They go back several generations to the early nineteenth century and to those who viewed the bourgeois society that was then emerging with
trepidation. How exactly does one make these observations relevant to our present society, which has changed more radically in the last two hundred years than
any classical conservative critic could have imagined in the wake of the French
Revolution? From whence comes the problem of applying a perspective that is
doubly distanced from our time—that is, from the latest "present age" that Nisbet
was already sketching in the 1950s?

Robert Nisbet and Russell Kirk (1918–1994) Compared

In 1953, according to George Nash's *The Conservative Intellectual Movement in
America since 1945*,[23] there appeared two epoch-making books, both of which
exerted imaginative power over postwar conservatism: Robert Nisbet's *The Quest
for Community*[24] and Russell Kirk's *The Conservative Mind*.[25] The two works are
often linked in their emphasis on lost social and cultural traditions, and their
authors, who were only five years apart in age, often encountered the same critics,

including some on the right. The populist conservative Willmoore Kendall went after both as adversaries of democracy,[26] whereas the Libertarian Frank Meyer denounced them even more vehemently as "statists," who would make short shrift of individual liberty.[27] Nisbet and Kirk were friends, and each received an Ingersoll Award from the Rockford Institute, Kirk in 1984 and Nisbet in 1985, in recognition of their contributions to thought.

The two figures also published books on education in the 1970s: Nisbet wrote *The Degradation of Academic Dogma*[28] and Kirk *Decadence and Renewal in the Higher Learning*.[29] These works make similar points about American universities and were generally thought to have come from kindred spirits. Perhaps Kirk would have adopted Nisbet's title for his disquisition if that label had not already been taken. Nisbet borrowed his title from *The Degradation of the Democratic Dogma*,[30] a work that had been written by someone who appealed to him and Kirk equally, the New England patrician and opponent of America's drift toward modern democracy in the 1870s, Henry Adams. Neither Kirk nor Nisbet had any sympathy for the student protest movement of the 1960s, but both highlighted the academic abuses that preceded the student protests. The growth of vocationalism, the bureaucratization of what had been higher education, the colonization of universities by government and politically partisan "institutes," and the process by which universities became big business were all problems in higher education targeted by Nisbet and Kirk.

From the distance of more than half a century, however, what is striking about their once frequently compared works of 1953 is how differently the two authors viewed the present age. Kirk's work—which was originally titled *The Conservative Rout* and which began as a dissertation at the University of St. Andrews in Scotland—is comparatively upbeat, despite its somber references to European ruins and eroded ways of life.[31] Most of the book, which consists of graphic portraits of Anglo-American literary figures, had no critical influence on postwar conservative thought, beyond the discussion of Burke's "Politics of Prescription" at the beginning and some well-phrased remarks near the end about Irving Babbitt and T. S. Eliot.[32] The favorable commentary on Eliot would later be turned into a full-length biography of someone whom Kirk had known and corresponded with.

The section on "conservatives' promise" at the close of the book seems mostly an attack on "collectivism" and planned societies, interwoven with passages from George Orwell, Christopher Dawson, and dozens of other writers who had warned about these troubling developments.[33] Surveying *The Conservative Mind*, one encounters a multitude of engrossing themes, but it would be difficult to prove that Kirk's comments on President John Adams, Secretary of State John C. Calhoun, Prime Minister Benjamin Disraeli, Cardinal John Henry Newman, Victorian literature, or Irving Babbitt's strictures about the romantic disposition have added even minimally to our scholarship on these topics.[34] Kirk's main points are made in the first few pages, particularly in "The Idea of Conservatism."[35] Here he suggests to the reader that conservatism remains a going concern, even though it was "frustrated" in the past, for example, when *nouveau riche* industrialists—that is, people who made their money through industry rather than through long-standing familial inheritance—held sway during the Gilded Age, and with the mushrooming of "liberalism" and "utilitarianism" in the form of the welfare state.[36]

Still, it is possible, or so Kirk contends, to rally the rising generation to the "principles of conservatism" for people today, just as in the past, to "respect the wisdom of their ancestors. Indeed, what else is the essence of social conservatism but the preservation of the ancient moral traditions of humanity?"[37] Kirk provides his readers with six principles of conservatism,[38] which are boiled down from the twelve that are featured in one of his favorite works, F. J. C. Hearnshaw's *Conservatism in England*:

1. Belief in a transcendent order or body of natural law, which rules society as well as conscience;
2. Affection for the proliferating variety and mystery of human existence, as opposed to the narrowing uniformity, egalitarianism, and utilitarian aims of most radical systems;
3. Conviction that civilized society requires orders and classes, as against the notion of a "classless society";
4. Persuasion that freedom and property are closely linked;
5. Faith in prescription and distrust of "sophisters [*sic*], calculators, and economists," who should reconstruct society upon abstract designs;
6. Recognition that change may not be salutary reform: hasty innovation may be a devouring conflagration, rather than a torch of progress.[39]

The standards that Kirk set down in his book are so general and placed against such grim opposites that they are plainly intended to elicit general consent. Who, after all, would hand over society to economic levelers or to those unleashing "a devouring conflagration?" The rhetorical phrases from Burke's *Reflections on the Revolution in France*[40] give the opening sections a certain archaic flavor, but this rhetoric against the excesses of the Revolution, or against what Burke thought this upheaval would engender, would not likely turn off Kirk's readers. After all, Kirk is not trying to resurrect the historical past. His statement of principles and his discussion of Burke's notion of prescriptive right are not attempts to defend status relations or inherited authority as they existed in England in 1790. The reader does not have to worry that Kirk is advocating the restoration of manorial relations or any return of power to an overbearing landed nobility.

Furthermore, this gray eminence of the postwar conservative movement soft-ened his formulation of principles as the years went on. Lest the defense of order and degrees, as originally stated in principle 4, take readers out of their comfort zone, Kirk explains in later editions that "equality before courts of law are recog-nized by conservatives, but equality of condition, they think, means equality in servitude and boredom."[41] One discovers that Kirk is making an esthetic argu-ment against an excess of equality, a condition that leads to boredom and unifor-mity and therefore should be avoided. Kirk's statement of principle is not about going back to any inherited hierarchical society. It is an appeal to individuals not to opt for more equality lest their lives become insufferably dull.

Even more important, perhaps, is that Kirk is addressing specifically those in an Anglo-American society who have an interest similar to his own in English letters produced during the late eighteenth and nineteenth centuries. Although he writes benignly about a few non-Anglo-Americans—for example, about Burke's "French disciples" and about Tocqueville, who "applied the wisdom of Burke to his own liberal ends[42]—his tolerance halts at the Rhine. Kirk is espe-cially exercised by the confusion of Burke's conservatism with German author-itarianism and rages against "Schlegel, Görres, and Stolberg and Taine's school in France," of whom all are "admirers of both Hegel and Burke, which perhaps explains the confounding of their superficial resemblance with their fundamen-tal inimicality."[43] Further, "Hegel's metaphysics would have been as abhorrent to Burke as his style."[44]

A bit of correction may be in order here: Schlegel, Görres, and Stolberg all belonged to the Catholic revival in early nineteenth-century Germany, a religious development that existed quite independently of Hegel's thought. None of these Catholic champions was known to have fallen under Hegel's spell. Although one certainly has a right to reject Hegel as a philosopher and to criticize works that are derived from his thought, one should first understand what one is rejecting. Then it might be a good idea to know who did and did not come under the sway of Hegel's ideas. Kirk's scattergun approach to a great thinker and his legacy is not the best way to engage either task.

Equally mystifying is the reference in *The Conservative Mind* to Hippolyte Taine, a French historian who wrote critically about the Great Revolution from a naturalist perspective. Here we find evidence of how little Kirk knew or cared about continental European thought, which may be a reason that he focused so single-mindedly on the Anglo-American conservative mind. Note that the ref-erence to "mind" in the title is a distinctly German touch that came from Kirk's Germanophile Chicago publisher, Henry Regnery.

Nisbet presents a dramatically different interpretation of social history from Kirk's overview of his literary and political predecessors. Indeed—except for their shared reactions to the Left and Burke—it would be hard to locate the two men in the same universe of discourse. Unlike Kirk, Nisbet was drenched in French social thought. His dissertation, completed under the renowned sociologist-historian Frederick J. Teggart at Berkeley in 1939, carried the title *"The Social Group in French Thought."*[45] In this very early work Nisbet examined French opponents of the French Revolution such as Louis de Bonald and Joseph de Maistre, with special attention being paid to their views about a changing class structure in early nineteenth-century France. Already at the beginning of his career Nisbet relished conservative thought, especially of the kind that originated on the European continent. Nisbet cited Burke on the danger of social leveling and abstract rights, but unlike Kirk, his thinking would have been the same even if he had not read Burke's *Reflections on the Revolution in France*. This difference may go back to what the two authors were looking for: Kirk was drawn to the rhetorical appeal of Burke as a critic of the Left. Nisbet was searching for a systematic analysis of his adversary, a lifelong project into which he poured his research energies.

Much of Nisbet's dissertation can be found in two essays dealing with the effects of the French Revolution on social theory[46] and with the counterrevolutionary origins of sociology, both of which were published in the *American Journal of Sociology*.[47] Nisbet would return in his later work, especially in *The Sociological Tradition*,[48] to the same counterrevolutionary figures. Given these interests, one should not be surprised that the section in *The Social Philosophers* that examines "conservative pluralism" features Burke, de Bonald, and Hegel.[49] Unlike Kirk, Nisbet read and appreciated Hegel's *Philosophy of Right*, and a description of Hegel's contribution to Nisbet's conception of conservatism is present in the following passage:

> Like Burke and Bonald, Hegel sees the vital importance of institutions and communities existing between the individual and the power of government, to serve as buffers, hence his strong advocacy of church, local community, profession, and especially occupational associations.[50]

In contrast to Kirk's invectives against Hegel's bad metaphysics and "authoritarian" teachings, Nisbet sums up Hegel's politics thus:

> Hegel, in short, is as apprehensive as Burke, Bonald, or any of the other conservative pluralists of the creation, through political centralization and other forces such as industrialization and commerce, of mass society devoid of relationships other than those of political power. Hence derives his preference for monarchy . . . over democracy: democracy, he believed, would lead more readily than would monarchy to the atomization of society and to centralization of political power.[51]

Significantly, Nisbet never shied away from continental thinkers who were unknown or unpalatable to the more strictly Anglophile Kirk. In *The Making of Modern Society*, for example, Nisbet points to outspoken antidemocrats of an earlier age who prefigured his warnings about mass democracy.[52] Nisbet also links these admonitions to the classical liberal Sir Henry Maine and to the feminist social democrat J. S. Mill:

> In the writings of Mill, Maine, Taine, Maurras, Burkhardt, Sorel, Nietzsche, and many others of the nineteenth century, there is a presentiment of a deculturalized, dehumanized mass of people whose incapacity for self-governance in the smaller things of life would evolve easily into incapacity of government in the larger and who would eventually become dominated by merchants of power and force.[53]

Nisbet cites here as elsewhere any available authority, including Marx, whose observations about "political bureaucracy" were compatible with his critical perspective.

Equally pertinent for a comparison with Kirk is the tenor of *The Quest for Community*.[54] Unlike Kirk, Nisbet is not reprising vignettes of Victorian personalities sandwiched in between comments on Burke and Eliot. Rather, he is constructing social criticism from a perspective heavily shaped by his contact with continental conservatives. A comment at the beginning of the chapter "Image of Community" epitomizes a recurrent perspective in Nisbet's book and warrants quotation:

> In the writings of such men as Edmund Burke, de Maistre, de Bonald, Hegel, and others we find premonitions and insights that bear an extraordinarily close relation to the contemporary ideology of community. The French Revolution had something of the same impact upon men's minds in Western Europe at the very end of the eighteenth century that the Communist and Nazi revolutions have had in the twentieth century. In each instance the seizure of power, the expropriation of rulers, and the impact of new patterns of authority and freedom upon older institutions and moral certainties led to a re-examination of ideas on the nature of society.[55]

Finally, Nisbet in *The Quest for Community* is not telling us how to be "conservative" or arguing that conservatism is less boring than its alternative. He is describing a modern social and political predicament for which he could find no way out.

Such critical methodological differences were overshadowed by the different personalities of the two post–World War II conservative writers. Kirk was a solitary figure who was painfully shy and lived with his family—which he acquired relatively late in life—in the pine barrens of Michigan. In his less guarded moments he would express reactionary thoughts about which side should have won the

American or English Civil Wars. Remarkably enough, Kirk sounded even more conservative than Nisbet in intimate circles,[56] but this was not the "hope breaking through" that informs "guides for conservatives" or the "speechifying" he did to support his wife and daughters. [57] Nisbet, by contrast, was an elegant, gregarious speaker, who was strikingly handsome and always tastefully dressed.[58] He thrived in high society and cultivated a wide circle of friends, including his collaborator on a book, the Marxist sociologist Tom Bottomore, and the neoconservative stars Irving Kristol and Gertrude Himmelfarb.[59]

Appearances here as elsewhere may be deceptive. As a critic of modern society, Nisbet was both more pessimistic and more deeply conservative than his friend and correspondent. Unlike Kirk, he did not feel impelled to write such partisan tracts as *The Intelligent Women's Guide to Conservatism*[60] and *A Program for Conservatives*.[61] Nisbet also never expressed Kirk's hope in the 1950s that they were living at the beginning of a "new Augustan Age." He doubted that the struggle against Soviet Communism would have the same conservative effect on the United States as the war against revolutionary France had exercised on British politics. In the conclusion of *The Quest for Community*, Nisbet sums up his unseasonable thoughts about modern centralized democracy.[62] With the modern administrative state, we are dealing with a "new classification." "Traditional labels—democratic, republican, capitalist, socialist, etc.—have by now become nearly as archaic as older classifications of monarchy and aristocracy."[63] Equally noteworthy is this statement:

> Government of, by, and for the people, for all its verity as an abstract proposition, becomes nearly as irrelevant in a world in which all despotisms rest upon foundations of mass acquiescence and where the arts of political propaganda are employed to sink the roots of government deeply in popular consciousness and participation.[64]

Going beyond the customary distinction between democratic and totalitarian states, Nisbet lets something fly that may have rattled his readers on the anti-Soviet Right: "We must conclude that all States in the future will be able to demonstrate, and will have to demonstrate attributes of socialism. But, by themselves, these will promise nothing in the way of freedom."[65] Nisbet has in mind a consolidated public administration that promotes "equality" when he depicts "the kind of state" that always seeks

> a higher degree of centralization in the conduct of its operation, always tending toward a wider measure of politicization of social, economic, and cultural life. [The state] does not do this in the name of freedom but of freedom from want, security, and minority tyranny.[66]

This attack on the type of state in which all human and social activities "are made aspects of the administrative structure of political government"[67] is not an allusion to something as remote as the Terror of the French Revolution. Nisbet is considering a specter closer to home; namely, an American government that no longer protects a "pluralism of functions and loyalties in the lives of its people."[68]

Nisbet warned against the perils of "democratic totalitarianism" quite early in the postwar years. His admonitions reflected concerns that went back to the surge of centralized power that began with the Progressive Era and that received added impetus from American participation in two world wars and the Cold War. Significantly, these admonitions came before the vast expansion of public administration that started in the 1960s in the United States, Western Europe, and the British Commonwealth. This development was only incipiently present in most Western countries until well after Nisbet had become an academic celebrity.[69] Later state projects such as fighting discrimination and punishing hate speech were barely around when Nisbet produced *The Quest for Community*. Yet he predicted the extension of public administration into forms of thought control that were limited to hard totalitarian states in the 1950s. The author of *The Quest for Community* also presciently notes that the democratic administrative state creates its own "consensus for change" by molding "popular consciousness" through its command of public education. In these observations, and particularly in his recognition that the expanding modern state always claims to represent an expansion of freedom, Nisbet was looking well beyond the post–World War II era.

Against Constructivism

If there is anything that shapes Nisbet's judgments about earlier social and political theorists, it is that he rejects the notion that civil society is a mere contrivance composed of potentially autonomous individuals. This may explain why Nisbet, a self-described conservative, could display an exceedingly broad taste in social theory, ranging from Louis de Bonald, Edmund Burke, Joseph de Maistre, Alexis de Tocqueville, and Georg Wilhelm Friedrich Hegel to the French Jewish socialist Émile Durkheim. All these thinkers dismissed equally the concept of an atomistic society and warned against a state that does not recognize the solidarity of family and communal relations.

Unlike his other heroes, Nisbet bestowed on Durkheim an entire intellectual biography; anyone who reads his *Sociology of Emile Durkheim* will recognize his debt to this French creator of sociological method.[70] Nisbet makes generous allowances for Durkeim's decidedly leftist politics and speaks positively about Durkheim's close friendship with the Marxist socialist Jean Jaurès. Nisbet valued his subject not for his socialist affiliations, but for certain qualities that he recognized in his scholarship. Already in his earliest major work, *The Division of Labor in Society*, Durkheim stressed the bonds uniting real people, whether through "mechanical solidarity in tribal societies" or through a more voluntaristic "organic solidarity" in the modern West.[71] The concept of individuals living apart from each other and trying to achieve autonomy outside of complex social relations seemed to Durkheim, as much as it did to Nisbet, a total fiction. Furthermore,

> Durkheim rejected individualism on every possible ground. He found it insupportable as a principle of social solidarity, as an ethic or moral value, as a cornerstone of the social order, and not least as the vantage point of social analysis. . . . Hence the specific criticisms of the individualistically oriented titans of his day, such as Herbert Spencer and Gabriel Tarde.[72]

Nisbet observes that in Durkheim's *Rules of Sociological Method*[73] and in the journal he founded in 1898, *L'Année Sociologique*, the distinguished Sorbonne professor, whom Nisbet clearly views as his illustrious forerunner, raised "structural functionalism" to the most respected form of social research. From the vantage point provided by Durkheim, the researcher must approach his investigation holistically. Neither an unadorned "biologism"—that is, a preoccupation with individual drives and instincts—nor an emphasis on individual action should guide social research; rather, we should be looking at how societies function collectively.[74]

Despite Durkheim's secularist, anticlerical politics, we are reminded of the fact that he published a groundbreaking work on religious sociology, *Elementary Forms of Religious Life*.[75] Nisbet does not stint in his praise of this study:

> Of the eternality of religion resting as it does on man's differentiation of the sacred from the profane, there is not the slightest doubt in Durkheim's mind. Durkheim may well have been atheist and disbeliever. *The Elementary Forms of Religious Life* is nevertheless one of the most powerful statements of the functional indispensability in society ever written.[76]

A religious skeptic, albeit formally a High Church Episcopalian with a German Jewish grandmother, Nisbet recognized in Durkheim his oft-stated appreciation of religion as a social phenomenon. He and Durkheim were equally aware of the value of the "sacred" in man's collective existence. In the long section on the sacred in *The Sociological Tradition*, one can easily detect the ideas of the French Jewish author of *The Elementary Forms of Religious Life*.[77] Equally apparent in this work are the thoughts of Durkheim's teacher at the Sorbonne, the classicist and historian Numa Denis Fustel de Coulanges.[78] Although none of these three

notables could be described as a traditional believer, all were impressed by the
pivotal role of religious belief in creating and sustaining community. Unlike the
anticlerical Durkheim, however, Nisbet was not opposed to established churches
where they already existed.

Nisbet's "historical pessimism" was already present in his subject, who pointed
out "the rents in the social bond" and "the ever-larger numbers of individuals
existing in social and moral isolation."[79] In these forebodings, which Nisbet
admits were often nearly concealed in his writings, "Durkheim is in a striking
degree the philosopher or sociologist of what we today call social disorganiza-
tion."[80] In his focusing on the "twin forces of social disintegration and individual
alienation in modern society," Durkheim is declared to have been a prophet of the
present times.

Impressed by these "premonitions" in Durkheim's work, Nisbet celebrates in his
French subject a precursor of his preoccupation with the "Twilight of Authority."[81]
This was the title of a book that Nisbet was already composing while finishing his
study of Durkheim.[82] Supposedly Durkheim had already glimpsed what Nisbet
was analyzing, "the fragmenting effect of modern industry on social authority."[83]
Durkheim too had recoiled from "the desiccating effects of centralized political
power upon authority."[84] Durkheim's famous study *Suicide*, we are told, is not just
about the anomie besetting isolated individuals, but also about the breakdown of
authority structures.[85]

This bridge building to Durkheim in the biography is not always convincing,
particularly in view of Durkheim's overt political commitments, which were markedly different from those of Nisbet. Durkheim belonged to a party of militant
secularists and self-styled progressives, favoring state control over the forces of
production. Although Nisbet revered this pioneer in sociology, the political gulf
between them may have been greater than his biographer acknowledges. But this
difference, in Nisbet's judgment, was outweighed by their overlapping views about
the sacred, their holistic approaches to the study of social phenomena, and their
understanding of organic relations as a prerequisite for mentally sound individuals. Finally, as Nisbet never tires of mentioning in the closing section of the biography, he and his precursor both understood the effects of fragmented authority.

There is, however, another link between biographer and subject. Like Durkheim,
Nisbet was searching for a modern basis for community that would not lead
to the dangerous collectivism warned against in *The Quest for Community*.[86]
Solutions that stemmed from European counterrevolutionaries, Nisbet sensed,
would no longer command respect in the modern world. There was no going
back to a system of "personal authority" and status relations of the kind envisaged by de Bonald or de Maistre. The social bond had to be preserved or renewed
in some other way, particularly in the face of an interventionist-happy public

administration and given the fact that the democratic idea of equality found ever more bizarre ways to express itself. Nisbet did not believe that the end of the Soviet Union and the eclipse of Marxist-Leninism as an ideology for Western intellectuals would render the egalitarian idea less appealing. Rather, he assumed that it would become even more irrational and even more emotive without a coherent Marxist framework to restrict it.

Nisbet's preoccupation with Tocqueville's observations about communal and familial association as the substance of American democracy in the 1830s, his focus on Durkheim's notion of mechanical solidarity—as well as his detailed references to seigniorial authority among classical conservatives—were all intended as responses to the problems of the "present age." But which if any of these visions still had purchase in modern America? In *The Social Bond*, which "strongly emphasizes the corporate solidarity of the group," Nisbet declares that "a revolution in the nature of authority" that began centuries ago culminated in having "personal authority superseded by territorial authority."[87] Given this unpromising historical situation, Nisbet looked for measures against further communal erosion, but they were rarely his preferred choices.

Nisbet as a Reluctant Libertarian: An Excursus

A self-described Libertarian and Calvinist theologian, Gary North wrote a thoughtful review of Nisbet's *Conservatism: Dream and Reality*[88] that demonstrates once more that politics makes strange bedfellows. North concedes that no one disagreed more fundamentally on principle with Libertarians than Nisbet, who

> was a lover of medievalism. So were most of his conservative prototypes. Classical liberals [read Libertarians] did not like medievalism. It was much too ecclesiocentric for their tastes. It was much too anti-cosmopolitan.[89]

Not surprisingly, many of Nisbet's more publicized disagreements were with avowed Libertarians. These altercations went back to the 1950s, when he first fell into the crosshairs of Libertarian polemicists, whom he attacked vehemently in return.

Despite these exchanges, according to North, overlaps can be detected between Nisbet and some Libertarians.[90] Nisbet was no friend of the warfare state. He decried this "Leviathan" as passionately as any Libertarian. He also favored "decentralization," which North considers to be a Libertarian position. According to North, there is much in such renowned works as *The Present Age*[91] and *Conservatism: Dream and Reality*[92] that Libertarians might read with profit. North explains that Nisbet "was never a partisan." Indeed, "there are few men of letters who have made so great a contribution to any intellectual tradition yet who gained so few enemies in his lifetime."[93] It is easy to imagine that North was dishing out these tributes in order to win support for Nisbet among his fellow Libertarians.

Here one may distinguish between what one could apply for one's purposes from Nisbet's corpus and the thinker's real sympathies. Although much of Nisbet's critique of the present age would appeal to Libertarians, he never wrote positively about their persuasion. In American politics, he was by his own admission a pre–New Deal Republican, and as a student of European social history, he was drawn to premodern social authorities. Libertarians were too atomistic and too egalitarian for his taste, and he always remained at a distance from a group that his friend Russell Kirk mocked as "chirping sectaries." Albeit with deep reservations, Nisbet voted Republican. He preferred the GOP, he once confessed to me, as the lesser of two unspeakable evils. Never to my knowledge was he tempted to vote for a Libertarian candidate for any office.

In the end there may be no fit between what Nisbet envisaged as a "good society" and what he identified as the distinguishing marks of the present age. What he left behind was not voting advice, but a body of social criticism, which was drawn mostly from sources on the Right but which he also leavened with insights from the classical Left. In no sense was his worldview subsumable under the journalistic enterprise that today calls itself the conservative movement. Nisbet occasionally enjoyed the company of representatives of this movement and was always ready to receive its accolades, but his own conservatism was too contemplative and too unalterably pessimistic to render him congenial to political activists. He tried not to notice what others celebrated as the "Reagan Revolution." As far as he could tell, this supposed watershed had not ended what in the United States was politics as usual. Although he accepted a resident scholar's position at the neoconservative American Enterprise Institute in 1978, he complained in conversations with me about how alien he found this atmosphere.[94] The political types whom he encountered in Washington, D.C., were less thoughtful than those whom he celebrated in *The Sociological Tradition*.[95] In his growing estrangement from the present age, Nisbet may have been what Germans call a *Grenzgänger* and Americans an "outlier."

3

Defining Right and Left

THIS CHAPTER TRIES TO EXPLAIN with appropriate distinctions what Right and Left are. For those who have no interest in hearing an activist's harangue, one should point out that "conservative" is not being equated with a member of the Republican Party or with the viewing habits of FOX News junkies. Being a Republican and dutifully reciting party talking points will not be treated as being on the Right, nor will the disinclination to do either be taken as definitive proof of leftist loyalties.

A classical or essentialist Right is hard to find in the contemporary Western world, where journalists and other assorted intellectuals rush to denounce its bearers—or even partial bearers—as "fascists." That may be one reason that such types rarely come into public view, outside of certain European parties that have been able to survive in a multiparty electoral system. Being on the essentialist Right is deadly in an academic or journalistic milieu that features almost exclusively quintessential leftist values. There are some isolated intellectual groups in the United States that betray a right-wing gestalt. But these groups are usually cut off from the conservative mainstream lest they endanger "conservative" institutes or publications by expressing improper ideas. This is entirely understandable given the prevalence of leftist influences in Western societies and the extent to which the establishment non-Left has absorbed leftist values and attitudes that have come from a predominantly leftist culture and educational system.

Contrary to a widespread misconception, the Right is not that side that plays up "values" in opposition to a "relativistic" Left. It is truly remarkable how tenaciously the Left fights for its "values." Leftists believe fervently in an overshadowing vision of universal equality. Though those of a different persuasion might differ with leftists over its highest value, it is evident that a moral vision infuses the Left's political concerns. It also makes no sense to define the Right as the side that wishes to move mountains in order to confer "human rights" on the entire world. Both the notion of human rights and the mission to impose them universally are derived from the classical Left, going back to the French Revolution. The fact that such a global mission is now thought to characterize the Right underscores the utter confusion into which Right-Left distinctions have drifted.

Finally, one does not join the essentialist Right by wishing to get off the train of progress just before the present moment. As a practical position, one might find the civil rights legislation of the 1960s to be less intrusive than its later additions, or an earlier phase of the feminist movement to be less intrusive than what has been called by its critics "gender feminism." I would be the last to question someone's right to choose a less drastic rather than a more extreme form of government social engineering, given what came later. But one does not prove one's rightist credentials by making such choices—save by the standards of a Left that is perpetually trying to move political debate further into its energy field.

There is also the problem of an inflated use of "conservative," a term that is applied to whomever the media choose to bestow it on. This form of certification complicates the semantic problem. Each time I see an adolescent blogger or pubescent columnist introduced to the viewing public as a "leading conservative," I crack the same joke to whoever is around: "Does this teenager follow Burke or Maistre?" By now, "conservative" signifies what certain journalists and certain news commentators decide to advocate. Journalists who take Republican policy positions are sometimes described as conservative theorists, although I am still struggling to find out what exactly makes such people "conservative" or "theorists." Presumably by defending the last Republican chief executive, President George W. Bush, the speaker gains recognition as a "conservative" thinker.

On a practical level, I can sympathize with Libertarians, who believe there is "too much government," and I have given my vote more than once to proponents of this stance. When Libertarians speak of "limited" government and constitutionally guaranteed freedoms, they almost always catch my ear. The problem begins when someone rises to defend Libertarian ethics or Libertarian anthropology. The notion of individuals defining their values and identities—while inhabiting an imaginary state of nature—does not seem to be a convincing account of where we come from as human beings. I've noticed, pace some Libertarian individualists, that a wide range of nonvolitional forces shape our individual lives. These are forces we most definitely have not chosen for ourselves, but which nonetheless shape our beings and belief systems. We bring with us a context, even if it gratifies our vanity to think that we fashion our personalities and give ourselves "values" by dint of personal will. The range of our life choices is far more determined by culture, heredity, and geographic location than someone who is addicted to Ayn Rand mega-novels might wish to believe.

Even more relevant to my argument is that there is nothing right-wing or even vaguely conservative about the way Libertarians approach the question of liberty. Unlike the essentialist Right's reading of Aristotle or Burke, Libertarians understand freedom as a universally shared good to which everyone everywhere is entitled by virtue of being an individual. Although I would not prohibit others, even if I were in the position to do so, from espousing such a view, it is not clear what renders this Libertarian understanding of social relations specifically right-wing. The classical conservative view of liberty flows from the legal implications of someone's standing in a particular society, held together by shared custom and distributed duties.

From this view that obtained among opponents of the French Revolution there arose a concept of socially situated liberty, which stands in vivid contrast to the Libertarian idea of unfettered individual liberty. Libertarians are seen from the Right as promoting a leftist position, which presupposes the idea of universal equality and even universal citizenship. It is therefore no surprise that Russell Kirk, Eric von Kuehnelt-Leddihn, Robert Nisbet, and other twentieth-century conservative thinkers eschewed Libertarians. The doctrinaires they scorned rejected the conservative notion of the social bond and were proclaiming principles that issued from the French Revolution. Libertarianism is here being defined as a body of dogma. Conservatives would have no quarrel with the often salutary results that may arise from Libertarian-minded citizens rallying against administrative tyranny.

Having clarified what a conservative or rightist would not believe, it may now be time to identify the real article. In the preface to his anthology of essays *Liberalism, Ancient and Modern*, Leo Strauss sets out to define the essentialist conservative worldview circa 1960.[1] Its exponents "regard the universal and homogeneous state as either undesirable though possible, or as both undesirable and impossible."[2] They do not like international bodies, which they identify with the Left, and "look with greater sympathy than liberals on the particular or particularist and the heterogeneous."[3] This honest, accurate definition seems all the more remarkable given the fact that Strauss's disciples have often worked to make American conservatism synonymous with a crusade to spread what they extol as universal democratic values.

Strauss's thumbnail characterization of "conservatives" would certainly apply to the genuine Right, yet his definition should be expanded for the sake of completeness. The Right affirms inherited hierarchy, favors the particularistic while being suspicious of what claims to be the universal, aims at preserving social traditions where possible, and opposes the Left by every means at its disposal. The Left takes the opposite positions on the first three points out of a sense of fairness, a passionate commitment to the advancement of equality, and a conception of human beings that stresses sameness or interchangeability. Whereas the Right believes in what Aristotle defined as the order of the household—in which elaborately defined distinctions are deemed "natural"—the Left recoils from nonegalitarian arrangements. Its advocates are delighted to have state managers and judges abolish the vestiges of inherited hierarchy.

The view that the Left considers us to be interchangeable individuals, who can be made to behave according to a socializing plan, may overstate the case. Yet something like this idea informs the leftist worldview. All good societies from this perspective are what Michael Oakeshott called "enterprise associations": frameworks of human interaction in which all members are encouraged or forced to think and act alike. The Left seeks to impose such an order, and the more thoroughly it engages this work, the better off, it is hoped, all of us will be. This is because the Left is committed to removing, as far as humanly possible, social, racial, and gender inequalities. Furthermore, the more control it accumulates, the easier it is for the Left to reconstruct or recode those who resist its planning. German social theorist Arnold Gehlen was struck by how younger Germans in the 1960s exhibited what he called "hypermorality."[4] Contrary to the opinion that such youth, who frequently turned into militant antifascists, suffered from a lack of values, Gehlen noticed their hysterical moral zeal spilling over into their entire lives.[5] This was partly due to a prolonged reaction to the Nazis, who were depicted by German educational institutions as conservatives. But Gehlen also linked the culture of moral indignation in his homeland to being cut off from any traditional communal association. In Germany, this process started with the Nazi revolution, was accelerated by a lost war, and then continued through a postwar occupation, which weakened even further any traditional German national identity.

Lest there be any confusion on this point, it seems necessary that we distinguish here between highest principles and instrumental goods on both sides of the ideological spectrum. Various values or value-references punctuate the Left's discourse—depending on time and circumstance—such as scientific truth, secularism, or freedom. While leftists may revere all these ideals, they assume their importance in relation to the *summum bonum* of universal equality. "Science" is to be advanced insofar as it discredits Christianity, which includes a dark side that sanctions gender distinctions and privileges heterosexual marriage. Science may also be pursued as a learning or discovery activity, providing it does not operate to the detriment of the Left's highest good.

In the nineteenth century the Left opposed organized religion[6] because it was allied to the aristocracy or to what it saw as an oppressive capitalist class, as defined by Marx.[7] Religion, more specifically Christianity, was thought to be hindering social change that intellectuals were working to achieve. The Left also exalts freedom, but—as Linda Raeder[8] and Maurice Cowling[9] demonstrate in biographies of John Stuart Mill—reformers who once embraced "liberty" and science espoused them as a means toward a higher end. In Mill's case—and here he may not have been unusual among Victorian reformers—science and liberty were esteemed as tools for emancipating those who were still not freed from the shackles of "superstitions." Mill, as Raeder explains, looked forward to a world of scientifically engineered progress, in which women would be "emancipated from bondage."[10] In this age of humanity, liberated from the past, everyone would presumably think like feminists and social democratic reformers.[11]

Science, however, remains instrumental for the Left and is meant to serve the march toward equality. If, for example, someone cited research evidence substantiating socially significant genetic differences between genders or ethnic groups, that scientist and/or author would likely encounter considerable difficulty in academic life or as a government consultant. In the leftist universe biological science may be called on, but only as long as it does not conflict with the proper ideological ends, which is promoting approved egalitarian teachings. In the same way, the theory of evolution is fine for the Left if the information being gathered can be directed against religionists or social reactionaries.

The Darwinian hypothesis about nature hits a snag, however, as soon as someone brings up the social significance of deeply rooted gender differences that may have been necessary for the perpetuation of human and animal life. There may be no reason here to belabor the obvious, which is the selective character that evolutionary theory has assumed for the Left. The philosopher of science David Stove has addressed this topic in his instructive work *Darwinian Fairytales*, in which he deals with the mythic as opposed to scientific aspects that evolutionary theory has assumed for intellectuals and journalists.[12] Stove's book highlights evolutionary theory's continuing value as a polemical tool rather than scientific hypothesis.[13]

The Right has sanctified its own version of an instrumental good. Having sometimes defined itself as the political expression of the doctrine of original sin, the Right has invested heavily in certain aspects of Christianity, just as the Left has made an equal investment in its selective conception of science. Although there is no evidence that many of the great conservative theorists of the eighteenth and nineteenth centuries, starting with Burke, were orthodox Christians, their political worldviews would have been unthinkable without some kind of Christian theological foundation.

The concept of hierarchy that conservatives defended went back to the Catholic Middle Ages, in which feudal relations were freighted with sacral significance. Temporal forms of command corresponded to the order of the church that was ultimately based on the structure of Roman authority. The notion of human fallenness was invoked in an empirical as well as theological fashion to drive home the point that human beings lack the capacity or right to reinvent themselves and their social contexts. Indeed, such experiments were sinful or hubristic and likely to result in disaster. Traditional conservatives were fond of quoting Saint Paul's

Epistle to the Romans, which affirmed that all authority is from God.[14] It is not for naught that God delivered the sword into the hand of the magistrate.[15] Needless to say, the "arche" or authority here invoked by conservatives was one that was handed down from one generation to the next.

The Left has also benefited from being rooted in a Christian heritage. Friedrich Nietzsche famously scorned Christian religion as the source of the "slave morality" that begat feminism and egalitarian democracy. While the Right saw in Christianity a justification for settled authorities, the Left drew from it the vision of a world in which "the first would be last" and "the meek would inherit the Earth." Such ideas of "social justice" could be derived from the Hebrew prophets, the Gospels, and the sharing of worldly possessions in the primitive church. Unlike the Right, however, the Left worked studiously to hide its debt to the Western religious tradition, claiming that its teachings were scientifically grounded or came from immaculately secular sources. This denial of paternity has gone so far that Marxists and cultural Marxists have tried to root out any explicitly Christian influences in their societies. Rarely does one find a more dramatic illustration of the Oedipal complex. Christopher Dawson and Mircea Eliade have both observed that the modern Left would be unthinkable without its distinctly Christian, even more than Judaic, matrix.[16]

Right and Left have historical identities and essentialist definitions, and it may be necessary to go into each one's characteristics in order to make sense of our reference points. It is usually brought up in a discussion of this type that the distinction between Right and Left was formalized during the French Revolution, in accordance with where political factions were seated in the French National Assembly. Those who favored further revolutionary change swelled the left side of the amphitheater; those who felt the ferment had raged too long and had to be quieted sat on the right side. In the (classically) liberal July Monarchy of King Louis Philippe I—set up in 1830 and overthrown to make way for the French Second Republic in 1848—there were two major parliamentary factions: a party of resistance and a party of movement. This distinction encapsulates what may be seen, in an oversimplified fashion, as the basic difference between Right and Left: one is the party of standing pat or making only necessary changes, while the other party is intent on pushing change further.

But there was a more ideologically based division that entered European politics, and it was reflected in what parties in England, Germany, France, and other European countries stood for during the course of the nineteenth century. These divisions coincided with recognizable classes and were driven by differing visions of the social good. The divisions created separated on the right the parties of the aristocracy, peasantry, and established churches from, in the middle, the self-styled liberal parties of the ascending bourgeoisie and from, on the left, the socialist and social-democratic parties of the urban working class. As the German Hungarian sociologist Karl Mannheim demonstrates in *Ideology and Utopia*[17] and *Das Konservative Denken*,[18] the political-social forces that became significant in the nineteenth century left behind distinctive worldviews. These views were ideal constructions but drew strength from being tied to partisan positions, and those for whom they were devised recognized in them anchors for their personal and social identities.

The traditional Right stood for an agrarian way of life that reflected a traditional authority structure that was typically allied to the Catholic Church or to Protestant state churches and entrenched monarchies. This conservative Right turned to the past for what the southern agrarian Richard Weaver called its "vision of order." But it also offered assistance to the urban working class, which was then becoming a "social problem."[19] The conservative Right felt no reservations about seeking an alliance with those at the bottom of the social ladder. It went about this task at least partly in reaction to the upper-middle-class leaders of commerce and industry, who were then replacing the aristocracy as a dominant political force.

Not surprisingly, the data that Karl Marx cited in *Capital* to prove the growing impoverishment of English workers came from accounts that had been collected and distributed by the Tories.[20] A party of landowners, Anglican clergy, and Oxford dons, the Tories dwelled on, and sometimes even exaggerated, the suffering of those who were subject to their political foes in the Liberal Party. Tories called on the state to impose limits on the working hours of factory laborers and to put child labor on the road to extinction. But as the career of Benjamin Disraeli proves, advocating tariff protection for English grain and the English squirearchy could not hurt a Tory political career in the mid-nineteenth century. Although Disraeli styled himself a "Tory democrat" and worked to forge an alliance between the English Right and the English working class, he was far from consistent in his support of the lower orders. He rose to political prominence in the 1840s as an opponent of the repeal of the Corn Laws, the effect of which kept the price of bread higher for the urban poor than would have been the case if foreign grain had been available at lower prices.

All political-ideological groupings in the nineteenth century had accompanying social foundations. Liberalism was the "idea of the bourgeoisie," just as socialism attracted the working class and sympathetic intellectuals. Conservatism originated in modern European history as an aristocratic reaction to the French Revolution, while the Left defined itself initially as a defender of this revolutionary process—together with the rationalist thinking that supposedly fueled the engine of progress. The sides that were taken were both social and ideological, and the two characteristics traveled together. In an earlier age it would have been difficult to think of distinctive worldviews apart from the concrete interests of the groups to which they were attached. Ideologies, however, eventually assumed a life of their own. Such theorists as Edmund Burke, Joseph de Maistre, Adam Müller, Benjamin Constant, John Stuart Mill, and Karl Marx erected conceptual foundations for political fronts, which finally assumed an existence that was independent of the social situations that gave birth to them.

A direction in which the Right and the Left have been moving for several generations, and perhaps most vigorously in the last fifty years, has been the uncoupling of worldviews and value from their earlier social grounding. Ideas that were once attached to classes and ways of life have been cut loose from their moorings and have taken on changing forms within a succession of movements. Equally noteworthy is that those who invoke what are already untethered worldviews are often nostalgic for reference points that have ceased to exist. Such Americans of conservative inclinations as Russell Kirk, Robert Nisbet, Richard Weaver, and Melvin E. Bradford all held up model conservative societies in which their preferred ways of life were practiced. They tried to relate their idealized order to what they saw as still existing in some form, but such searches for a continuing past may be becoming fruitless when a ubiquitous form of the Left is coming to dominate our lives.

There is an additional conceptual problem that warrants consideration here: the United States was founded in the eighteenth century as a liberal republic and does not have what Burke called an "ancient constitution" of a kind that could once be found in Europe. The social world that gave birth to classical conservatism was more ancient and more medieval than the government that America's founders set up for posterity. Although one could locate in this American past landed aristocracy or clusters of reactionary patricians, it may be idle to push this excavating venture too far. Earlier Americans who owned slaves or indentured servants or who expressed grim Calvinist theology did not prefigure the long-term direction of American history. And they would not be attractive to our society, which more than earlier ones values equality and socioeconomic mobility. For good reason most excavators of America's classical conservative pedigree have been men of letters. They have refurbished a moral-aesthetic vision rather than offered detailed histories of America as a classical conservative country.

The Left has faced a problem similar to that of the Right, since its worldview became uncoupled from its nineteenth- and early twentieth-century social framework. The Left has ceased to be a movement of the urban working class, fighting for higher wages or nationalization of productive forces. In the last quarter of the twentieth century the European Left was occupied by most of the same forces that have occupied it in the United States: lifestyle radicals, cinematic celebrities, public sector employees, ethnic minorities, feminists, and academics. Cultural radicals have replaced real Marxists. The protests of aggrieved feminists and the gay community have become far more important for the Left than the complaints of unemployed factory workers.

Communists in power persecuted religious institutions, and sometimes harshly. They did so because they thought independent churches threatened Communist political power and because Communism, like American liberalism, turned atheism or secularism into a state religion. But the social values inculcated by the Communist leadership and the moral attitudes it worked to propagate among its subjects had a recognizably bourgeois character. Despite early experimentation in free love, the Soviet Union eventually turned to enforcing a strict social ethic. Annie Kriegel—in what has become the authoritative history of the French Communist Party—pointed to the residual Catholic influence in how the party cadre viewed women and marriage well into the 1960s.

If the traditional French Communist Party were still around, its members would likely have marched in those demonstrations against the legalization of same-sex marriage that took place in Paris in May 2013. Recently the onetime Marxist Israel Shamir, who lives in Paris, denounced in his newsletter the decadent bourgeois supporters of gay rights.[21] At the time I proclaimed to a friend half-jokingly that this is a Marxist I could happily endure. Shamir praises Lenin for treating "women's issues" dismissively and commends the Russian Communists who already in the 1980s were "interacting" with the Orthodox Church "to stop the attempt to enforce the gay agenda."[22] Next to our "conservative Republican" journalists who have advocated same-sex marriage, Shamir and Lenin held almost medieval views about the nature of the family.

Despite its changing forms, unlike the Right, the Left has remained politically and culturally potent, and a recognizable variant of its worldview is flourishing throughout the onetime Christian West. Part of the Left's strength can be measured by how thoroughly its ideas have seeped into what is now considered the Right. One encounters the Left's worldview even in those who claim to be resisting its advances. In a modern world of contending wills, moreover, the Left has fought without giving quarter, unlike a "conservative" establishment, which is certainly an establishment but not necessarily of the Right. A warning that issues from establishment "conservatives" is that we should do nothing risky to offend the Left, for example, by ignoring the Left's accelerating standards of political correctness, because "we conservatives" face hostile media. This may be at least partly a case of putting the cart before the horse. The Left holds its present advantage partly because it has been able to impose its vision in the face of a timorous, vacillating opposition. Willmoore Kendall's observation that "the Right never retrieves its wounded" may be truer now than it was fifty years ago; that is, before the would-be Right became predictable in running away from its wounded comrades, unlike the more principled Left, which shields its own.

The Left, however, holds the high ground for reasons other than a caving opposition. Universalism, equality, human rights, and managed democracy will likely remain the order of the day in first-world countries. Freedom will be allowed to survive to whatever extent it can be made compatible with equality. Christian institutions will be tolerated to whatever extent they teach the required values and instill obedience to a leftist state. This will happen—at least partly—because the modern state has expanded its power base at the expense of intermediate institutions, including churches and communities. But this success also stems from the now triumphant leftist vision, which encompasses every aspect of human life. The Left strives to expand its power not primarily because those who lead it hunger for government favors. Although there are careerists among the present generation of leftists, in the 1960s many on the Left risked their lives and fortunes working to revolutionize America. By contrast, Republicans in the 1980s held their "Reagan Revolution" by lining up as office seekers in the Beltway. Unfortunately leftists, who often show a boldness that one can admire, bring with them principles that are both toxic and totalitarian. Further, they no longer have to worry about being stopped, if present trends continue to unfold.

The Right, that is, the authentic one, is far more splintered than the Left for a number of reasons. It controls few if any institutions in Western countries and, even worse for its future, possesses no identity that its current representatives would all recognize as their own. The Right is not only untethered but also burdened by the infighting of its constituent groups. Mainstream "conservatives" in the meantime have become an integral part of the public discussions in the national media. These designated "conservatives" enjoy journalistic acceptance as the respectable opposition and provide televised sound bites and political best sellers in an age of mass communication.

The success of this artificial Right stems at least partly from the backing of moneyed interests, whether in the form of corporate donors or leaders of the Republican Party. Those who receive this largess are now the sole recognized occupants of the visible opposition, and they have been sedulous in keeping out of their political conversation unseemly reactionaries. This media-approved Right has nothing to fear from what lies outside the mainstream. The nonaligned or classical Right, call it what one will, cannot even agree on what defines its "Rightness." Its competing representatives are all holding tight to fragments of what was once a pristine conservative worldview. But that may be where the common ground ends. The traditionalists are beset with quarrels about what exactly the "true teachings" are.

All claimants are holding on to at least some fragment of the old doctrines that they seek to represent. They each assert a pedigree of descent from some generative conservative worldview, and their ranks now include cultural traditionalists, right-wing anarchists, imitators of the European revolutionary right, exponents of human biological diversity, and Christian theocrats. While all these groups can claim to hold some part of the original conservative worldview, not all of them cherish the same fragments. Also, not all of them are pining for the same lost world. Some insist that the West has been going to the dogs since the Reformation, and that we should be trying to return to something at least faintly resembling a medieval Catholic society. Meanwhile, others lament the disintegration of the Protestant bourgeois order that once dominated Northern European societies and the influence of which spilled over into the United States. Still others on the essentialist Right identify their vision of order with some ideal communal life that now belongs to the past. All these visions entail narratives centered on a fall from grace. Those who articulate them point to various fateful dates when everything is thought to have gone off the skids. Nonetheless, the claimants to this conservative legacy differ about whether this slide can be reversed and about the extent to which the past can be reclaimed.

We are not speaking here about the Right as it emerged from its original context, namely, as the worldview that accompanied the birth of European conservatism. Rather, we are noting the end of a process, one in which a particular worldview has been separated from its original home and absorbed piecemeal into other movements. This fragmented response to a broken past has characterized a Right that has survived the vanishing of the world of classical conservatism.

A heavily frequented website in the United States, under the care of the pseudonymous Mencius Moldbug, addresses "neoreactionaries."[23] Moldbug and his followers profess principles that are recognizable as the essential beliefs of classical conservatism, starting with the defense of hierarchy, inherited cultural particularities, and traditional gender roles. But the affirmation of these principles does not lead those who profess them into political engagement. Moldbug and his group revel in aesthetic stances, characterized by the invocation of reactionary artistic figures and the posting of intricate theoretical discourses. We may infer from their acts of avoidance that reactionary politics are only seen as sustainable as a kind of *esoterica*: a safe zone outside of the political world controlled by an all-pervasive Left. The continued existence of reactionary mind-sets depends, or so it is believed, on keeping their bearers insulated from a situation that the Right cannot hope to master. This may be a correct assessment at the present time.

Although the factions of the fractured Right continue to shun each other like rival Anabaptist or Hasidic sects, they are united by three characteristics. All reveal some conceptual link to an original worldview. When they defend inherited authority they appeal to endangered or broken traditions as the source of community and rooted identities. Finally, all groups of the genuine Right share an instinctive dislike for the Left's highest value—equality—and each is reacting to the lack of restraint with which the Left implements that value. Unfortunately for their survival, the marginalized groups on the Right cannot agree on a strategy that would allow them to counteract the Left's conception of social progress.

The Left has a vision, but the Right has only the fragments of one. The Left believes fervently in the triumph of a "Religion of Humanity," based on a universal state in which the human condition can be standardized and homogenized through sensitive management. The Right by contrast has no picture of a happy future. It differs from those conventional Republicans who wish to go back to the halcyon days of President George W. Bush or perhaps to the glory days of the Reagan administration. The true or essentialist Right simply wants to stop what is generally viewed as the train of progress and, if possible, reverse its direction. Although there were once unifying visions of order among classical conservatives, these orientation points have disappeared and been replaced by pure desperation.

This continuing loss of ground is disheartening for those who are struggling against a hostile age, and comparable developments have overtaken the independent Right—or those groups that comprise one—in Western European countries. In Germany at the time of national reunification in the early 1990s, the national Right vibrated with excitement over the prospect of a unified country. Germans would at last be able to put off their sackcloth and ashes and would no longer have to view themselves as a pariah nation. Their reference point as a people would no longer be their humiliating defeat in 1945, nor would they would have to talk in a ritualized fashion any longer about the "burden" of their entire history, as a prelude to Auschwitz. Once again, Germans could be a proud nation, as they were at the time of their unification in 1871.

Never did national conservatives anywhere miscalculate so badly. Former Communist functionaries and agents of the Communist secret police streamed into government positions in the Federal Republic, exchanging their pro-Soviet Communist identities for cultural Marxist ones. A party of the Left became a major force in German politics, and it was made up of hastily disguised Communists like the leader of the Party of Democratic Socialists, Gregor Gysi. Indeed, even the current chancellor of Germany, Angela Merkel, turns out to have been an obliging Communist, almost up until the moment when the Berlin Wall fell.[24]

Hoping to protect themselves against the anxieties voiced by Western journalists and politicians about a resurgent German nationalism, German chancellors from Helmut Kohl down to Angela Merkel have put funds and energy into a government-organized "crusade against the Right." This enterprise has turned out to be little more than a witch hunt against the opposition directed by embattled Leftists—including longtime Communists—but no significant outcry against this intimidation has been raised. Furthermore, no politician hoping to make a career in Germany would express patriotic sentiments too loudly or suggest that he or she is not eagerly awaiting Germany's further absorption into the European Union (EU). German elites have been pushing their country dramatically toward the Left ever since reunification.

This piece of contemporary history holds a valuable lesson: what may start out as the project of an unauthorized Right will inevitably fail in the absence of the necessary resources. Respectability, or even sustained visibility, is by no means guaranteed, even if one manages to unite like-minded people who can agree on a shared program. Those who are made to look like dangerous or troublesome outsiders need more to effect a breakthrough. Political and media elites in some Western societies are so impervious to any genuine Right that its representatives have absolutely no chance of becoming part of the authorized political discussion. In such societies, "Right" and "Left" will continue to function as labels for distinguishing rival claimants for political patronage, but will have no other real significance.

For those who don't want such a Right to be noticed, which includes the conservative establishment in the United States, this ban of excommunication is entirely welcome. The media establishment has survived and prospered without an essentialist Right by favoring what may be called "litmus test conservatism." In this opportunistic jockeying for position, a particular stand becomes associated with the Right or the Left depending on which national party and its affiliated media decide to defend it. These positions have no intrinsic connection to one-time established worldviews, but assume ideological meaning situationally; that is, by virtue of which party or media agents uphold these particular stands.

For example, a liberal internationalist foreign policy stressing American export of "human rights" was a signature Left-Center position in the United States for generations. Today it is a "conservative" one because the Republican Party, its neoconservative funders, and the party's attachment to the military-industrial complex favor a position that conservative Republicans would have emphatically rejected seventy years ago. In interwar Europe ecology was a central theme of the Right; in the United States today it has been turned into an identifying mark of the Left. The demonstrative support for the Zionist cause and for what is summed up as "Israeli security" issuing from Republican news sources and commentators has no real connection to the Right or the Left; however, since the GOP is now eager to pull away Jewish voters and donors from the Democrats, a fervent enthusiasm for Israel as "America's closest ally" has become integral to what advertises itself as the Right. It is not even the case that being for the military has a clear ideological connection to the historic American Right. Traditionally, those on that side of the spectrum have been critical of military "crusades for democracy" and complained about the costs of maintaining large standing armies.

A flourishing classical conservatism does not exist in the United States, where what is left of any traditional Right may already be on oxygen support. Those who represent this eroded Right would be even less visible were it not for self-styled "antifascists" and "antiracists" who warn us against "right-wing extremism."[25] Although this intellectual Right, or what remains of one, works hard to look "relevant," it can't kick old habits, such as recycling rhetorical scraps from certain authoritative authors. Devotees of this Right are particularly fond of ceaselessly quoting Russell Kirk and the southern agrarians. This practice brings to mind what Nietzsche once mocked as "antiquarian history," a rote repetition of what resonated in the past but no longer has appeal.

The most incisive criticism of this antiquarian Right has come from the social theorist Samuel T. Francis in his anthology *Beautiful Losers*.[26] Never has a more devastating attack been launched from the independent Right against the failure of American conservatism.[27] According to Francis's work, "archaic conservatives" have been marginalized by late modernity, and the fault lies at least partly in the refusal of the withered Right to undertake radical adaptation in a postconservative age. A Right that hopes to survive, according to Francis, must become populist as well as reactionary and seize on divisive issues that it can use to isolate the Left. These censures that emanate from a form of the revolutionary Right recall Nietzsche's warning in *Thoughts Out of Season* about the antiquarian mind-set: "As far as history serves life, we should wish to serve it. But there is a form of history that some feel driven to pursue that causes life to atrophy and deteriorate."[28]

Nietzsche's broadsides against a life-atrophying *passéisme* are recycled in Martin Heidegger's *Time and Being* "as a false sense of history that no longer has a connection to a life project pointing toward the future. Someone who surrenders to this defective time dimension loses his determination to carry forth his project or to pursue any fate issuing out of the past."[29] No less than Nietzsche, Heidegger is underscoring the stupefying obsession with a particular past that leads to the cessation of vital energy. We know that for counterrevolutionaries of the nineteenth century, "history" and tradition were interconnected; both were thought to be present in the continuing organic existence of peoples and classes.[30]

Throughout my career I have earned the reputation of being a spoilsport when speaking about positions I respect but that seem unlikely to gain ground in unreceptive times. In my defense, there is value in assessing one's obstacles before beginning a steep climb. In this chapter attention has been directed to the obstacle course that confronts any genuine Right that seeks to gain influence. My approach has been that of a generally sympathetic observer but not a prospective participant. At this late point in my life, I am hardly fit for the rigorous journey that I have tried to outline for others.

4

The Problem of Historical Connections

Bismarck and the German Empire

In a heavily researched biography of Otto von Bismarck (1815–1898), the German statesman and architect of the German Second Empire, historian Jonathan Steinberg observes that his subject was an "irresistible political figure and a disastrous one."[1] According to Steinberg, "Bismarck's legacy passed through [World War I German general and later president] Hindenburg to the last genius statesman that Germany produced, Adolf Hitler, and the legacy was thus linear and direct between Bismarck and Hitler."[2]

The question that might be asked, but rarely is when the subject is modern Germany, is how "linear and direct" the connection was between Bismarck, who dominated politically the first twenty years of the German Empire, and the later Nazi regime. Together with other participants in the state-building process, Bismarck helped create a constitutional monarchy for the newly established Germany. This German empire was given less of a modern constitutional government than the one that existed in England, but it was nonetheless a regime that provided for religious and academic freedom. The imperial constitution also authorized a popular assembly elected on the basis of universal manhood suffrage, and the assembly that came out of this state building, the *Reichstag,* was given power over the purse.

Steinberg leaves the impression that Bismarck's insincere or inadequate devotion to nineteenth-century liberalism and his reliance on military power led ineluctably to Hitler's savage tyranny.[3] Bismarck, according to Steinberg, bullied his political opponents and never really accepted the principle of parliamentary supremacy. The German chancellor also made no secret of the fact that he had welded together a single German nation through wars, even if other countries, especially the French Second Empire under Emperor Napoleon III, had contributed to this course of events. Although his real métier was desk work, the chancellor loved to prance around in military uniforms. Germany's greatest social scientist, Max Weber, lamented the direction that he saw the imperial regime taking, and he criticized Bismarck's highly personal style of rule for having "deprived Germans of a political education."[4] Presumably the chancellor should have stepped aside and allowed the parties in the *Reichstag* to determine the future of the German imperial state.

Steinberg also suggests that before the appearance of his biography, historians were writing indulgently about his subject. It took his arduous work of scholarship to make us aware of Bismarck's dangerous impact on German history. But this assertion may be difficult to square with the fact that critical biographies of Bismarck now abound.[5] As a college student I was assigned two such works, one by Otto Pflanze[6] and another by A. J. P. Taylor,[7] neither of which could be accused of celebrating Bismarck's stewardship of Prussia and later Germany. Both works examined Bismarck's career in light of the Nazi catastrophe.

A Bismarck biography published by Christian Graf von Krockow in 1997 and still widely quoted in Germany dwells on the failure of Germany's unifier to push his country in the direction of a modern democracy.[8] Graf von Krockow is fond of the German term *Verhängnis*, meaning an unpleasant fate, which is used to describe Bismarck's legacy. Another recent work on the German Iron Chancellor, by Christoph Nonn, which came out, not coincidentally, on the two-hundredth anniversary of his birth, highlights Bismarck's disparaging references to Jews.[9] These gibes are thought to demonstrate Bismarck's link to the racial policies of the Nazi regime. But the *Frankfurter Allgemeine Zeitung* points out that Nonn's "prelude to Auschwitz" was considerably less ominous than he intimates.[10] Bismarck's comments about Jewish parvenus were then widely heard among social elites throughout the Western world. Despite making remarks that would raise eyebrows today, Bismarck had close working and social relationships with German Jews.

A more balanced biography of the Iron Chancellor in his home country only appeared a few months ago. This one, by distinguished diplomatic historian Hans-Christof Kraus, focuses on Bismarck's achievements as well as failures and questions the attempt to treat his subject as Hitler's forerunner.[11] Kraus's book is particularly thorough in explaining how after German unification Bismarck erected an alliance system in which the German Empire was made the cornerstone.[12] Bismarck's system was created not to aid German expansion but for the defensive purpose of preventing war between Germany and its neighbors. Kraus points out that Bismarck viewed Germany after 1871 as a "saturated power." He tried to mediate disputes between other countries, albeit also occasionally taking advantage of these altercations when it served his country's interests.[13]

The chancellor was also not categorically opposed to strengthening the parliamentary side of the monarchy that ruled Germany after 1871. Yet he also believed, according to Kraus, that since a seemingly united Germany was still a collection of principalities and free cities, a chancellor's government was suitable for the German Empire for the time being.[14] Kraus does not however deny that Bismarck favored a German constitution that rendered him essential to its functioning.[15] This overshadowing role held by the chancellor became a liability once Bismarck was dismissed by the young Kaiser Wilhelm II in 1890 and his position taken by less competent, more impulsive successors.

Kraus expands on the contingency plans that Bismarck constructed during the period of German unification.[16] None of the wars that Prussia fought was viewed as necessary from the beginning, and Bismarck always operated with alternative possibilities, providing that certain desirable situations could be brought about. Until the final break with Austria in 1866, the Prussian minister president and future German chancellor hoped to achieve a shared domination with the other major German power over Germany. Only when it became obvious that Austria would block any arrangement aiming at shared rule—and by force if necessary—did Bismarck consent to a military solution. Moreover, even after war broke out Bismarck sought a lenient peace, provided it would leave Prussia with a free hand in Germany. The Prussian chancellor may even have seen during the war a future ally in a temporary foe.

Whereas Bismarck exploited the heated quarrel unleashed by French foreign minister Antoine Agenor, Duc de Gramont, when a Catholic cousin of the Prussian king sought the vacant Spanish throne in July 1870, he did not plan from the beginning to fight a war against France. Bismarck watched as the Duc de Gramont and his superior, Emperor Napoleon III, humiliated King Wilhelm I over the candidacy to the Spanish throne. He then produced for the press a vivid description of the hectoring of the king by the French ambassador, knowing how recklessly France's upstart emperor would act. He then sat back until the French declared war. But Bismarck originally hoped, says Kraus, to grab the Spanish throne for a relative of the Prussian king, who would be amenable to Prussian influence.[17] Although Bismarck took the war that came, bloodshed had not been his preferred option.

World War I and German War Guilt

The treatment of Bismarck, as illustrated by Steinberg's work,[18] points to a problem that I myself encountered as a young man writing about German history. The difficulty of my task was already evident when I was doing graduate work at Yale in the mid-1960s. No matter what aspect of German history was under consideration, we were expected to uncover a path leading to the Third Reich. All German history was considered "tragedy" or—as underlined in A. J. P. Taylor's *The Course of German History*[19] and William M. McGovern's *From Luther to Hitler: The History of Fascist-Nazi Political Philosophy*[20]—the prelude to a disaster inflicted on the world by an unusually nasty people who had been perpetually taken in by horrible leaders and diabolical intellectuals. From Bismarck to Hitler, a world historical catastrophe was always just around the corner between the Rhine and the Elbe. We were also urged to assume that the Germans and Austrians were exclusively responsible for the Great War.

According to Fritz Fischer, who pioneered studies stressing Germany's pre-meditated plan to unleash a European-wide war on the way to becoming a world power, "Hitler was no operational accident."[21] From Fischer's perspective, all of German history since Bismarck's work of unification had been preparation for the Nazi catastrophe.[22] As a graduate student I was treated to the less than friendly admonition that believing any other account of the outbreak of World War I was to belittle the German problem.[23] Such a move would send a dangerous message—or so the German philosopher Jürgen Habermas has underlined for more than forty years—that the Germans were not required to abjure their national identity as a precondition for world peace. According to Habermas, nothing less than a repudi-ation of the German past would cleanse his country of its inherited evil ways and protect surrounding countries against further eruptions of Teutonic violence.[24]

In my periodic discussions with teachers and later, colleagues, it seemed that veracity mattered less than moralizing. Stress was placed on the therapeu-tic effect of certain narratives, although this didactic approach to history raised more questions for me than it solved. I then inconveniently stumbled on works that contradicted the imposed dogmas. Among Anglophone writers, the one who pointed me most directly toward the revisionist path was the interwar his-torian Harry Elmer Barnes (*The Genesis of the World War*,[25] *In Quest of Truth and Justice: Debunking the War Guilt Myth*,[26] *Perpetual War for Perpetual Peace: A Critical Examination of the Foreign Policy of Franklin Delano Roosevelt and Its Aftermath*[27]). From reading Barnes and similarly oriented scholars, I concluded that my teachers had exaggerated the links between the Central Powers and Nazi Germany.[28] They also overemphasized the belligerence of the German govern-ment before World War I while understating and even ignoring the aggressive designs of Germany's and Austria's neighbors.

Barnes's summary explanation for the outbreak of the Great War comes closest to my present view on the subject:

> The basic causes of the war were general ones such as nationalism, imperialism, militarism, for which no single country can be held either uniquely or primarily responsible. They were fanned and intensified by both future belligerent sides and

sprang from German militarism, French revenge aspirations, British navalism and imperialism, the century-old Russian ambition to get control of Constantinople and the Straits. Whatever the case earlier, Germany was far less prepared for war in a military sense in 1914 than Russia and France. General Buat [a French commander] admits that in 1914 the French active army was 910,000 to 870,000 for Germany with nearly twice the population of France; and Repington, the English military critic, admits that the German army in regard to equipment, military manoeuvres, and leadership was inferior to the French. This was especially true in the artillery branch. The active Russian army [at the time] numbered 1,284,000.[29]

Although Barnes made regrettable statements after World War II that downplayed Nazi atrocities, these indiscretions do not detract from his understanding of World War I. All too often, his positions taken at different times about different events are dishonestly run together in a way that makes Barnes's defensible views on World War I appear to be a prelude to his later depreciation of Nazi crimes.[30]

A solid research historian, Sean McMeekin, has demonstrated exhaustively, on the basis of Russian and Turkish documents, that the tsarist government before World War I was strongly committed to weakening Germany, Austria, and the Ottoman Empire. According to McMeekin, Russian foreign ministers from the late nineteenth century on were trying to wrest from Germany's Ottoman client the Straits and Constantinople. The Russian government also incited the Serbs and other client powers against the Turks in pursuit of its expansionist ends.[31] Russian leaders did not rule out a war with Germany and Austria, providing such an undertaking helped them gain control over the Dardanelles. The more than a million Russian troops that appeared on the Austro-German border just before the outbreak of war were not placed there for decoration. The Russians were preparing for a conflict with the Central Powers, and with special vigor after French president Raymond Poincaré promised military assistance from his country during a visit to St. Petersburg during the third week of July.

The respected Cambridge historian Richard J. Evans has pointed out that McMeekin may exaggerate the determination with which the tsarist government pursued the conquest of the Dardanelles as a paramount territorial objective.[32] Yet the Russians, as McMeekin shows, were trying to take territories from the Ottoman Empire that would aid Russian naval expansion, particularly around the Black Sea. This led the tsarist government into stirring up anti-Austrian and anti-Turkish sentiments in the Balkans, a dangerous indiscretion that the French and British, who regarded Russia as an ally against Germany, did nothing to prevent.

Although McMeekin's work may overstate the Russian government's determination to seize the Dardanelles, his overall interpretation of the Russian role in precipitating war in 1914, and particularly the actions of Russian foreign minister

Sergei Sazonov, widens the focus of responsibility. Unlike those who stress almost exclusively German and Austrian responsibility, McMeekin has read in the original languages the relevant archival documents that led to his conclusions. He also takes on the Fischer thesis with statements like the following:

> Convincing as it is in its own terms, even a watered-down version of the Fischer thesis set against what we now know about Russia's early mobilization and French collusion in helping Sazonov dupe the British, can stand no more. There were at least as many men in St. Petersburg who wanted war in 1914 as there were in Berlin—and the men in Petersburg mobilized first.[33]

Further, Sazonov and his confreres, including Russian army commander V. I. Sukhomlinov,

> chose consciously to mobilize Russia's colossal armies in full knowledge that they were risking war with Germany by doing so, while Sazonov deliberately concealed all this from London. We should also spare a critical thought for Ambassador Paléologue and French liaison General Languiche who each with or without formal authorization from Poincaré and Viviani, gave France's imprimatur for Russia's secret mobilization against Germany.[34]

Such counterevidence does not exonerate the Central Powers from obvious blunders that they committed before and during August 1914. The gravest German mistake may have occurred decades before the Great War: the unfortunate acquiescence of Europe's premier statesman, Bismarck, in a then-popular demand in his country, which was seconded by the military, that Prussia take from a defeated France two of its valued provinces, Alsace and Lorraine. In retrospect, it is difficult to see how this forced cession would not have led to another war, just as the Carthaginian peace imposed on the fledging German Weimar Republic at Versailles in 1919 stoked German desire for revenge.

Noting shared responsibility for the war does not require us to defend the Schlieffen Plan—as modified by the chief of the German General Staff, Helmuth von Moltke—in 1914.[35] Moltke's success in getting the German government to move its armies through a neutral country, Belgium, in order to carry out a flanking motion around the bulk of the French forces, led to predictable disaster. Indeed it may have doomed the German side during the first week of the struggle.[36] This strategy required the occupation of an intensely hostile Belgian population, a reaction that might have been expected since the Germans were obliged to move through a fervently Francophile region of Belgium.[37] Moltke's military venture also provided the English war party with an excuse to declare war on the

Central Powers. The English Conservative Party in 1914 expressed its resolution to stand by France even if the German armies never crossed into Belgium. Kaiser Wilhelm II's government, however, provided English foreign minister Edward Grey with an acceptable justification for entering the war, by violating Belgian neutrality. Equally ominous for the Central Powers, once England joined the war, it may have been no more than a matter of time before Anglophile elites in the United States pushed their country into the struggle on the English side.[38]

The Germans stumbled into a war they were bound to lose, one in which the victors produced what became the standard accounts of what had happened. Grey evokes in his memoirs a German threat in 1914 that later historians would take at face value: "In Germany in the centre of Europe was the greatest army the world had ever seen, in a greater state of preparedness than any other."[39] The French stood in terror of this force that was intended for aggressive purposes: "The immense growth and strength of Germany had smothered all French interest in attempting a revanche" for the loss of Alsace and Lorraine.[40] Supposedly the Russians and French were "justified" in mobilizing during the July crisis, since they understood that for Germany mobilization was not "the first but the last step" on the way to war.[41]

A few corrections may be in order here. In 1914 France and Russia both had larger armies than Germany, and France had superior artillery. England's continental allies mobilized ahead of the Germans, not after them. There is no evidence that President Poincaré, the French envoy to St. Petersburg, Maurice Paléologue, or any other French political actor in July 1914 ever renounced "interest" in recovering their lost provinces; rather, they were hoping that Russia would strike the first blow against Germany. Grey's assertion at the beginning of volume 2 of *his memoirs*—that Germany was "aiming at world predominance and built the greatest army the world had ever seen"—combines falsehood with conjecture.[42]

What makes the view of German history as a doom-and-gloom narrative particularly striking is the unwillingness to recognize contingency, or what the ancient Greeks called *tuxē*. A musicologist friend of mine has remarked jokingly that the building plan for a Nazi concentration camp was already foreshadowed in J. S. Bach's *St. Matthew Passion*.[43] So deterministic have accounts of the "course of German history" become that we are made to believe that Nazism was always about to surface in the country in which it finally erupted. Hitler's accession to power was the predictable outcome of the cumulative German past.

Never mind the reservations and qualifications that could be thrown up against this view! Before 1933 Germany had been a parliamentary republic, and before that a constitutional monarchy that prided itself on being a *Rechtsstaat*, a state under law, whatever preliberal residues remained attached to its constitutionalism and however insensitively Bismarck attacked his political opponents. Although anti-Semitism had surfaced in Germany—as in other European countries—in the late nineteenth century, it would have been difficult to predict before the Nazis took power the vicious, murderous policies carried out by the Third Reich. The reason so many German Jews were understandably shocked by Nazi brutality is that there was little in the society in which they grew up that portended what would happen after 1933.

Moreover, the Nazis were not simply, or even primarily, social reactionaries, but as Rainer Zitelmann documents in his studies of Hitler and his movement, proudly and even ferociously revolutionary.[44] There was no love lost between Hitler and the German monarchy, and the future Führer openly rejoiced at the overthrow of the old order and deplored the fact that this upheaval was not even more thorough. The Nazi regime worked to modernize the German economy, pushed women into the workforce, and tried to replace Christianity with its own neo-pagan religion. It treated traditional legal codes with utter contempt and depended on terror to maintain order. The treatment of this regime as a continuation of the rule of King Frederick the Great or of Bismarck has been vastly overdone. It ignores the overshadowing modernity and unprecedented character of the Third Reich.

A Jewish refugee from the Nazis, Hannah Arendt was one of the first to analyze systematically the radical nature of totalitarianism, and the insights that went into her classic *The Origins of Totalitarianism* may have come from observing the Beast firsthand, before she fled Nazi Germany.[45] But Arendt's emphasis on the modern character of Nazism and totalitarian rule holds little appeal for those who are trying to save us all from our reactionary natures. Arendt's analysis is also a bad fit with the politics of indignation that has been especially favored by "progressive" German intellectuals. And by no means has everyone in this last category, for example the antifascist littérateur Gunter Grass and the antinational historian Fritz Fischer, been free of Nazi association.

In *Hitler's Thirty Days to Power*, the late Yale University Sille Professor of History Henry Ashby Turner Jr. outlines the lucky chances that broke for Hitler in the month preceding his appointment as German chancellor on January 30, 1933.[46] Turner is far from a defender of the German national state founded by Bismarck, and his work abounds in conventional references to "German militarism" and the "autocratic" ruling class under the Second Empire. Precisely because he is so critical of the German past, far more than he has to be to prove his point, his arguments seem all the more cogent. Although Turner acknowledges such conditioning factors as "the weakness and fragmentation of German liberalism, the strength of militarism, and the susceptibility of a part of the public to pseudo-scientific theories of race," as well as "the shock of defeat in a war the Germans had been led to believe they were winning, the draconian Versailles Treaty, the hyperinflation that destroyed the value of the country's money and the crush-ing impact of the Great Depression," he warns against simplistic, deterministic explanations in answering the question "Why Hitler?"[47] The Nazi takeover was not "bound to happen."[48] Indeed, the "improbable reversal of Hitler's fortune" after it had begun to wane came from "the actions of other persons, for although imper-sonal events make events possible, people make events happen."[49]

Turner introduces us to a rogue's gallery of scheming *Helfershelfer* (accomplices) who assisted Hitler in taking power, from *Reichspräsident* Paul von Hindenburg, who elevated "the Bohemian corporal" to the chancellorship; to Hindenburg's chief of staff, Otto Meissner; to former chancellor Franz von Papen; to Lieutenant-General Oskar von Hindenburg, the president's son, whom the Nazis were then blackmailing; down to the vain General Kurt von Schleicher, Hitler's immediate predecessor, whom the Nazis manipulated and later assassinated.[50] None of these figures was trying to preserve the Weimar Republic, which was already totter-ing under the burden of the Great Depression and a Nazi-Communist majority that blocked any attempt at a parliamentary solution to ravaging unemployment. Despite their deviousness or susceptibility to manipulation, however, none of Turner's actors yearned to live under a government imposed by Hitler and his underlings. In fact some of those who helped install the tyranny that followed were killed on Hitler's instructions in June 1934, during the so-called Night of the Long Knives.[51] What Turner wishes to emphasize through this description of key actors is the role of unintended consequences.[52]

My own interest in such accounts stems from my desire to free the study of history from two interrelated temptations: the tendency to find exaggerated or misplaced continuities in events that come about because of dramatic turns and the presenting of history as moral lessons, in which judgments are rendered by reference to who brought about or hindered the present age. In this second case we would do well to recall the obtrusive presentism that Herbert Butterfield exam-ines in *The Whig Interpretation of History*. Like Butterfield's subjects, historians today are given to obsessing about "how much wiser we've become since the bad old days" and "how all the good people in the past were just like us." Presumably those whom we don't choose to honor by regarding them as our precursors either didn't count or were the baddies in the march toward the present.[53]

Examples of this glorification of the present moment and the singling out of villains and heroes in relation to our privileged present are numerous and instantly available, but perhaps we should pick an example in what is directly related to the argument of this essay. Two historians of ancient Greek wars, Victor Davis Hanson[54] and Donald Kagan,[55] view the struggle between autocratic impe-rial Germany and "democratic" Great Britain as foreshadowed in the conflicts between Greek city-states of the fifth century BC. Although Hanson and Kagan have written competently about some aspects of ancient history, their sloppy comparisons between modern and ancient history leave much to be desired. In their more popular writings, Athens and Thebes are depicted as forerunners of the Anglo-American democratic world, while Sparta is treated as a stand-in for the kaiser's Germany. Hanson drags into his comparisons strictures about how the "democracies" must act in the face of undemocratic foes. For example, they should have crushed the modern German-speaking Sparta when they had a chance, that is, before Germany moved from its unprovoked aggression in World War I to the crimes of the Third Reich.

To make his position even clearer, Hanson has written newspaper commentaries on the mistake of the United States and Great Britain in not having occupied Germany after November 1918. Among other measures, we should have forced on the Germans our democratic values, although it is not clear whether we should have inflicted on them our values circa 1919 or those we fancy right now. Pressure should also have been applied to get the Germans (never mind their shattered economy!) to cough up reparations to the French.[56]

In Hanson's case, it is unfortunate that his public fame derives less from his study of Greek hoplites[57] than from his obliging performance as a purveyor of certain popular prejudices. His syndicated columns are full of drive-by shootings of now familiar targets, along with Hanson's wooden homages to President Abraham Lincoln, Prime Minister Winston Churchill, Prime Minister Benjamin Netanyahu, and President Ronald Reagan. Readers of the *National Review*, the *Weekly Standard*, and other publications in which Hanson's effusions are featured may well mistake his stereotypes for self-evident truths.[58]

Presumed Bridges to the Present

Perhaps we should spell out those principles of the historian's craft that Herbert Butterfield, Marc Bloch, Leopold von Ranke, and other long-honored practitioners of their discipline have laid out. For example, history should not be practiced as a form of political advocacy; the area of study that the historian concentrates on should provide enough intellectual and emotional stimulation so that he does not have to yield to partisan enthusiasms; and someone doing history should aim at *Sachlichkeit*, objectivity, even if this ideal can never be more than distantly approximated in practice. Butterfield defined his discipline in such a way that he didn't think it had become what it should be until the nineteenth century, when figures like Ranke turned history into an organized research field. Up until that time—according to Butterfield—historians mostly told stories about whatever interested them in the past. The result was a literature of annals and exhortations but not "history" in the sense in which Butterfield wanted his field to be understood.[59]

Butterfield was also concerned with the loose and arbitrary connections that partisan historians made while looking for heroes and villains. He complained about the "Whig version of abridged history" and cited as a prime example of this oversimplification the Protestant Reformation:

> The Whig historian tells us for example that the Reformation is justified because it led ultimately to liberty; we must avoid the temptation to make what seem to be the obvious inference from this statement; for it is possible to argue against the Whig historian that the ultimate issue that he applauds only came in the long run from the fact that, in its immediate results the Reformation was disastrous to liberty.[60]

Further,

> Luther and Calvin were both alike in that they attacked the papal and medieval conceptions of the religious society; but it is doubtful that the Biblical Commonwealth for which they labored would have been less severe in its control of the individual or would have commended itself to these men if it had been less severe.[61]

Ironically, neither Martin Luther nor John Calvin enjoys standing any longer in our narratives about the making of the modern world. Luther, as portrayed in the pioneering interpretation of William McGovern, has been turned into the first villain on the road toward the Third Reich.[62] As for another Whig precursor, Calvin, perhaps this theologian is now best remembered as someone who bequeathed to white Anglo-Saxon Protestant society its particular sexual hang-ups. These and other figures who were once regarded as forerunners of nineteenth-century constitutional freedoms, certainly when Butterfield published his book on Whig history in 1931, have now lost their places of honor in our hymns to human progress.

All the same, Butterfield's criticisms are still relevant for identifying faulty lines of continuity. And these faulty lines have not always been drawn from the Left. For many years I debated a legal scholar on the contemporary idea of liberty. While I argued strenuously that the idea in question was largely a twentieth-century creation, my debating partner insisted that it was already implicit in the late medieval break from Catholic Aristotelianism. Once wayward philosophers like William of Ockham stressed the primacy of will over reason in religious and moral matters, the way was left open to contending individual wills. The Protestant Reformation gave religious substance to what my friend regarded as the will-driven perspective of modern thinkers. Society was conceptually reconfigured from an ordered whole, held together by assigned responsibilities, to one in which the aim of government would be to gratify individual wills and desires.

Such positions remind one of Martin Heidegger's brief against the "Socratic turn" in Western thought that took place over two thousand years ago. Because of this primal error, according to Heidegger, we as a civilization have closed ourselves off to existential reality. We have even taken the liberty of imposing our meaning on the world around us. Whatever the pleasures of such speculation, it does not amount to demonstrating historic causation. Looking for direct paths over millennia leading from one mind-set to another hardly reveals such a connection. There is a vast space that lies between late medieval philosophers and the fans of President Barack Obama and Bernie Sanders. Although the Socratic or medieval origins of late modernity may provide dinner conversation, they do not, in my opinion, yield very much else.

Moreover, there is even less scholarly value in neatly distinguishing between good and bad things in historical studies (although it may be allowable to make an exception here for such obvious villains as Hitler, Stalin, and Mao). Permit me, however, to come back to my World War I hobbyhorse (graduate school habits die hard). Unlike "democratic" France and "liberal" England, the German Empire, we are told, was "autocratic" and "militaristic" and therefore had no scruples about unleashing World War I. But as Barnes reminds us, France had a much larger and better equipped army, with a much smaller population, than did Germany in 1914. Although there was an established principle of ministerial responsibility in relation to the National Assembly, and although France held direct elections for its executive head, this did not prevent the French government before World War I from behaving militaristically and belligerently. French president Poincaré, who tried to goad Russia into war against the Central Powers, was more given to saber rattling than German chancellor Theobald Bethmann-Hollweg. Although Bethmann-Hollweg was technically only responsible to his sovereign, he tried in vain to conciliate the British—who viewed Germany as a dangerous rival—and even succeeded in scaling back the German naval program by 1912. Certainly the British had a better-developed parliamentary system than their German cousins, but this did not prevent a minority of the Liberal cabinet after 1905 from engaging in adventurous continental diplomacy in order to isolate Germany. Moreover, these "conversations" were carried out behind the backs of the Commons, that is, behind the backs of seventeen members of the ruling cabinet who would have opposed the actions of the war party.[63]

Nor should we assume, as Barnes and Walter Karp[64] point out, that the US government, which was supposed to be paradigmatically democratic and pacifistic, behaved in a restrained manner during World War I. Neither major party in the

United States stayed neutral in the war; both were demonstratively pro-British. Nor did our leaders—except for the principled secretary of state, William Jennings Bryan—make serious efforts to stay out of the European strife or push peace initiatives when they were still possible. Although President Woodrow Wilson and Secretary of State Robert Lansing—who took over for William Jennings Bryan after he resigned in 1915—were effusively pro-British and turned a blind eye to the starvation blockade imposed by the British on the German civilian population, their opponents attacked them as insufficiently pugnacious. Republican leaders were furious that Wilson waited until April 1917 before plunging his country into the war. The subsequent suppression of civil liberties in "democratic" America went well beyond anything that occurred in "autocratic" Germany or Austria-Hungary, where opposition to the war did not result in the protestor's immediate arrest and where enemy newspapers were still openly circulated.

A strong argument can be made for a limited executive as well as for ministers being subject to parliamentary majorities, but one might ask how these measures made Western governments less belligerent in 1914. From 1916 on, as German diplomatic historian Hans Fenske documents, it was Germany and Austria, not the "democracies," that were eager to make peace.[65] The British could have concluded a peace that gave Germany back its prewar borders, but British leaders wanted to reduce their major continental rival. Moreover, from their point of view they may have been right. They knew the Anglophile government of the United States would soon be sending armies to Europe. Besides, the British enjoyed unbroken naval supremacy and could draw on a vast colonial army. With the collapse of their Austrian and Turkish allies, the Germans were not in a comparable bargaining position, even if they were able to occupy the Western part of the rapidly disintegrating tsarist empire by the end of 1917, with their already overtaxed manpower.

Another example of the victor's history being given a Manichean twist has been the tendency of the recently deceased Harry V. Jaffa and his well-placed disciples to play off the "democratic statesmanship" of Winston Churchill and Abraham Lincoln against what was allegedly autocratic leadership. The heavies in this hagiography are predictably the Germans, the antebellum South, and the Muslim enemies of the state of Israel. Yet those who entered the democratic pantheon may have gotten there because of good fortune as much as for any other reason. What would have happened if Churchill, who pushed England toward the precipice before World War I, had been instrumental in pushing his country into a war it lost? Where would Lincoln's reputation be if he had not emerged victorious in the American Civil War? Why was Lincoln's conflict less blameworthy than the far more limited wars engaged in by Bismarck while uniting Germany? Today we glorify Lincoln as the Great Emancipator. But in his time Lincoln, like Bismarck, saw himself as a nation builder, or in Lincoln's case as a nation preserver. He also explained in a letter to journalist Horace Greeley that he was fighting against the secessionist southern states not to free slaves, but to preserve the Union.[66] If Lincoln became the Great Emancipator, it was in the course of fighting a war of suppression against secessionists, most of whose leaders were slave owners. As is also widely known, Lincoln freed the slaves in states that were in rebellion against the Union mostly as a military measure.

The attempts in the nineteenth century to compare Bismarck and Lincoln were fully understandable. But we must also consider that one of these giants was obviously more successful than the other in gaining the admiration of a later generation. This may have been partly due to the vagaries of fortune rather than humanitarian behavior. Bismarck, who is now far less admired than Lincoln, shed far less blood in achieving his national goal. Let us say counterfactually that Lincoln saved the American Union at an enormous price, but did not free slaves after he sent armies to quell the southern rebellion. Would he still enjoy his present divine-like status?

What would have happened if the South had managed to gain its independence after a protracted conflict? Would Lincoln nonetheless have become the center of a national cult? We might also ask whether Bismarck would be remembered differently if the Germans had not lost World War I, or if the Nazis had not climbed to power through a series of contingencies. Some wielders of force are viewed as good and others as evil. Furthermore, our judgments in both cases may be related to how historical figures have fared in the court of public opinion after their deaths for reasons they could not have foreseen. Admiring people in the past is often the result, as Butterfield maintained, of the belief that "right-thinking" people always thought like progressives in our time.[67]

All this is by way of differentiating between justified and unjustified historical connections; in the end, the historian has to make causal connections, in accordance with his work. The historian should also consider "conditioning factors," which Turner does when he tells us that Germany in 1932 was less resistant to a political leap into the dark than, for example, England. Although this conditioning does not predetermine a course, it does indicate higher or lesser degrees of susceptibility. A conditioning factor may also work in more than one way; for example, because Germany in 1914 had the largest socialist party in Europe, probably the world's best educated working class, the highest wages in Europe, and the best organized workers' unions, it could have developed like its Nordic neighbors even if it had kept its monarchy. Sweden—which once had a more autocratic monarchy than the German imperial government, together with a strong work ethic and collective identity—went from being a military power to a centralized social democratic administrative state. This is an alternative path that Germany might have taken in the twentieth century.

Such an outcome, or other imaginable futures, was possible even after the Germans lost World War I, if other things had not intervened. Turner proposes that if those conspirators who were trying to replace the German republic with an authoritarian, nationalist state, but not a specifically Nazi one, had succeeded, they would have established some kind of generic military dictatorship.[68] Although this would not have been a pleasant regime, it would have spared "humanity the shame of the Holocaust" and have "averted the carnage and destruction of the Second World War."[69] Note that Turner is not offering a happy ending to the subversion of the tottering Weimar Republic, but suggesting what might have happened if circumstances had worked out differently in January 1933.

Another suggestion for improving the quality of historical works would be to spare readers an exuberance of moralizing. Such a perspective detracts from historical analysis, even if it confirms someone's partisan prejudices. Avoiding tasteless flattery is possible even if one is doing an "authorized" biography and even if one adores one's subject. Dumas Malone's study of Thomas Jefferson is a multivolume investigation of the life and accomplishments of someone whom Malone deeply esteemed.[70] But Malone did not gild the lily for his subject, even if he spent nearly forty years researching his life. In Malone's voluminous study, we learn about President Jefferson's views on racial inequality, reservations about immigration, and revulsion for urban life, all opinions that are now out of fashion. Jefferson's opinions may not have been entirely shared by the biographer, when he was writing in the 1940s and 1950s. Yet Malone never hides Jefferson's real views or tries to fit them into a progressivist American culture.

Polybius and the Grand Design

A final suggestion that brings us back to our major theme is that one should avoid conjuring up "grand designs" where none can be proved. This practice can be discerned as far back as in Book One of *The Histories* of the Hellenistic historian Polybius (200–118 BC).[71] A scion of a prominent Greek family, Polybius was sent as a hostage to Rome, where he stayed for most of his long life. There he became a tutor to the sons of a Roman patrician and consul, Lucius Aemilius Paulus Macedonicus, and eventually the close companion of Aemilius's son, Scipio Aemilianus. (The latter was also known as Scorpio Africanus-Minor, the Roman military commander who sacked the city of Carthage at the end of the Third Punic War in 146 BC.)[72] Polybius's patron, to cite even more ancient genealogy, was the adopted son of the eldest son of Scipio Africanus-Major, the victor over Hannibal in the Battle of Zama in 202 BC. A friend of Roman notables, Polybius venerated the Roman constitution, which, as he famously explains in

Book Six, allowed the Roman government, depending on the occasion, to function as a monarchy, aristocracy, or democracy.[73] In line with this interest, Polybius set out to compose a *historia pragmateia*, a factual history showing how Rome, through its successful wars against the Phoenician maritime empire of Carthage, extended its rule across Europe, Asia, and Africa.[74] This study claimed to be drawing on eyewitness accounts and to be recording political and military events as dispassionately as possible.

In Book One, which deals with the First Punic War between 264 and 241 BC, Polybius sketches his method of sifting through data and tells us how his study would differ from earlier chronicles of the same events.[75] Unlike less reliable chronicles, his history would be based on *historia apodeiktikē*, provable facts. It would aim at delineating the full sweep of events and

> link activities in Italy and Libya to those in Asia and Greece, referring everything back to one central purpose. We shall thereby be establishing the beginnings of their actions in these events. For the Romans having conquered the Carthaginians in the aforesaid war and seeing that they had acquired the dominant and greatest part of what was their overall goal, they then looked with confidence toward the future point at which they would extend their hands and cross with all their military might into Greece and various regions of Asia.[76]

While planning his histories, Polybius decided to begin

> with this book and with the one that follows, so that no one who pauses to read this explanation of events should be in the dark and have to search elsewhere in order to familiarize himself with the multitude of deliberations, powers, and resources through which the Romans pursued their purposes, [namely, those purposes] by which they came to control the land and sea throughout the known world.[77]

Finally, it is only by reading Polybius's account that readers would

> become acquainted with the well-considered *aphormai* [starting points] by which the Romans advanced toward their purpose and achieved the completion of their rule and their domination of all things.[78]

Reading sections 3 and 4 of Book One in the Greek text, one is struck by the frequency with which words for purpose or intent—for example, *prosthesis, epiboulē, epinoia*—are interspersed with descriptions of the growth of Roman power, *dunasteia*.[79] This Roman expansion, resulting from the struggle against the Carthaginians and from subsequent wars against the Seleucid dynasty in the

Middle East, did not take place accidentally, according to the *Histories*. Although Polybius mentions *tuxē*, it is not fortune but Roman drive and an "overall purpose," as described in Book One, that explain Rome's rise to intercontinental supremacy.[80] Polybius attributes this design, which he thinks was there from the beginning (*echs arxes*), to a world power whose leaders knew where they wanted to go. Furthermore, he admired the leaders who thought in this manner. It is therefore unlikely that he undertook his work to run down Carthage's conquerors. Unlike Hanson, Steinberg, or Fischer, who emphasize a supposedly straight path leading from the Second Empire, or even earlier, to the Third Reich, Polybius believed that he was praising the Romans by ascribing to his host country and patrons an imperial design.

We may nonetheless question this ascription of an overall expansionist design to the Romans. Contrary to what is suggested, the overall plan was not at all demonstrable, *apodeiktikē*. Polybius may have invented his "design" because he wished his reader to believe that unlike others chronicling the same events, he was providing a "panorama," a truly big picture. He was not only documenting his assertions, but presenting a view that was "truly broad." He was dealing with political and military "actions" by placing them in the framework of "the completion of an overall purpose." Further, it may have been difficult for Polybius to grasp why the Romans had spilled so much blood and treasure to wage the "longest, most continuous, and greatest war" in history, lasting twenty-four years in its first phase, unless they were pursuing fixed goals. This protracted conflict did not take place accidentally or involuntarily, but allegedly reflected deep commitment; this was evident from the first moment the Romans began "carrying out their intent (*kathēkonto tes protheseos*)."[81] Polybius does urge the reader to notice in Rome's imperial ambition "what is most beautiful and most significant in this enterprise of *Fortuna*," but then he returns to his leitmotif by telling us that whatever "occurred and whatever contests were waged in the past, Fortuna never allowed these to be brought to completion with greater speed and urgency than in our generation."[82]

This leads back to my remarks about Butterfield and to my complaints about conventional Germanophobic commentators. It should be obvious to those who have been following my gist that I am now switching perspectives. If the historian is seeking a mass readership, perhaps he should ignore all my warnings about biased history. Taking these warnings to heart will not aid the sales of a work of "history." Like the search for grand design, certain fixations become popular at particular times, and the able, market-oriented storyteller must know how to appeal to his public. Historians do well by offering a narrative that their target readers would like to imagine is true. Although in a better world historians would not be driven by partisan passions or indulge such passions in others, taking this high ground will not likely bring huge financial rewards.

I used to gripe (and perhaps still do) about a lightweight book published by Republican Party journalist Jonah Goldberg, *Liberal Fascism*.[83] I was annoyed by the attention this work received in a field in which true researchers usually labor for a pittance. Unlike diligent but largely unrecognized scholars, Goldberg drew copious comments from the national press and parlayed his writing efforts into big bucks. I was especially turned off by the ludicrous comparisons of prominent Democratic politicians to Italian fascists and by the forced parallels between Hillary Clinton and German Nazi officials. Most horrifying of all, this screed remained on the *New York Times* best-seller list for nonfiction from February 2008 through April 2008 and even reached first place by March 8, 2008.[84]

Since then it has dawned on me that there is nothing about this publishing coup that should have offended me. Goldberg produced propaganda for his party masked as historical analysis and sold his well-packaged product to FOX News junkies and Republican Party loyalists. Recently, Republican presidential candidate senator Ted Cruz (R-TX) paid homage to Goldberg's interpretation by accusing the Democrats of being "the home of liberal fascism."[85] It was as a Republican commentator, not as a scholar of fascism, that Goldberg achieved mass sales and obtained lucrative invitations to speak. The author achieved what he was hoping to accomplish in a media culture. To paraphrase an old adage, nothing succeeds as thoroughly as success.

5

Liberal Democracy as a God Term

WHEN I WAS A YOUNG FACULTY MEMBER at Rockford College forty years ago, my divisional chairman, who was a devout disciple of Leo Strauss, once complained that a colleague he had just spoken to did not believe in liberal democracy. I've no idea how my superior came by this knowledge, but he was deeply upset that his colleague didn't praise "liberal democracy as being better than other forms of government." Our divisional chairman then shared with me a text he was working on that proved that Marx "rejected liberal democracy." Up until that moment I had never encountered the term "liberal democracy," and when I first heard it mentioned, I thought it was a reference to Democrats who endorsed Senator George McGovern.

I thereupon researched the operative term and learned that it was of fairly recent origin. James Madison and Alexander Hamilton didn't apply it when they described the nascent American regime in *The Federalist*. Appeals to "democracy" by Presidents Thomas Jefferson and Andrew Jackson were to a populist spirit, not to a hallowed form of government. President Abraham Lincoln may have come closer to defining a democratic commitment bottomed on natural rights, but one has to understand the Gettysburg Address for what it was, wartime rhetoric that invoked universal ideals to justify the suppression of a regional secession led by slaveholders. Such ideals and the move toward a government structured around a collective end were implicitly present in Lincoln's view of democracy. But despite these intimations of strong executive power, one should not read more than is warranted into Lincoln's re-founding of America as a consolidated state standing for universal principles. Presidential administrations in the 1880s, under Chester Alan Arthur and Benjamin Harrison, were generally no more overbearing than ones that had existed before the Civil War under Presidents Martin Van Buren and Millard Fillmore.

Although the United States ultimately became a more ideologically infused political society as a result of the Civil War, as late as at the beginning of the last

century, according to Robert Nisbet and Forrest McDonald, the major involvement of the federal government in our lives was the collection and delivery of
mail. This was long after the southern states were prevented from seceding, with
devastating force, and long after President Lincoln had proclaimed a "new birth"
for a nation "dedicated to the proposition that all men are created equal."[1]

A visit to *Wikipedia* indicates that the concept "liberal democracy" came
into vogue during the Progressive Era, with the efforts of Presidents Theodore
Roosevelt and Woodrow Wilson to reconfigure American republican government according to the needs of an urban, industrial society.[2] In my book *After
Liberalism*, I undertake to examine this fateful conjuncture and offer reasons for
its emergence.[3] But in researching my book, I couldn't trace any widespread usage
of the term "liberal democracy" even as far back as the early twentieth century.
Except for some fleeting references to it by English Hegelian Thomas Hill Green
around 1910, "liberal democracy" did not make an appearance during the early
twentieth century. When I asked a young friend, Keith Preston, who has written critically on the subject, when "liberal democracy" first became a popular
term, he told me that in a tract in the 1980s, Catholic neoconservative Michael
Novak paid tribute to it. Keith also read references to the term ascribed to me and
assumed that I knew when it came into general use. In point of fact I did not.

What I do know is that as late as April 1918—when William Tyler Page produced "The American Creed," which Congress more or less adopted as a "national
creed" in the midst of America's entanglement in World War I—the United States
was thought to be "a democracy in a republic, a sovereign nation of many sovereign states, a perfect Union one and inseparable." Although this farrago of bor-
rowings from Secretary of State Daniel Webster, President Abraham Lincoln, and
the Declaration of Independence was composed during a military crusade waged
in the name of "democracy," significantly the American Creed does not describe
America as a "liberal democracy." Presumably what my superior at Rockford
College wanted his colleagues to worship became a popular concept later than
either of us realized.

Note that *Webster's Unabridged Dictionary* provides a definition of "liberal
democracy" and six instances in which the term has been applied.[4] It refers to a
"democratic system of representative government in which individual rights and
civil liberties are officially recognized and protected, and the exercise of political
power is limited by the rule of law."[5] Except for the adjective "democratic" inserted
into the first line, this definition could apply to a variety of regimes limited by the
rule of law and by the toleration of peaceful minorities.

There are only three references in *Webster's* to "liberal democracy" before the
1930s. Around that time our key term was contrasted to Italian fascist rule in

the *Journal of Modern History*, which gives the impression that Mussolini popularized "liberal democracy" as a usage when he opposed the efficiency and supposed incorruptibility of his government to its Anglo-American rival. But Mussolini did not come up with "liberal democracy" when he drew this contrast. In a well-attended speech that he delivered in Berlin in September 1937, in which he declared a family relation between fascism and Nazism, Il Duce attacked the "capitalist democracies." According to historian Renzo de Felice, Mussolini later replaced this term with the adjective "demoplutocratic (*demoplutocratiche*)."[6]

Two of the six references to "liberal democracy" that are found in *Webster's* only date back to the year 1992. The last is from the *New York Review of Books* in 2009 and associates "liberal democracy" with the protection of minorities.[7] Given the source, we may assume that those groups we are urged to protect are neither fundamentalist Christians nor the Little Sisters of the Poor. By 2009 "liberal democracy" had acquired such favorable connotations that it served as a generic compliment for a regime that was agreeable to the speaker.

The only reference to "liberal democracy" that seems especially worth noting is from President John Adams's *A Defence of Constitutions of Government of the United States of America*, a narrative that recounts Adams's visit to the Basque region of Spain, then known as Biskaia, in the 1780s.[8] The future president expresses his admiration for the resolve of the native population to acquire more regional independence from the Kingdom of Spain, but complains that what appears to be "liberal democracy" in the view of Basque separatists is really "a contracted aristocracy."[9] Unlike Americans, the inhabitants of Biskaia were not eager to create a true representative government, but were only interested in restoring the hereditary privileges of their landed class. Whether or not this was a fair characterization of the political aspirations of the Basques is beside the point. What stands out is Adams's favorable reference to something that he chooses to call "liberal democracy."[10]

Two points should be made about this quotation. One, the writer is not delineating the features of a future American federal union, but rather indicating what the proposed Basque self-rule was not. Basque autonomists were not democrats, nor did they intend to protect minorities who settled in their region. Two, John Adams was no unqualified fan of popular rule. As he grew older, he surpassed even European counterrevolutionaries in his disdain for government by the people. In an oft-quoted letter to John Taylor in 1814, Adams states these choice opinions:

> Democracy, while it lasts, is bloodier than either aristocracy or monarchy. Democracy never lasts long. It soon wastes, exhausts, murders itself. There was never a democracy that did not commit suicide.[11]

Passages like these would hardly encourage an American dedication to democracy as a sacred value. Least of all would they make one think of Allan Bloom's exhortations to Americans in *The Closing of the American Mind* to impose "democracy and human rights" on unreceptive societies as "an educational experience" if necessary by military force.[12] Adams, who was writing soon after American independence was achieved, should not be confused with an American liberal internationalist in the 1980s invoking America's duty to bestow his preferred values on the rest of the human race.

"Liberal democracy" as a term or concept has gained currency primarily for two reasons. One is its vagueness; it can be made to mean what the speaker wants it to signify. Not surprisingly, one finds online numerous meanings given to "liberal democracy," from freedom and equality combined with some kind of representative government protecting minority rights, to a government that redistributes income in accordance with the needs of the majority. We are further led to believe that democracy and liberalism fuse at a certain point, on the way to becoming social democracy. Sometimes "liberal democratic" government is linked to a linguistic, geographic context. It is made synonymous with the political practices of the Anglosphere, an appellation that embraces the United States, Canada, United Kingdom, and other English-speaking regions. These regions are seen as blessed with a shared political culture, which is styled "liberal democracy."

This concept or term has geographical and ethnic reference points. It can mean the political practices that now prevail in certain regions of the Western world and in its cultural extensions elsewhere. Those who apply this term often gloss over the fact that political arrangements in England and the United States looked different hundreds of years ago from how these institutions later evolved. Fans of the Anglosphere sometimes apply the label "liberal democratic" to English-speaking peoples, no matter whether the regime being referred to was an aristocratic oligarchy, bourgeois liberal monarchy, or modern public administration. They thereby designate either our present political system or something that is thought to have led, however tortuously, in its direction.

There is a second reason that "liberal democracy" has caught on: it expresses a value judgment about what the speaker intends to praise. It suggests the political equivalent of the traditional Catholic idea of "no salvation outside the Church." No one but a fool would imagine that the term is purely descriptive. It is a god term, on the altar of which the worshipper can never slay enough fattened calves. Although the term "liberal democratic" has been made to serve a number of political purposes, it has also, not incidentally, been raised to sacral significance. It is a concept or rallying cry that the neoconservatives bestowed on the Republican Party as they made their historic journey from the Left to become the American conservative establishment.[13]

An example of the honorific use of "liberal democracy" can be found in University of Virginia professor James W. Ceaser's *Liberal Democracy and Political Science*.[14] The author sets out to demonstrate the necessary conceptual bridge between liberal democracy and a "special kind of political knowledge" that can help "maintain" the ideology that is energetically defended.[15] Neither *The Federalist* nor the American founders, we are told, were indifferent to the question of moral character, yet they focused mostly on the mechanics of government. It awaited Tocqueville—who is considered "the first political philosopher of liberal democracy"[16]—to fill in the blanks and provide an appropriate ethic for a liberal democratic dispensation. Tocqueville explained the requirements for a successful democratic regime, which he hoped would result in a way of life. He stressed the need to combine "a degree of civic-mindedness, which is fairly widespread among the citizenry,"[17] with a "jealous spirit of independence."[18] He knew this combination was difficult to achieve, and so his other accomplishment as a "political philosopher" was to call for the "active engagement in society of a certain kind of knowledge."[19]

Ceaser calls for a renewal of "political moderation," seen as "the proper arrangement of the political institutions" and "a separation of power, which forces ambitions to counteract ambition."[20] Such a balance among the parts of the constitutional system would "teach leaders a sense of their limits." But even more important, Ceaser argues, is the "quality of life" that is needed to sustain liberal democracy. Although some may imagine that once put into operation the desired regime will continue to function, according to Ceaser, "liberal democracy requires constant superintendence even if its political institutions have been wisely designed."[21]

Supposedly Alexander Hamilton and James Madison wished to establish a "liberal democracy," even if they never chanced on this felicitous term. The union they worked to achieve was to be "complex and skillfully contrived," and because of this complexity, the mode of government they favored "has greater need of political science."[22]

Unhappily liberal democracy "often fails to generate enthusiasm for itself as an integral whole."[23] That is because intellectuals are too fixed on particular aspects of this regime and fail to show sufficient respect for "the compound" that resulted from the founders' efforts to achieve a mixed regime. Finally, liberal democracy—in what may be a lapse of judgment on the part of the governed—bestows on its critics "status and acclaim, elevating some to the very highest positions in the intellectual world." This we are told is a grave problem that needs to be addressed. Academics should be rising to a task that they have so far ignored, which is creating a "social enterprise" "devoted to understanding the nature of democracy and bringing that knowledge to bear on its behalf."[24]

Ceaser recycles a charge that his teacher at the University of Chicago, Leo Strauss, directed against the American Political Science Association in the 1960s. Strauss was then targeting "value-free analysis" and the failure of his colleagues to recognize that "democracy is the tacit presupposition of the data."[25] Particularly when democracy has come under fire, maintains Strauss, professors should not be "teaching the equality of all values" and scorning the truth that "there are things that are intrinsically high and others that are intrinsically low."[26] Ceaser's comments about political science as a social enterprise basically restate Strauss's indictment of political scientists. Academics have shirked their duty by not instilling love of "liberal democracy" in those who come under their influence.

Ceaser offers in the last two sections of his tract a sensible plea for a limited, decentralized government. His intended reform for "liberal democratic" government—and particularly his plan for the re-empowerment of localities— would have the effect, if properly implemented, of limiting runaway centralized administration.[27] Less attractive, however, are the attempt to redefine the original American design through the loaded term "liberal democracy" and, finally, the effort to transform political science into a Straussian enterprise. A thinker of a different stripe, George W. Carey, subtitled his learned study of *The Federalist* "*Design for a Constitutional Republic*."[28] In a letter to me that accompanied a gift copy of his monograph, the author indicated that he was trying "to ignore the Straussians." Nowhere in his study does Carey even mention the term "liberal democracy."[29] He considered that term to be extraneous to any attempt to understand the justification for the Constitution offered by its architects. There was no need, according to Carey, to drag in a concept devised long after America's founding to describe the government brought into existence in the 1780s.[30]

Another illustrative tribute to liberal democracy is a work by Hudson Institute Fellow John Fonte, which centers on the supposed struggle between the forces of "sovereignty" and "submission."[31] Although Fonte raises a justified call to protect American sovereignty against what he calls "transnational progressivism," the battle lines may not be as clearly demarcated as his book suggests. The author's allies and their adversaries, whom he sees as located mostly in nonprofit organizations that claim global reach, embrace overlapping human rights doctrines. Both sides consider government to be a means for bringing equal rights to the entire human race. But the two sides differ in one critical respect that Fonte calls to our attention: unlike the new globalists, American liberal democrats view the sovereign American state as a necessary vehicle for working toward the universal practice of human rights. This task cannot be left to free-floating intellectuals speaking for humanity. Although this judgment may be deemed more realistic than the object of Fonte's criticism, we should recognize the common ground that he and the nonprofit advocates of world community share. All of them embrace the same vision of a democratically transformed world, with all that entails culturally and socially. Unlike Fonte, however, the transnational progressives are globalists in a hurry.

The term "liberal democracy" is often brought up in a polemical context. Whether that context is antifascists of the 1930s, Cold War liberals like National Security Advisor Zbigniew Brzezinski writing about the "totalitarian" threat to democracy, or Straussians and neoconservatives devising a pedigree for their political preferences, a common feature persists: the glorification of liberal democracy takes place in opposition to what we are made to believe is a cosmic evil.

Keith Preston examines these tendencies in a collection of essays, *Attack the System*, which assails those who are protecting their accumulated power by focusing on disempowered enemies.[32] Preston attributes the endless celebration of "liberal democracy" to the propagandistic efforts of a ruling coalition, which marginalizes unwanted critics.[33] Those in charge of our "democratic capitalist welfare state"—to borrow a phrase from Irving Kristol—view their power base as being so broad that those relatively few who dare to question the assumed consensus are turned into enemies of liberal democracy.

Preston speaks of an interlocking power base, consisting of multinational corporate interests, the teachers of the doctrines of political correctness—who dominate educational institutions and the media—and a vast administrative class.[34] Although there are continuing tensions among those in this power-sharing structure, the parts of the whole cooperate more often than they fight. Preston identifies liberal democracy with "democratic capitalism" and its attendant ills: egalitarianism, consumerism, and therapeutism, as opposed to merit, responsibility, and frugality.[35] The state is authorized to provide everyone with "equal rights" and not only with the pursuit of happiness, but happiness itself. Theoretically, this is to be done through a generalized ethos of materialism and consumption to the point of gluttony; endless psychological conditioning; and a "Nanny State" resolved to protect everyone from falling into "unhappiness" as a result of poverty, illness, racism, sexism, or drug addiction. Preston sees this dynamic at work in mass democracy, which "requires the radical expansion of the state in order to satisfy the demands for state assistance from all of these groups and the creation of massive bureaucracies in order to manage the distribution of state services."[36]

The modern constellation of powers that is coterminous with liberal democracy allegedly goes back to an early mercantile republic, which Preston links to the original constitution and which points forward toward a "more egalitarian system of government, an increasingly diverse population base and a broad consumer economy."[37] Preston views this system as veering inescapably toward "PC totalitarianism," when it imposes the kind of thought control that is only mini-mally opposed.[38] The ruling class, however, has no problem with throttling incon-venient thought and opinion:

> The radicals of the sixties have gotten older, grayer, and wealthier, they have gone on to form a new kind of cultural and intellectual establishment, largely by securing their own dominance within the worlds of academia, media and entertainment. Further, the end result of this dominance has been that this new Cultural Left Establishment has formed an alliance with the older, pre-existing political, economic, and mili-tary establishment. What the proponents of the sixties cultural revolution have, in essence, done is rather than overthrow the U.S. empire, they have seized control of that empire and are using it for their purposes, which may or may not overlap with the interests of the older establishment. The creeping totalitarianism we see evolving today is an outgrowth of Marxism, not necessarily in the orthodox socialist sense, but in the reapplication of Marxist theory in cultural matters, where the "official victims" of western civilization replace the proletariat as the focus of a Manichean struggle for political power.[39]

Supposedly we can grasp the "ideology of the Western, particularly American, ruling class" by looking at its essential features:

> Militarism, imperialism and empire in the guise of human rights, corporate mer-cantilism or state capitalism under the guise of 'free trade,' 'totalitarian humanism' [empowers an] all-encompassing and unaccountable bureaucracy to peer into every corner of society to make sure no one anywhere, anytime ever practices "racism," sexism, smoking, "sex abuse" or other such Leftist sins . . . a police state designed to protect everyone from terrorism, crime, drugs, gangs, or some other bogeyman of the month.[40]

Any "competing institution" that stands in the way of this "liberal democratic" ruling order, says Preston, will have to be cut down to size or abolished.

It is open to question whether the "system" that Preston examines functions as harmoniously as he suggests. One might ask whether those who coexist as parts of the ruling class necessarily see themselves as being on top of the heap. And do all the participants actively cooperate? Does a government enforcer of laws against sexism view himself as being in a broad coalition with Mitt Romney, Donald Trump, and Rupert Murdoch? Feminists and corporate moguls may be accidental allies in a sociopolitical or cultural system in which they are not even aware of their partners. Advocates of multicultural transformation, corporate executives, and public officials may not grasp their shared interests and may be hostile to others who share their power system. Only those outside the interrelated power structure may be able to understand how the parts fit together.

There is also no compelling reason to believe that corporate executives take leftist social positions principally because of bedrock moral conviction. They may well be expressing their "positions of conscience" in order to sell their products with minimal inconvenience or because they are afraid of the consequences of offending the government. I doubt that I'd be offending anyone but a few rich relatives if I observed that businessmen do not seem on the whole to be ideologically driven. Was Mitt Romney, a former governor of Massachusetts and corporate executive, who ran for president on the Republican ticket and who in his wordy debates with President Obama endorsed feminist ideas, committed to feminist ideals? A more obvious reason for Romney's path of accommodation is that he was hoping to win a presidential election by appealing to his opponent's base. Did the executives at Coca-Cola withdraw their financial contribution from the Boy Scouts of America because they were outraged by this organization's unwillingness to accept openly homosexual scoutmasters? Or were they trying to avoid a confrontation with the social Left that might have affected the sales of their teeth-rotting beverage? Going along with a particular ideology need not signify an enthusiastic expression of support. It may be the result of a desperate effort to avoid damaging attacks.

A feature article by Jeff Guo in the *Washington Post* in 2015 underscores the growing failure of small commercial enterprises together with the success of larger ones in the United States over the last thirty years.[41] A major reason offered for these trends, on which the Brookings Institute has done detailed statistical studies, is the building of close connections on the part of corporate executives to politicians and public administration. Surveying these signs of "crony capitalism," we need not assume that corporate heads love big government on principle, or that they vibrate to the multicultural ideology proclaimed by the state and public educators. They simply jump through whatever hoops thy have to in order to obtain government assistance.

Further, certain interests can work together, as they do in "liberal democracy," without necessarily being entirely in sync. Historian Renzo de Felice cites the case of Italian fascism, which managed to bring together in loose alliance the Italian upper and lower-middle classes. This was unprecedented in Italian politics since the unification of the country in 1871, and Mussolini managed this feat by appealing to all elements of the bourgeoisie as a figure of order, who would protect Italy against social violence. The fascists, however, also promised social programs that attracted the lower-middle class and even some members of the working class; however, as Felice notes, there is no reason to imagine that Mussolini was really reconciling social classes. He was marketing himself as a leader who could safeguard order while pursuing a policy of collective social responsibility.

In the coalition of forces that dominate liberal democracy in its present incarnation, there is no reason to assume deep friendship among the constituent members. It is a coalition held together by interests that sometimes intersect and that can be made to work together in particular circumstances. Public sector employees, culturally radical journalists, and academics may loathe fat-cat businessmen and call for marching on Wall Street to punish malefactors of great wealth. But they must realize, if they are at all rational, that their own power and influence would be endangered if capitalists did not generate revenues and keep the public happy with consumer goods. An active market economy is necessary for all participants in the coalition to prosper, however vehemently some elements within this coalition may vent against sexist, racist, or homophobic businessmen and bankers.

The business and corporate community cooperate with their imposed allies because they have no choice. The government and the culture-education industry treat them in public statements as pariahs, while our two parties shake down the rich for contributions or await their donations with a sense of entitlement. Republican donors like Sheldon Adelson and the Koch brothers may be extracting from the party that they help finance support for their pet causes, but the fervent endorsement of the Israeli Right and the reduction of marginal tax rates are positions that the party would likely take because of its electoral constituency, even without the additional fillip. Donations given to the Democrats to sway them on these issues would not likely have that effect.

Although cultural leftists earning large incomes and pursuing sybaritic lifestyles are found on Wall Street and on corporate boards, one may dispute whether everything that the Left pushes suits the wealthy and commercially oriented. Cheap foreign labor and massive immigration do provide profits to the wealthier elements of the business class, and so conceivably does having women in the workplace generating incomes that can be spent on consumer goods. But do corporations want the government investigating them for gender or racial discrimination, vetting the composition of their workforce, or requiring them to spend large sums on sensitivity-training classes? Are corporate executives waiting in line to make contributions to activists like Jesse Jackson, who threaten to expose them as "racists" unless they cough up "antiracist" bribe money? Big business puts up with other members of its coalition just as store owners used to pay the mob to "protect" them against disaster. Occasionally the "bribe recipient" did protect his clients, but only if some other group tried to muscle in and become the new enforcers.

Allow me to make one exception—and one could, of course, cite other exceptions—to this description of how the business sector relates to the rest of the ruling coalition in "liberal democracy." Here we are speaking about the defense industries and their neoconservative promoters, which Preston mentions as leading beneficiaries of the system he delineates. These groups prosper when the country is fighting a war or being edged into one. The neoconservatives, according to Preston, are particularly adept at accelerating the journey leading toward military engagements. They are usually intent on employing military power, no matter which American national party may happen to be in power. Equally important, they enjoy a lock hold on foreign policy in the Republican Party and flex their media power in keeping a potentially uncooperative GOP presidential candidate from even getting close to the nomination. Multiple attacks issued by neoconservative commentators and foundations helped sink the presidential hopes of libertarian Republican senator Rand Paul. The mortal sin of this hapless candidate was to have displayed ambivalent attitudes toward military actions advocated by neoconservative "policy experts" and news commentators. The same motive may also lie behind the nonstop attacks from the same quarters that were vented on GOP presidential candidate Donald Trump. As a candidate Trump expressed reservations about foreign entanglements and opposed the granting of amnesty to illegals, both signature neoconservative positions.

One reason neoconservative advocates do well is that they pitch their belligerent rhetoric to whatever special concern the political class may be highlighting. Whether the emphasis is on freedom, global democracy, or—more recently— the need for internationally recognized gay rights and the inviolate human right of half-naked exhibitionists to desecrate Christ the Savior Cathedral in Moscow, neoconservative proponents of direct and indirect intervention present themselves as battling the enemies of the "West."

This all-purpose trope means what those who wield it would like it to mean. It belongs to an assemblage of terms that enable a politically and journalistically powerful group to enjoy continued public exposure. It furthermore represents the idiom of what Franco-Italian Marxist Constanzo Preve characterizes as *la théologie interventionniste des droits de l'homme*, the interventionist theology of human rights, a vocabulary that justifies America's unconditional right to intervene with force internationally as an exercise in self-validating virtue. "The West," "human rights," and the defense of "liberal democracy" all fit into this peculiar mode of discourse and invariably into a context of unending struggle shaped by the sociopolitical elite.

Before ending this appraisal of the essays of a generally unknown anarchist thinker, I should indicate why an examination of Preston's arguments seems a worthwhile endeavor. Preston recognizes that even in a country of over three hundred million people with multiple information sources, certain groups stay in positions of authority and actively cooperate with others in the same power orbit. He also understands that there is ideological compatibility among the power sharers, seen, for example, in their efforts to keep others, including Preston and myself, out of the public discussion.

This does not happen by accident, and although contingencies may account for why such events as World War I or the French Revolution broke out, they do not account for the widespread agreement on political values and social sentiments among interlocking elites in the United States. Groupthink, as illustrated, for example, by the very rapid turnaround of public opinion about same-sex marriage and the public affirmation of feminist principles, takes place because well-placed, media-effective elites are calling the shots. These shots do not threaten corporate capitalist or military interests, which obligingly go along with the moral values of educational and cultural elites. One may note the harmonious interaction of the parts of what can be described as a system, together with the lack of widespread criticism outside of an imposed framework of values and concerns.

Preston is aware that earlier attempts have been made to explain how the parts in his system operate in relation to the whole. The more prominent of those who have done so have been Marxists or quasi-Marxists, such as C. Wright Mills, William Appleman Williams, and A. Noam Chomsky. Although these scholars have helped illuminate our historical situation, they have focused perhaps too one-sidedly on economic forces, while treating cultural, religious, and even political factors as either incidental or reflective of material structures. But there have also been critics of the "liberal democratic" system who stress the centrality of political control, and here one could cite, among others, the libertarian economist Murray N. Rothbard and the theoretically inventive follower of James Burnham, Samuel T. Francis.[42] Such critics have treated the growth of the modern administrative state as a major determinant in the creation or reconstruction of cultural and social attitudes. An attentive reader of *After Liberalism* may notice to what extent analysts of the managerial revolution have affected my thinking about social and political dynamics.[43] Although there are obvious limits to this interpretive perspective, those who apply it do shed light on contemporary power structures.

Other critics of political modernity have emphasized cultural and religious values as a key to understanding political developments. Not all of these critics have been equally informative, and some of them have now been reduced to churning out electoral propaganda intended to persuade us to vote Republican or Democratic or to lavish donations on Beltway think tanks. But implicit in this recruiting effort is recognition that cultural values impact people's lives. One has to credit the cultural Left with grasping its transformational reach when it assails most visible reminders of the white southern heritage or marginalizes opponents of gay marriage.

Unlike corporate executives and business-as-usual Republicans, these cultural transformers act with deliberateness in discrediting what stands in the way of their vision. They incite hundreds of thousands of believers to pour into the streets to dramatize their key issues. Presumably the followers of leftist opinion makers share their moral fervor, coupled with their loathing for the society that they are working to bring down. Among the opponents of the cultural Left, only the Right to Life movement has been able to generate comparable energies and to mount mass demonstrations, but with the significant difference that the Left can swing into mass action on the spur of the moment on behalf of the causes and groups its organizers choose to highlight.

All of this is by way of underlining the need for synthetic approaches to understanding the role of elites in contemporary Western societies. To his credit, Preston suggests such approaches, despite the sketchy and sometimes imprecatory manner in which he names his players. In his criticisms of "liberal democracy" he provides comprehensive lists of those who establish the conditions for "everyone going along."[44] He also properly assumes that "stability" within the system does not entail having the people always holding the same opinions about every issue or media talking point. "Stability" requires that the masses do not perceive the extent of cataclysmic changes undertaken by elites. Instead they are made to view those changes in the context of implementing certain fashionable values, such as "fairness" and "sensitivity."

The fact that a Democratic president had Congress pass the Defense of Marriage Act in 1996, which strictly limited marriage to heterosexual union, and then totally turned around and called for the courts to legalize same-sex marriage in every state less than twenty years later, is now not widely regarded as an inconsistency in American leadership. Rather, it is interpreted as a sign of moral "growth" on the part of former president Bill Clinton. The public will go along with moral upheavals, providing that the media, educational establishment, and government administrators all act in concert to bring about the change.

A weakness in Preston's thinking—which is also characteristic of more famous critics of modern-day elites, such as Christopher Lasch—is the belief that one can somehow be rid of the problem of systematic control by "empowering the people." It is, for me, inconceivable that the "people" would stop following their present elites just because Preston and like-minded critics are pointing out to a handful of readers how the public is being manipulated. Why would I think that most people would opt for Preston's independent thought rather than their present leaders? Can Preston point to a single instance in recordable history in which a society has survived or even come into existence without new elites taking power? What Preston is offering us is a Sorelian myth, in which—following the model of the French anarchist and later protofascist Georges Sorel—society can be cleansed morally and spiritually by pursuing a revolutionary path to political redemption. The truth of a vision, according to Sorel, is less critical than the collective action to which the vision leads. Perhaps this is what Preston has in mind when he presents himself as an anarchist calling for resistance to power. It is doubtful, however, that he truly believes that the "people" will rise up against the elites once shown the true path.

It is also unlikely that "people" would follow any would-be elite. Those who lead them must promise material plenty and make it appear that they are working toward greater human equality, even if that does not result from their actions. Different elites arise in different historical circumstances, and the ideological or religious justifications attached to them cannot be exchanged simply because those in power wake up one day and decide to change the dominant narratives or values. Contrary to a position that I have argued against for decades, elites do not simply "manipulate" symbols and myths. They themselves are imbued in varying degrees with the ideologies they transmit. The connection of political myths to their bearers is more than adventitious or opportunistic. It is unlikely, for example, that Hillary Clinton is merely cynical about those "women's issues" she has spent decades championing. It is equally unlikely that President Obama does not share the grievances of black civil rights activists and just pretends to embrace them.

There are undoubtedly opportunists in politics, and most CEOs may take moral stands mostly on the basis of what helps their careers and corporations. But those who enter politics must take a side on the basis of professed beliefs, which mirror a particular worldview, be it the historic or cultural Marxist Left or the latest tenets of the religious Right. The media lay down what become prescribed ideological positions and, from all appearances, those engaged in this art of persuasion or browbeating believe in what they are trying to impose. One should not mistake the varying degrees of intensity with which politicians affirm their hegemonic values for mere cynicism or imagine that everyone in politics is simply pretending to believe what he or she really scorns.

Certain principles and values replace other ones as the "people" and those who rule them posit the winning values of the time. Although far from everyone affirms these values with the same zeal, those ideological positions that become widespread provide a public religion. Finally, to repeat a point made earlier, while elites may change their minds radically on certain questions, they can only win acceptance for their volte-face by meeting two conditions. As in the conversion of Presidents Clinton and Obama to same-sex marriage as a federally protected right, a politician who changes his mind must appeal to the goal of fuller human equality. Finally, the politician who takes a "progressive" turn can only prevail if he brings on board a preponderant part of the American elite. The others will then be induced to follow.

6

Origins of the State

ROM A RECENT READING of Woodrow Wilson's *The State*,[1] it became clear to me that this work rejects certain entrenched American views about the source of political rights. Wilson provided a view of the "state" that differs from the conventional American understanding of rights as inhering in the individual from the moment of birth. His argument about the state is previewed in the opening sentence of his work, in which he addresses the "probable origin of government."[2] The state's origin "is a question of fact, to be settled not by conjecture, but by history."[3] The inquiry then moves to "such traces as remain to us of the history of primitive societies."[4] The societies involved in this investigation are ancient Indo-European, Turanian, and Semitic ones, although not Far Eastern civilization, and Wilson concludes that the state's origin cannot be located in any of these hypothetical beginnings. In all the societies surveyed, it is possible to find complex family patterns, patriarchal authority, and/or Germanic tribal chieftains, but no inklings of the modern state.[5]

Wilson is not impressed by explanations for the state's development featuring a social contract theory. He is profoundly skeptical about certain rights of nature that supposedly were developing in primitive political societies. He treats these imaginary rights with the same doubt with which he approaches narratives about the divine origin of the state or an original lawgiver, whose life remains shrouded in mystery. But a shadow of truth, according to Wilson, may cling to all of these already commonplace explanations:

> Although government did not originate in a deliberate contract and although no system of law or social order was ever made out of hand by any one man, government was not at all a spontaneous development. But one having arisen, government was affected, and profoundly affected, by man's choice; only that choice entered not to originate, but to modify, government.[6]

Wilson did not identify the state with enumerated natural rights that supposedly came from a very remote past. Like Hume and Burke, he regarded government
as a cultural-historic artifact that arose out of definable needs and that originated
in a particular time and place. He expresses a debt to the German historical school
of the nineteenth century, which emphasized the state's rootedness in specific historical circumstances. Members of this school focused on the state as a historically
determined institution and on the complex conditions that engendered this political arrangement. In his opening chapter Wilson traces the origin of the modern
state to an Indo-European society that emerged from patriarchal authority and
that substituted contractual for status relations.[7] Here the future president may
have been thinking about the English jurist Henry Sumner Maine, who famously
observed in 1861 that modern civilization had moved "from status to contract."[8]
Like Maine, Wilson assumes that the state as a historical institution had the power
to alter social relations.[9] Kinship and feudal patterns faded in importance as the
state and its sovereign came to dominate what in the new dispensation were individual subjects or citizens.

   Not surprisingly, Thomas Hobbes in his defense of the sovereign state never
refers to nations or classes. In Hobbes's *Leviathan*, we meet only isolated individuals who would engage in perpetual warfare without a sovereign, who is there
to maintain peace and "promote commodity."[10] The assumed lack of collective
identities prior to the social contract in Hobbes's scheme serves his defense of the
sovereign state as something that creates identity as well as a system of defense.
Because of the indispensability of sovereign authority for maintaining civil order,
Hobbes showed no tolerance for anything that might weaken the state. Neither
an intermediary social structure nor any religion that operates in defiance of the
unitary government, according to Hobbes, could be given a free hand, without
creating the threat of political dissolution. Hobbes took this position, according
to Michael Oakeshott, [11] not because he was in love with dictatorial government.
Rather, Hobbes was convinced that given the religious and dynastic wars of his
age, a minimal state would not function effectively, especially in the face of the
murderous discord unleashed by the English civil war.[12] This bloody commotion
was for Hobbes the natural condition that ran from the sixteenth century into
the second half of the next. Then religious and dynastic strife beset the Continent
even more destructively than in Hobbes's homeland. Oakeshott ends his introduction with this pregnant observation:

> What distinguishes Hobbes from earlier and later writers is his premise that man is a
> moving "body," that human conduct is inertial, not teleological movement and that
> 'salvation' lies in continual success in obtaining those things that a man from time
> to time desires. And certainly civil association has no power to bring this about.

Nevertheless, what it offers is something of value relative to his salvation. It offers the removal of some of the circumstances that, if they are not removed, must frustrate the enjoyment of Felicity. It is a negative gift, merely not making impossible what is sought. Here in civil association is neither fulfilment nor wisdom but peace, the only condition of human life that can be permanently established.[13]

According to Oakeshott, the goal of civil association for Hobbes was maintaining tranquility, whence the need for a sovereign state. This institution was a utilitarian necessity beyond the frills that came with inherited power. German legal theorist Carl Schmitt engaged another side of Hobbes's project when he characterized the author of *Leviathan* as "*der Vollender der Reformation*"; that is, the thinker who extracted from the Protestant Reformation its fullest political implications.[14] In contrast to the medieval chain of authority that culminated in the pope or in both the pope and the Holy Roman emperor, the Reformers consigned most religious matters to the civil authorities. There would be no permissible appeal for the clergy beyond national, or in some cases local, magistrates. The papacy, according to the last part of Hobbes's *Leviathan* and in most European monarchies, would also be denied the privilege that the Jesuit cardinal Robert Bellarmine claimed for the bishop of Rome in the sixteenth century. Popes would no longer be allowed to exercise "indirect power" over the Catholic conscience. Hobbes lets it be known that subjects of the state were residing not in a "Christian commonwealth" but in a sovereign state. Only through the disciplining of church authorities, according to Schmitt with reference to Hobbes, did the state system evolve.

For Schmitt, the European nation-state that emerged with the early modern period was a unique historical phenomenon. It belonged to a system of states held together by accepted legal practices, which Schmitt called the *jus europaeum politicum*, that is, European international law.[15] European states held territories that more or less coincided with where their ancestors had settled. This marked out regions culturally and linguistically even before the creation of modern states. Although bloodshed continued to occur after the Peace of Westphalia that followed the Thirty Years' War, armed confrontations would no longer take place over religious differences. Each state would have its own religion that accorded with the wishes of the ruler and eventually with those of the majority of the population. Territorial disputes leading to armed conflict would break out periodically, but these would be contained by diplomatic means and by the recognition that there were no longer "just wars" but only "legally appropriate enemies." In any case, wars for a time would no longer escalate into struggles between those claiming to represent an absolute good opposing an absolute evil. Outbreaks of violence between standing and mercenary forces would be understood as unpleasant interruptions in the way international relations would otherwise proceed.

Needless to say, Schmitt's picture of Europe from the Peace of Westphalia to the eruption of the French Revolution in the late eighteenth century is noticeably idyllic. It sweeps under the rug lots of mayhem, particularly the bloody wars of conquest unleashed by Louis XIV from the 1670s through 1713 and the struggle for European dominance between France and England in the mid-eighteenth century. But what Schmitt may have had in mind when he evoked the old European state system were the generally peaceful conditions in Europe between 1815 and 1914. Then, a properly educated class—the members of which were able to stave off general wars and isolate troublemakers—conducted diplomacy. For Schmitt, as for others of his generation, this was truly *la belle époque*. Writing his magnum opus *Der Nomos der Erde* during World War II and at the beginning of the Cold War, Schmitt may have been pining for an age in which Europe still dominated world politics and in which European states had still not devastated each other.[16]

Like Wilson, Schmitt conceives of the state as a time-bound construction. It was a man-made creation shaped by circumstances, and according to Schmitt, its days were already fatefully numbered. The heyday of the state extended in its European homeland from the early modern period down to the Great War in 1914. According to Schmitt, various modern conditions militated against the survival of the inherited state system. These ranged from the rise and diffusion of modern globalist ideologies to the development of forms of warfare that render obsolete the conduct of limited wars between standing armies. Schmitt viewed modern democracy and internationalist movements as further solvents in weakening the old state system. In the European past states and nations had generally traveled together. As state rulers encouraged ethnic and linguistic cohesion as well as religious unity among their subjects, cultural identity and political rule were joined together in postmedieval Europe. Over a period of centuries the state system came to incorporate distinct nations, fixed territories, and recognizable ruling classes.

As an aside, it should be mentioned that Schmitt was not categorically opposed to democracies, but believed such governments did best when they rested on established national consciousness and a shared history. He considered true constitutions to be not the work of bodies of experts, but documents or traditions that arose from self-conscious peoples. Above all, he scoffed at the idea that a culturally and morally fluid society could produce what he understood as a state. Not surprisingly, he conceived of this invention within the framework of the classical European state system, a system that he saw unraveling by the early twentieth century.

Other illuminating views about the erosion of the state can be derived from, among other authors, Martin van Creveld and Wolfgang Reinhard. Although both these interpreters, perhaps Reinhard more consciously, follow Schmitt in locating the birth of the state in early modern Europe, neither author attributes the state's weakening to those issues that were central to Schmitt's work. The modern democratic welfare state, according to van Creveld, has doomed the state as an institution, because it has made unwise commitments to lobbies and constituencies.[17] A wide range of demographic and age-related problems has hastened this erosion. Van Creveld is particularly thorough in looking at the shrinking mass of taxpayers in relation to those who are living from or will soon become dependent on the public purse.[18] As a military historian, he is also keenly aware of the effects of modern warfare in making national borders a thing of the past. Van Creveld notes that terrorism and partisan tactics have ended the era in which war was a symmetrical exercise of force between sovereign states. The combatants in this new type of warfare do not represent sovereign entities that are engaged in armed conflict with each other; many contemporary warriors are operating outside of any traditional state system.[19]

Reinhard observes that politicians have made extravagant promises to gain votes, with financially ruinous effects. He then underlines a specifically German issue that Germany's intellectuals continue to agonize over—and even give the impression of being obsessed with. The German state, remonstrates Reinhard, deserves to vanish because of its glaringly wicked history and because of the evil it has inflicted on the rest of the world. In his major study *Geschichte der Staatsgewalt*, the author reminds the reader that in Germany the operation of the state culminated in an administration that served the Nazis.[20] Being optimistic, however, the author believes that past German practices of submitting to tyranny are no longer a problem. Since the 1960s a "better socialized" generation of German administrators has replaced those who were there before.[21] Does this mean that Germans have become less servile, or that they have transferred their allegiances to a politically correct regime?

Although Reinhard does not answer this question directly, he doubts that in view of its thousand-year "irreversible structural development . . . the state can now be anything but absolute." Accepting such a protector of our freedom, he explains, may be like "allowing the goat to protect our garden."[22] Still, it might be useful if Reinhard indicated which forms of control he would recommend once the state was encouraged to wither away. Nothing he writes leads one to believe that he wishes to remove political authorities entirely. From his hints, it would seem that as a properly reeducated German he might give the nod to the EU or the United Nations (UN) as a suitable replacement for the old European state system.

Reinhard creates the impression that the state has remained much the same over many generations. Surely there is a difference between dynastic, aristocratic regimes and democratic welfare administrations, or between nation-states in the European sense and what our journalists mean when they praise the United States as a "global democracy" and "propositional nation." In his defense, Reinhard could point to certain features of the modern state that have been around for centuries. Common to all states have been centralized administration, the attempt to subject everyone in one's territory to the same legal code—which is imposed and enforced from above—and the attempted or achieved monopolization of violence by a sovereign authority. Equally noteworthy is that a transmission process is at work by which certain Western administrative features have been carried elsewhere. This export of a Western political structure has been accompanied by another assimilated gift: nationalism. The result has been a hybrid, a mixture in which specifically European features have been grafted onto the political culture of non-Western countries. But this is not the same kind of state building that took place in Europe in centuries past. A recent Third World development, this grafting entails a selective borrowing from Western political life by non-Western elites.

Another relevant question: Are we still dealing with the same political genus when a state that maintains public order, protects national borders, and seeks to preserve the character of a nation shifts gears by devoting its energies to promoting equality and ethnic and lifestyle diversity? Mind you, I am not passing moral judgment on either arrangement. Rather, I wish to note that these forms of governance are not the same, even if both engage in public administration and conduct international relations. And pace Reinhard, were all German administrations more or less interchangeable, because some German administrators had working careers spanning several different regimes?

College administrators of my acquaintance have always appeared to believe in the last thing that they were expected to espouse. One day these functionaries line up to cheer academic freedom; the next day they work to stuff political correctness down everyone's throat, or discover that the driving moral issue in their lives has been creating need-adapted dorms for transgendered persons. Why should we single out German administrators who tried to hold onto their jobs in rapidly changing political circumstances as uniquely opportunistic? The failure to comply with commands in Nazi Germany could bring far stiffer penalties than the fate of losing an academic sinecure in contemporary America. The fact that administrators will mechanically enforce laws does not mean that all governments are interchangeable, or that Hitler's regime was an extension of the Weimar Republic or the German Second Empire. What we are describing here is not Nazism per se, but bureaucracy, as a form of administering people and things that not only served the Third Reich but also serves modern welfare state democracies.

Curiously, European traditionalists have expressed concern that the state may be withering away. One Hungarian Catholic conservative, Thomas Molnar, lamented in his political writings "l'usure de l'état," that the state's power and scope are eroding from one generation to the next. This complaint can still be encountered among French Gaullists; old-fashioned German, Spanish, and Italian nationalists; and others on the European Right—but not necessarily on the neo-fascist right.[23] Such fans of "the state" by no means believe in the ends of government as conceived by the Obama administration, nor from all appearances are they hooked on gay rights or, if they happen to be American citizens, pulling for Hillary Clinton in the presidential race. A positive attitude toward the state has long been characteristic of the historic European Right and is amply evidenced by the statements of Edmund Burke and those of the classical conservatives of the nineteenth century about venerating political authorities. The present identification of the Tea Party patriots and Libertarians with calls to shrink the size of the government would have puzzled such figures.

Real conservatives were never in favor of what our journalists and politicians would consider to be an inclusive democracy. Traditionalists have looked back fondly to an earlier time, that is, to a time in which Europe's political development still revealed the contours of their preferred regime. In this archetypically conservative mind, state, nation, and social tradition all belonged to a bundle of inherited authorities. Perhaps the most recent, halfway acceptable political model that these conservatives would regard with any favor is the Western nation-state, before it began coming apart in the second half of the twentieth century.

Despite this harping on the past, one key assumption of the traditional Right is undoubtedly correct: what we now call the state is not an intact heirloom bequeathed from some very distant past. It is the end point of a transformation by which an older form of political organization became divorced from national and/or traditional hierarchical associations and came to center its energies on massive economic redistribution, social engineering, and the universalization of citizenship. The question remains whether the survival of certain administrative procedures from the past means we are still dealing with what classical conservatives or nineteenth-century liberals understood by the state. The answer is an emphatic *no*. The changes that have occurred in government during the last century do not indicate mere technical advances. Our late modernity has brought forth new structures and new justifications of authority, in which both ends and means have changed significantly.

In *The Old Regime and the French Revolution*, Tocqueville famously posits a relation between the centralizing tendencies of the revolution in France and the earlier consolidation of government under the Bourbon monarchs.[24] The efforts of French kings going back to Henry IV to end aristocratic privilege and increase the taxing, administrative, and judicial powers of the central government culminated in a revolutionary regime that pushed forward the same processes under republican auspices. The reconstruction of France's political structure under the Revolution and Napoléon Bonaparte—according to Tocqueville—had its origins in an earlier monarchical consolidation of power.[25] Although this genealogy is certainly defensible, Tocqueville never mistook the eighteenth-century French monarchy for its revolutionary successor. The revolutionary government spoke about the rights of man and proclaimed its mission to bring these tokens of the new order to a then mostly benighted humanity. It practiced an accelerated consolidation relative to its predecessor and drafted all citizens into a revolutionary army with the *levée en masse*—that is, the mass uprising of the people, but better understood as the large-scale conscription of able-bodied Frenchmen—in 1793. Revolutionary France brought with it a highly administered form of democratic government and tried to reeducate its population in doctrines that came out of the Enlightenment. In *Democracy in America*, Tocqueville announces that he came to the New World to learn about its way of life and whether it provided a variant on democracy that was not accompanied by the extreme centralizing proclivities accompanying the French experiment.[26]

Those tendencies that Tocqueville identified with revolutionary France have survived more or less in the form of the current democratic model. The more we expand the suffrage and the more extensive immigration becomes here and in other Western countries, the more transformative modern democracy becomes. That is neither incidental nor accidental. There may be a close connection between the dissolution or destruction of national or regional communities—which usually bring with them undemocratic inequalities—and the accumulation of administrative power for the purpose of leveling human disparities and banishing discrimination. The march of equality is exactly what modern administered democracy claims to be advancing. The expanded freedom that public administration promotes, as seen in same-sex marriage and feminist self-actualization, is inextricably linked to an expanding egalitarian mission. One can only effect those changes that certain clienteles desire by vastly expanding the custodial role of the government.

Modern mass democracies involve a collective enterprise that seems to defy any restraint or countervailing power. It is not, as Libertarians would have us believe, the latest incarnation of the same demon that has been around since ancient Mesopotamia. We should notice these differences rather than fabricating false or exaggerated continuities. Current critics of the "state" would do well to understand the time-bound characteristics of what they imagine to be their timeless enemy. Finally, I would disclaim any intention of trying to convert anyone to an earlier form of political domination, whether to the state as a concentration of monarchical power or to the nation-state that peaked in the nineteenth and early twentieth centuries. Past models of the state may no longer be historically relevant, and it would be foolish to try to convince others to accept what may no longer be retrievable. Rather, I wish to indicate that politically we are in uncharted waters.

7

Reexamining the Conservative Legacy

Two recently published books, Yuval Levin's *The Great Debate: Edmund Burke and Thomas Paine and the Birth of Right and Left*[1] and Domenico Fisichella's *La Democrazia Contro la Realtà: Il Pensiero Politico di Charles Maurras*, deal with conservative thought in an equally thoughtful manner.[2] The authors of these studies are familiar with the whirlwind of political life, Levin as a transplanted Israeli who contributes regularly to both the *National Review* and the *Weekly Standard* and founded *The New Atlantis*, and Fisichella as minister of culture in the first cabinet of Italian prime minister Silvio Berlusconi and a longtime senator in the Italian National Assembly. Given their preoccupation with political affairs, we may wonder how these individuals found time to produce their scholarly studies.

Both authors believe that their subjects have something to teach the present generation. They maintain that their ideas remain relevant, although in the case of Levin's second subject, Thomas Paine—a critic of Burke, an enthusiast for the French Revolution, and an advocate of the "rights of man"—we are shown what Levin does not consider to be sound political views. A complaint against Levin's work in *The Guardian*, that he is not entirely even-handed in his treatment of Burke and Paine, may be wide of the mark. It is doubtful that the author intended to present his two subjects as equally worthy of our respect. Levin is writing as an exponent of Burkean principles, who presents Paine as a foible to the wiser Burke. Although Levin portrays Paine as a spokesman for an eventually triumphant progressive cause, he sees no reason to join in the celebration, even while acknowledging Paine's effect on posterity.

Fisichella may have a harder row to hoe in eliciting respect for his subject. Charles Maurras was a leading figure of the antidemocratic Right in France for more than fifty years, and his highly polemical newspaper *Action Française* was bitterly critical of everything that the Western world now pays homage to, whether cultural pluralism, political equality, or what Maurras mocked as the human rights heritage of the French Revolution. From his stand in the Dreyfus Affair from its outset in 1894, particularly his insistence that the Jewish Captain Alfred Dreyfus, who was at the center of the affair, should be found guilty of treason for the sake of the French military even if the charge against him was never proven, to his post–World War II condemnation by a French court as a collaborator during the German occupation, Maurras has suffered from a truly bad reputation. But not all of this bad press may be deserved. Maurras's biographer Stéphane Giocanti demonstrates conclusively that the charges heaped on him as a Nazi collaborator were largely unsubstantiated. They represented payback by the French Left, including the true accessories in the fall of France, the Communist Party.[3]

It was not Maurras and his followers in Action Française, many of whom fell in the Battle of France, but rather Communists who refused to take up arms against the invader as long as Nazi Germany remained allied to the Soviet motherland. A lifelong adversary of the "German Menace," Maurras had already called for a French preventive war against Hitler in 1936, when the German government remilitarized the Rhineland. Although Maurras was hailed by the Vichy regime as an intellectual pillar of the new order and wrote in defense of its leader, Marshall Philippe Pétain, he derived no tangible benefit from this association. By the early 1940s Maurras had become a recluse suffering from extreme deafness, although he was dragged out of retirement at the end of the war to stand trial on trumped-up charges.

One may even doubt whether Maurras had any significant influence on the revolutionary Right in France during the late 1930s. By then his monarchist cause had been overshadowed in members and disruptive potential by, among other movements, the Parti Populaire Français, founded in 1936 by the former Communist Jacques Doriot. By the time Hitler invaded France, Maurras's movement and paper (both called Action Française) had drifted into political irrelevance. During the war, as noted by Giocanti, Maurras, who was one of France's leading literary scholars, wrote mostly on belletristic topics.

Although Maurras had long been popular among Catholic traditionalists in France, in 1926 Pope Pius XI, the same pontiff who had Joan of Arc canonized while reaching out to French Catholics, placed Maurras's tracts on the Index of Prohibited Books. Pius discovered to his consternation that Maurras, a freethinking dandy, was not a devout coreligionist but promoted the church for mostly political reasons. Thereafter, such onetime loyalists as Jacques Maritain and Georges Bernanos defected not only from Maurras but also from the Right, evolving over time into politically left-wing Catholics. Another longtime admirer of Maurras was French president Charles de Gaulle, whose family had approved of his promilitary positions. But de Gaulle, a towering figure of the Resistance, was powerless to prevent Maurras's trial, even if he managed to have his death sentence commuted to life imprisonment, which meant five years out of the octogenarian's by then considerably shortened life span.

In any case, Fisichella's attempt to clarify Maurras's statements of "political realism" would seem a harder task than pointing to the merits of Burke's conservative principles, or so it would seem from examining Levin's forcefully argued work. Levin marshals sound points for Burke's "prejudice" in favor of aristocracy as rule

> formed under special social condition. And there is no condition in preferring for rule those who are better formed for making judgments . . . as society sustains itself through inheritance, it will sustain certain social and political inequalities, too, for its own good. And these inequalities have crucial added benefit, beyond elevating the best qualified.[4]

These inequalities, as Levin and Burke both tell us, provide "a strong barrier against the excesses of despotism, by establishing habits and obligations of restraint in ruler and ruled alike grounded in the relations of groups and classes in society."[5] Besides defending the value of this "uneven social topography," Levin explains his subject's misgivings about democracy and "abstract rights." Rights for Burke were part of the "inheritance" of a people, not the invention of a single generation, and while democracy could be a "legitimate part of a government," democracy by itself was ruinous to both prescriptive liberty and a balanced regime.[6]

Levin stresses Burke's indispensable conceptual role in defining what the political Right became by the time of his death. Here the author is stating what is not only axiomatic but true in a sense that goes beyond what he says. Almost all continental critics of the French Revolution and the architects of European conservatism in the early nineteenth century cited Burke's *Reflections*, which have been called "the breviary of the counter-revolution."[7] By the first decade of the nineteenth century French, German, and Italian opponents of the Revolution—as well as defenders of a society of orders and degrees and historical rather than abstract human rights—were quoting Burke with approval.

Even before Friedrich von Gentz, a later adviser to the Prussian monarch Friedrich Wilhelm III, translated the *Reflections* into German in 1793, there were already hundreds of references to the English text among incipient German conservatives. The same was true for French émigré communities that had fled eastward to escape the tumult in their home country. The ideas that German sociologist Karl Mannheim designates as "conservative thinking" would probably have been far harder to formulate if Burke had not lived to see the French Revolution and if he had not been driven by nonconformist minister Richard Price to pen his eloquent diatribe.

More problematic than his formative influence for the Right is whether those ideas that Burke expressed in response to the French Revolution are still pertinent. Levin treads the path already taken by Russell Kirk and Peter Stanlis when he stresses the congruence between Burke's teachings and our own dispensation. We are given the impression that Burke's picture of a sound society and polity is reflected in our present American situation. But one may challenge a statement by Peggy Noonan of *Wall Street Journal* in a review of Levin's book, namely that his work "brilliantly brings out the richness of the tradition underlying our politics."[8] According to Levin, our parties answer to the same "general descriptions" as did the debate between Burke and Paine, which is between "progressive liberalism" and "conservative liberalism."[9] If the Democrats inherit Paine's basic disposition, but seek to liberate the individual in a rather quixotic and more technocratic way than Burke, the Republicans, who stand for "the Right," have "a deep commitment to generational continuity."

Levin correctly notes that Burke's counsel of prudence in politics, which is also, not incidentally, found in Aristotle's *Nicomachean Ethics*, allows us to deal with the "given world."[10] The question is whether this shared Aristotelian reference point establishes a conceptual link between Burke's vision of the good society and our current regime. It may be difficult to pull out of Burke's picture of a well-ordered, hierarchical society and a state built on settled traditions the contours of our present government. One may be forced to agree with the late Frank Meyer when he criticized Russell Kirk's depiction of America in the 1950s as a society that resembled the one Burke was defending in 1790.[11] Meyer warned against confusing an America that had been largely created by the modern administrative state with eighteenth-century England. In *In Defense of Freedom*, he asked rhetorically whether "the whole historical and social situation in which they (America's Burkeans) find themselves, including the development of statism, collectivism and intellectual anarchy" parallels Burke's delineation of a solid constitutional order.[12]

Of course the older America targeted by Meyer may now look almost as archaic as the Old England described by Burke. And this renders even more apposite the question of whether the world that Burke saw himself as upholding pointed toward our own state and society, which claims to be committed to the ideals of human rights and social equality. Would Edmund Burke in observing our society have penned these lines: "Our political system is placed in just correspondence and symmetry with the order of the world and with a mode of existence decreed to a permanent body composed of transitory parts"?[13] I won't add to this rhetorical question by asking how Burke would have responded to whether same-sex marriage should be advanced by the courts or through state legislatures. Neither our continuing struggles for "equal rights" nor a state dedicated to removing social and legal distinctions between genders could conceivably have entered Burke's mind when he denounced the far more modest democratic changes introduced by the French Revolution.

Pace Levin, it is doubtful that our two gargantuan institutionalized national parties are descended from those factions of landed aristocrats who in eighteenth-century England formed cabinet governments. It is also likely that a "conservative movement" promoting universal human rights would have been for Burke a total contradiction It is not even clear that the "liberalism" defended by Levin in his conclusion corresponds to our latter-day understandings of that term.

For anyone who is struck by discontinuity in political life more than by "intergenerational continuities," Fisichella's exposition of Maurras's political theory has much to teach us. One certainly does not leave this book thinking that Maurras was an endearing figure. Much about his career is off-putting. His appeal to anti-Semitism as a populist weapon was anything but commendable. But Maurras spoke emphatically for the "Right," a designation that is not used here as a synonym for the GOP or its promoters in the media. By the 1890s, when Maurras appeared on the French political and journalistic scene, the monarchy, which could have been reestablished in the 1870s, was a thing of the past. In 1906, when Captain Dreyfus was pardoned but not entirely exculpated, France had a committed anti-clerical government, which appealed to the model of the revolutionary Jacobins of 1793. The triad of monarchy, army, and church around which Maurras built his movement was an improvisation. Even the attempt to yoke French nationalism, which was born of the French Revolution, to the Right, was a practice that only took off in the last few decades of the nineteenth century. Unlike Burke, who was a defender of a given world, the Provencal littérateur who founded Action Française invented his reality together with his "political realism."

Fisichella provides a genealogy for Maurras's rightist "logic," citing as his precursors the counterrevolutionary Joseph de Maistre, the father of sociological positivism Auguste Comte, and perhaps most intriguingly, the classical historian Numa Denis Fustel de Coulanges. A diligent student of antiquity, Fustel documented the far-reaching effects of Indo-European religion and customs upon Greek and Roman societies. In *La Cité Antique*,[14] Fustel put his painstakingly gathered material into a monumental study that is still widely read and appreciated. But there is a fact about his work that readers of Fustel (including myself until recently) are generally unaware of. This great classical historian was an ardent French nationalist, who "fixed his target" on Montesquieu and other exponents of the long-standing view that European liberty arose in "the forests of Germania."[15]

Fustel became an oft-cited source for those who wished to prove that European civilization was Greco-Roman rather than Germanic. Not at all surprisingly, Maurras, who underwent an epiphany of sorts while visiting Athens in 1896 and standing before the Parthenon, eagerly embraced Fustel's portrayal of Greco-Roman antiquity. According to Maurras, France was the bearer of Western civilization, in mortal combat with the anticlassical Germans and the only slightly less malign English. Although he made the Catholic Church a pillar of his right-wing nationalism, it was the classical antiquity, not the Jewish authors of the Gospels, as Maurras tells us, that he found worth preserving. Maurras despised Protestantism for its Germanic origin and its emphasis on individual will, and threw in for good measure as the devil's work romantic art and literature, which he attributed to hyperindividualism and a wayward imagination.

Fisichella dwells on the necessarily situational character of Maurras's theoretical construction of a French Right. Although his worldview indicates a Catholic monarchist commitment, Maurras also made accommodations to the age. He vigorously championed the concept of labor unions; acclaimed the Third Estate as the "backbone" of the nation; and was particularly sympathetic to the lower middle class, which in fact had played a pivotal role in the radicalization of the French Revolution and the creation of what for Maurras was the hated Third Republic in 1871. Maurras tried to integrate all classes into the "historic nation" and the "patrimony it bequeathed to posterity." Although a monarchist who praised the pre-Revolutionary France of "thirty kings and forty provinces," he pinned his hope of monarchist restoration on the Count of Paris, a descendant of the Orléanist collateral branch of the Bourbon dynasty. In the nineteenth century this branch of the Bourbon dynasty supported constitutional reforms and the ascending bourgeoisie. Far from being partisans of Action Française, Orléanist promoters were mostly bankers and businesspeople, at least some of whom were Jews and Protestants, two groups that Maurras conspicuously disliked.

Even if not quite the "democratic realist" that Fisichella claims to find in his subject, Maurras was remarkably adaptable in reconfiguring the Right around classes that were extraneous to French conservatives in the early nineteenth century. The template holding this ideology together and attesting to its European rightist character was Maurras's appeal to the French as a historic nation and to those traditions that preserve social cohesion. Maurras distinguished between traditions as "nothing more than collections of nonsense" and inherited practices that nurture families and stable human relations. The nation as he understood it was a physical entity but also a body of tradition that had to be "bequeathed intact." A proper state protected this body of custom and the social relations it upheld while exercising its sovereignty against national enemies. The task of a traditional state, however, was neither to refashion family relations nor to commit one's country to global crusades in the name of abstract universals. It was to preserve and protect what already existed, what Burke called "prescribed rights" and "historic entailments."

Against an ordered social and political life, Maurras pointed to the shambles of the French Republic, which he saw as a front for corrupt interests. Maurras ascribed those scandals to the lack of recognized authority in a government that never stood for the entire nation. To whatever extent the Third Republic had legitimacy, Maurras maintained, it acquired that by identifying itself with the French Revolution. This too bothered Maurras, who viewed the Revolution not as an extension of the French past, but rather as a traumatic break from the older traditions of his country.

Needless to say, one could argue just as easily for the opposite point of view, which Tocqueville did when he plotted the course of political centralization in France through the Bourbon dynasty down to the French Revolution. The Revolution expanded an administrative structure that had begun centuries earlier and which the aristocracy had rebelled against in the eighteenth century. One can also show that both the Enlightenment and romanticism had strong roots in France and, pace Maurras, did not depend for their existence primarily on the thinking of German or English Protestants. Maurras had the tendency to blame on a foreign contamination what was often quintessentially French.

One can also recognize in Maurras's defense of a monarchist regime above partisan interests Rousseau's appeal to the general will in *Du Contrat Social* (*Of the Social Contract*).[16] Like Rousseau, Maurras distinguishes between what most people think they want and "what one in a hundred understands as the general good." Although it is possible that Maurras came up with this formulation on his own, more likely he picked it up while reading France's most famous proto-romantic. Another concern shared by Maurras and Rousseau was the poisonous effects of moneyed interests on political life. The passages that target this pollutant in *Social Contract*, for example—"where there is money, there are also chains; the term 'finance' is a servile term that is unknown in a true political organism"—might well have come from Maurras's numerous tirades against the Third Republic.

These observations are not meant by any means to be an uncritical endorsement of Maurras's plan for French counterrevolutionary reform. Some of his positions are now hopelessly dated, and others, starting with his campaign against Dreyfus, were intemperate even by the standards of his time. On the positive side, however, Maurras was aware of the difficulty of survival that confronts the Right in uncongenial times. Given the will to survive in unpromising circumstances, the Right, or what remains of one, must improvise to remain a political force. It must try to be creative but also true to itself, without sinking into becoming a mere appendage of the Left and without having to draw fictitious distinctions between itself and the other side. The Right must also be able to differentiate between traditions that can provide social stability and intergenerational connections and those that are merely historical excrescences, such as witch hunts or the binding of women's feet in Imperial China. For all his misjudgments and rancorous invective, one can recognize in Maurras's thought, however cobbled together it may have been, a distinctively rightist *gestalt*.

8

Whig History Revisited

HAVING RECENTLY REVISITED Herbert Butterfield's *The Whig Interpretation of History*,[1] I experienced second thoughts about what for me was once a mind-changing book. The occasion for rereading the text after fifty years' absence from it was an invitation to participate in a conference on Butterfield, a Cambridge University Regius Professor who had questioned some of the commonplaces of modern historiography. Butterfield published his short but significant book in 1931 to challenge a historical view that had been formulated by "Protestant gentlemen of the nineteenth century" and predicated on a self-satisfied conception of human progress.[2] The past in this view was seen as a prelude to our modern age and was full of "origins" pointing toward our own moment in time.

It is clear why Butterfield's tract would appeal to someone who has grown tired of a certain historical narrative. A distaste for history as a morality play may be even stronger in some critics today than it was in Butterfield's time, especially among those of us who instinctively recoil from history as the record of designated victims struggling for recognition through the modern enlightened state. Butterfield was addressing an older generation of relatively sober Whig historians of the stature of G. M. Trevelyan and Lord Acton. But his critical observations seem all the more relevant for our age when some of the practices he lamented have become even more grievous than they were a hundred years ago.

Butterfield was not indifferent to what he considered the "big questions," and despite his unhappiness with the idea that Luther and the Reformation had led the West toward "religious liberty"—albeit along a circuitous route—he was not a religious indifferentist or a moral skeptic. Kenneth McIntyre's compendious biography of Butterfield underlines his religious commitment as a Protestant Christian. Whatever his objections to moralizing, they did not involve a rejection of religious principles. In fact, Butterfield offered his criticism as a moral stance. He was plainly upset by those who used the past to create political platforms while pretending to offer nothing but the facts. In contrast to their approach, he urged historians to focus on the complexity of circumstances and the interaction of contending sides to understand historical change. There should be no heroes or villains if history is properly done. What should be sought are clarifications, which require meticulous, dispassionate research.

Herbert Butterfield was asking for a tall order, and he himself expressed reservations about it in a work that he published in 1943, *The Englishman and His History*.[3] Here he was rehabilitating one side of the Whig tradition, which could be found in Edmund Burke and other critics of revolution. This was the search for and possibly invention of an "ancient law" out of which the "historic liberties" of the English people were said to have issued. The jurist who may have been most responsible for this "ancient law" was the chief justice of the King's Bench during the reign of James I, Sir Edward Coke. It was Coke who, in trying to limit monarchical caprice, claimed that kings were subject to a law that went back to time out of memory. The common law that arose from these supposedly ancient practices took precedence over royal statutes.

Coke, who was an amateurish historian, managed to convince the public, and to some extent the monarch himself, of his interpretation, and he enshrined in his posthumously published *Institutes of the Lawes of England*[4] the reconstruction of the Magna Carta as a national document, which guarantees the liberties of all Englishmen. Coke reinterpreted a forced agreement between a cornered monarch, or regent, and his overbearing vassals and managed to turn the extorted concessions into the cornerstone of English liberties. His reformulation furnished the substance of the Petition of Rights that the House of Commons imposed on King Charles I[5] and the rights later demanded by the American colonies on the eve of the American Revolution.

Butterfield was not suggesting that Coke was doing good history. He was merely observing that the idea of ancient liberties, going back before the Norman Conquest, had benefited English society, even if it rested on an invention. But he was also admitting that he himself had been an "impenitent Whig" all along, that he reveled in those liberties that belonged to Englishmen, and that it was that legacy—as he tells us in the final chapter of *The Englishman and His History*[6]—that his nation was fighting for in World War II.

The critical question then is: What part of Butterfield's strictures about the Whig interpretation are we supposed to take seriously, presuming the author was not hiding his real views in 1943 in order to support the British war effort? At the very least, Butterfield's work offers useful advice against moralistic and present-minded history writing.[7] This remains the case even if the author, as he himself reveals, was at least a qualified Whig historian. Butterfield correctly warns against any narrative that is telescoped into a Whig version of abridged history. . . . We have to be on guard when the Whig historian tells us, for example, that the Reformation is justified because it led ultimately to liberty; we must avoid the temptation to make what seem to be the obvious inferences from this statement; for it is possible to argue against the Whig historian that the ultimate issue which he applauds only came in the long run from the fact that, in its immediate results, the Reformation was disastrous for liberty.[8]

Indeed, looking back at the fanatical hatreds of the sixteenth century, Butterfield concludes: "The real seat of the tragedy lay in the ideas that Luther and Calvin and the Popes held in common and held with equal intensity—the idea that society and government should be founded on the basis of the one authoritative religion." Impervious to such facts, the Whig historian "likes to imagine religious liberty issuing beautifully out of Protestantism when in reality it emerges painfully and grudgingly out of something quite different, out of the tragedy of the post-Reformation world."[9]

Historians may also benefit from some of those elegantly worded maxims that Butterfield strews throughout his book, for example:

> The true historical fervor is that of the man for whom the exercise of historical imagination brings its own rewards, in those inklings of a deeper understanding, those glimpses of a new interpretive truth, which are the historian's achievement and his aesthetic delight.[10]

Whereas the self-restrained historian refrains from glorifying the present in the past, he also "goes out to meet the past."[11] "By imaginative sympathy he makes the past intelligible to the present," and he does this by being open to "those complications that undermine our certainties and show us that our judgments are merely relative to time and circumstance."[12] The proper historian understands the meaning of this truism:

> If we turn our present into an absolute to which all other generations are merely relative, we are in any case losing the truer vision of ourselves which history is able to give; we fail to realize those things in which we too are merely relative and we lose a chance of discovering where in the stream of the centuries we ourselves, and our ideas and prejudices, stand.[13]

Some examples of moralistic history writing adduced by Butterfield are so egregious that they place the offenders in an exceedingly bad light. Butterfield may be right when he tells us "in Lord Acton the Whig historian reached his highest consciousness" and "in his writings moral judgment appeared in their most trenchant and uncompromising form, while in his whole estimate of the subject the moral function of history was most greatly magnified."[14] Except for its Victorian padding, this sentence that originated with Acton could have come from a feminist historian declaiming against the sexist past: "It deems the canonization of the historic past more perilous than ignorance or denial, because it would perpetuate the reign of sin and acknowledge the sovereignty of wrong."[15]

Despite these admonitions against present-minded, progressive historiography, we are still forced to notice the Whiggishness in Butterfield. Perhaps we should consider him a chastened member of this school, who recognized its limitations but could not escape its grasp. Even in *The Whig Interpretation of History*, Butterfield praises the achievements of Whig history, which show "that prejudice and passion can make a contribution to historical understanding."[16] The problem is, this genre "brings the efforts of understanding to a halt."[17] The Whig historian "stops the work of imaginative sympathy at a point that could almost be fixed by a formula."[18] Butterfield surely understood that his prime example, Acton, represented the extreme in Whig historiography. Other British historians in the nineteenth and early twentieth centuries, some of whom were Butterfield's teachers, embodied a less triumphalist, more reflective form of Whiggishness.

It might also be instructive to move from the type of Whig history in which, according to Butterfield, we see the "transference into the past of an enthusiasm for something in the present, an enthusiasm for democracy or freedom of thought or the liberal tradition," to a less partisan search for origins.[19] Even without the Whig prism, we can view Luther or Calvin as transitional figures to the modern age, without having to ascribe to them the values of the nineteenth or twentieth centuries. There are things about the Reformation—for example, Luther's rejection of monasticism and stress on the "priesthood of all believers" or Calvin's favorable view of commercial loans—that point toward a postmedieval society.

The historian can note these bridges without misrepresenting Luther or Calvin as a vindicator of religious liberty or as a modern individualist. In his comments about the Whig search for origins, Butterfield defined his target too narrowly by citing the association of religious liberty with the Protestant reformers. But he does observe that Luther and other Protestant reformers of the sixteenth century, whether consciously or not, were engaged in a work of transition toward a later age. Despite their focus on the early church, the reformers were departing from older habits and ways of life, for example, when Calvin defended the charging of interest on commercial loans or when Luther attacked monasticism and urged the clergy to marry.

A final critical point that might be addressed is whether historians can or should avoid "judgments of value," a practice that Butterfield warns against in the course of criticizing Whig historians. Butterfield's defense of this position, as we have seen, jars with some of his underlying assumptions. Clearly he values religious freedom and thinks that the strife that religious differences generated in the sixteenth and seventeenth centuries was an unmitigated evil. It is impossible to read the following sentence without noticing the outrage that drenches every word:

> I do not know who could deny that the Reformation provoked a revival of religious passions, religious fanaticism and religious hatreds which were unlike the world to which things seemed to be moving in the year 1500; and when we look at Erasmus and Machiavelli and the spirit of the renaissance we must wonder whether freedom of thought and modern rationalism might not have had an easier course if Luther had never resuscitated militant religion.[20]

Who would believe these sentiments came from someone who seeks to remove "value judgments" from the study of the past? And what do we do with this oft-quoted aphorism from Butterfield's *Christian Diplomacy and War*?[21] Here the author tells us that "the great menace to our civilization is the conflict between giant organized forms of self-righteousness."[22] In this aphorism Butterfield is once again mixing value judgments into the writing of history.

Admittedly some prominent historians, many of whom Butterfield admired, tried to do exactly what he urged, by composing historical studies from which presentist themes and moral judgment are generally kept out. The medievalist Marc Bloch and the father of nineteenth-century historical research methods Leopold von Ranke worked to achieve this goal. But history, even at the highest level, is rarely done in that manner. As a statement of what drives historians at most times, one should consult John Lukacs's *Historical Consciousness*.[23]

Although Lukacs may overemphasize the subjective nature of historical investigation, his work does locate what is usually an incentive for historical scholarship. Lukacs is correct to pay attention to how existing concerns shape the study of the past. Rarely do historians approach their activity as a detached scientific exercise. Far more often they are led to their subjects by their engagement with their own age. Such historical classics of the mid-nineteenth century as Theodor Mommsen's *Roman History*,[24] especially the fifth volume on the pivotal role of Julius Caesar as the restorer of Roman order; Fustel de Coulanges's *The Ancient City*;[25] and Francis Parkman's *France and England in North America*[26] are unimaginable absent certain nonscholarly preoccupations that influenced their authors. One need not share these preoccupations to recognize the achievements to which they led, nor are these monuments to research in any way diminished by the fact that Parkman set out to celebrate Anglo-Saxon Protestant civilization, that Mommsen was looking for a German unifier, whom some imagine that he had found in Bismarck, or that Fustel de Coulanges wished to glorify the Greco-Roman basis of French civilization.

We may also have to note, like nineteenth-century Whig historians, that the Western world has abandoned what most people would consider to have been unpleasant practices. It would not be inconsistent with the historian's profession to welcome the disappearance of slavery in the West, even if one regrets the carnage of the American Civil War and even if one believes that human bondage might have been abolished in the United States in a less disastrous manner. A historian can hold such a view without descending into the preachiness of Acton or into the hand-wringing of the latest academic advocate of women's studies. Butterfield himself bewails the evils of religious strife, even while urging the historian to put away his present-mindedness. Yet his warnings about Whig history do not prevent him from deploring the religious intolerance of the sixteenth century.

This does not require us to believe that Butterfield or his mentor at Cambridge, G. M. Trevelyan, would have endorsed whatever has been done in our age to advance the secularist project. Whig historians can sympathize with past human reforms without having to applaud every social or political change that has occurred up until the present moment. We should observe that Butterfield, even in his assault on Whig history, writes in a recognizably Whiggish spirit. Although we are told that human achievements are "the result of interaction; they are precipitated by complex history," Butterfield also invokes the broad panorama of "the evolution of constitutional government and religious liberty."[27] Indeed those with any sense for human development should be able to "see this evolution as the cooperative achievement of all humanity, Whig and Tory, assisting in spite of themselves."[28] Should we not also notice here something that resembles Hegel's World Spirit working through our apparent mistakes to bring about happy outcomes?[29] That would not be to read too much into a text, even one that warns against the Whig interpretation of history.

9

The European Union Elections, 2014

WHILE RESEARCHING A BOOK on fascists and antifascists, I noticed the antifascist anxieties mounting after the elections for the European Parliament in May 2014. In those elections, the "Far Right" Front National and its dynamic, attractive leader Marine Le Pen captured one-quarter of the vote in France and helped limit the share of the popular vote won by François Hollande and his leftist coalition to 14 percent. In Britain the United Kingdom Independence Party (UKIP) gained more votes than Labour, the Conservatives, or Liberal Democrats and, like the National Front, obtained about one-quarter of the votes cast. The UKIP, through its leader Nigel Farage, calls for limiting social benefits to immigrants, removing Britain from all EU control, and introducing a school voucher plan similar to one touted by American Republican politicians.

These elections changed nothing internally in the countries in which they took place. Although a barometer of changing public opinion about immigration, the elections did nothing to alter the balance of power in the United Kingdom or France. Those who were in charge before the elections are still running Western European governments. Moreover, the victory of the UKIP in Britain cannot possibly be seen as a triumph for what the media decry as the "Far Right." Neoconservative columnist Seth Lipsky correctly points out that the election in the United Kingdom in May 2014 favored Thatcherite, pro-Atlanticist moderates, who are entirely different from the backers of continental European "hate parties."[1] When approached after the election by Marine Le Pen, who asked him to join the rightist alliance that was crystallizing in the European Parliament, Farage pointedly turned down the offer. The American media are quite right to view Farage and his party as a continuation of the Conservative Party, before it lurched to the left after Thatcher and with particularly dramatic clarity, during David Cameron's tenure as prime minister.[2] Farage's party has not developed the sharp social edge associated with more explicitly anti-immigration or more explicitly nationalist parties in Europe.

The mainstream media have noticed a pattern in how such parties as Fidesz—also known as the Hungarian Civic Alliance—and Jobbik Magyarországért Mozgalom—also known as the Movement for a Better Hungary—in Hungary and the National Front in France blend reactions against the Communist or multicultural Left with opposition to Third World immigration. These parties draw heavily on the youth vote, in contrast to what is happening in the United States, where the young overwhelmingly favor the Left and are molded by what passes for popular culture. Since there was nothing two years ago like a serious, organized Right in the United States before the rise of the populist Trump movement, except for such pale approximations as Tea Party activists protesting tax hikes or the medical insurance plan under the Obama administration, the rightist specter on the European continent makes intellectuals and journalists reach for certain unsettling connections. The nationalist Right is thought to mean fascism, which means Nazis, which in turn means Auschwitz.

This anxious thinking is not peculiar to the *Wall Street Journal* or *New York Times*, although both offered examples of this panicked reaction in the wake of the French election.[3] This reaction indicates growing concern about an enemy that the European and American Left is unwilling to leave in the past. More is at stake here than fear about the return of the Nazi past. The Left points to the resurgent Right to justify its own form of socialization. Any deviation from the Left's prescribed course of social-political control may lead us, or so we are made to believe, into spinning off into a fascist ditch. In this spirit of concern, German chancellor Merkel has assured the world multiple times that "Germany has no party on the right."[4] Indeed, such a party could not long survive in Merkel's reconstructed German society, because the German courts would ban such a presence as a threat "to the liberal democratic order."

Meanwhile, former Communist activists, including longtime Stasi informer Gregor Gysi, are allowed to enter German provincial governments and may soon be asked to join a federal coalition, as members of the Party of Democratic Socialists. A scandal that no one but right-wing politicians, like Prime Minister Viktor Orbán of Hungary, even bother to notice is that former Soviet collaborators, including those who informed on their people, have entered European governments as progressive democrats.[5] This receives scant coverage in the Western press. Such politicians, once they join leftist coalitions in France, Italy, Germany, Hungary, Romania, and so forth, become happy campers on the multicultural bus. Like Gysi in east Germany, they discover such trendy causes as expanded rights for gays and communal privileges for Muslim "new settlers." Longtime Communist myrmidons fit easily into a progressive Western culture and in fact are seen as good for American corporations, since they are open to foreign investment and offer an investment-friendly multicultural ideology.[6]

Perhaps the most frenzied reaction to the elections for the European Parliament in 2014 that I have thus far encountered comes from an acquaintance of mine, Tim Stanley, who blogs for the *Daily Telegraph* in England. For Stanley, the recent electoral results are confirmation of what he's long feared: "European fascism has returned? It never went away and it probably never will."[7] What follows this cri de cœur is a list of characteristics linking the European electoral Right to interwar fascism.[8] As a research scholar in this field, I am led to wonder about Tim's brief. Does the fact that wayward Catholic priests had boys castrated in Holland in the 1950s prove, as Tim seems to be arguing, that fascism was or is on the march in that country?

What conclusions should we draw from the fact that the Austrian Freedom Party had roots in an Austrian classical liberal party that the Nazi government "subsumed" into its movement? The Nazis went around "integrating" everything they could into their party structure. That's what *Gleichschaltung*, which was integral to the creation of a totalitarian regime, entailed. Another supposedly telling mark of the fascist presence that horrifies Tim is that in 1986 Austria elected Kurt Waldheim as president, "a lieutenant during the war who was attached to Germany [*sic*] units that killed partisans and deported Greek Jews."[9]

For the record, Waldheim, who was UN secretary-general from 1972 until 1981—that is, before he became Austrian president—was never a member of the Nazi Party, even if unbeknownst to his passionately anti-Nazi family, he joined a Nazi youth organization after the Nazis occupied Austria. Waldheim was later drafted into the German army and served in a Wehrmacht unit that shot Bosnian partisans who were fighting the occupying forces.[10] Although Waldheim was not directly involved in the shootings, in all probability he knew about them. That said, it is difficult to imagine what he could have done to stop these executions.

The Communist partisans whom the Germans were then fighting were equally willing to execute their enemies.[11] Their victims included members of the monarchist anti-German resistance force known as the Chetniks, with whom Josep Broz Tito's partisans were then struggling for power. One may challenge the claim made by Waldheim that he was ignorant of his unit's involvement in transporting Greek Jews from Salonika to Nazi death camps. All the same, there is no evidence that he assisted in this operation, even if he knew that a removal was taking place. Not exactly parenthetically, Waldheim, who became Austrian president after working for the UN, took office not as a Nazi sympathizer, but as leader of the inconspicuously centrist Austrian People's Party.

I'm also puzzled by Tim's charges about how "neofascism" polluted the postwar Italian government dominated by the Christian Democrats. A neofascist party, the *Movimento Sociale Italiano*, was organized in 1946, the remnants of which later merged with the Alleanza Nazionale, led by the president of the Chamber of Deputies, Gianfranco Fini, in January 1995. This party never entered an Italian government, and when it voted, was generally pro-Atlanticist, procapitalist, and demonstratively pro-Israeli. With regard to the right-wing "terrorism" in Italy noted by Tim, the sporadic examples I could unearth[12] did not compare to the massive violence unleashed by the Red Brigades in Italy in the 1970s.[13]

The charge made against the coalition partner of Orbán's Fidesz Party in the Hungarian government, Jobbik Magyarországért Mozgalom, that it is a raging anti-Semitic force, has sometimes been exaggerated in what may be Tim's source for this accusation, the pro-corporate-investment but socially leftist *Economist.*[14] What is true is that Jobbik has taken a strongly nationalist Hungarian position, criticized the dual loyalty of Hungarian Jewish Zionists, and refused to accept Hungarian responsibility for collaborating in the deportation of Hungarian Jews after the occupation of their country by Nazi Germany in 1944.[15] When a verbally intemperate party member complained about disproportionately high Jewish support for the former Communist regime, this Jobbik official was quickly disciplined by the party leaders, and his remark was repudiated by the premier. But Tim may have to get used to an obstinate Hungarian electorate, which votes for the Right even when the Hungarian economy shows a less than 1 percent annual growth rate. In the EU 2014 election, Jobbik reached a new milestone by picking up 14.7 percent of the vote.[16] Moreover, there is a difference that Tim should note between not liking a parliamentary party in a foreign country and calling on everyone to treat it as an international outlaw.

It would take more space than I am willing to fill to refute all the evidence that Tim cites that Europe has been ripe for a fascist takeover for decades. There is, however, one European government that Tim continues to take pleasure in. It is the one that we imposed on the Germans after World War II, and this government, which our media still oversee, operates with usually obliging German officials. Germany watchers are driven by the fear that Germany could once again become what it was before it was reeducated, but Tim is confident this won't happen, at least not in the foreseeable future. The facts that Germany has "accepted personal responsibility for what it once did"[17] and is willing "to allow the Americans to dictate the terms of German democratization"[18] have been a blessing for the world. The only fly in the ointment, Tim explains, is the attempt to integrate into a west German society, which has been otherwise minutely protected against fascism, a formerly Communist-controlled region that was "fascist-influenced." Apparently the Communists didn't do as good a job as our guys and permitted "a parody of Prussian militarism" to survive on their watch.[19] By the way, Tim is not against the Right entirely. He refers to the zealously antifascist regime of Angela Merkel as "center-right," which may be an accurate way to describe the politics of a country in which no one as far to the right as Karl Rove could be elected dogcatcher.

Having clarified why I think that the fears expressed about fascism in European politics have been vastly overstated, perhaps I should explain why this alarm has been expressed. Like antiracism and antihomophobia in the United States, antifascism is the ideological cement that holds together the political-cultural order in Western "liberal democracies." It forms the ideological mission of the ruling class, in the same way that fighting for an uncorrupted Catholic faith provided a moral justification for the rulers of sixteenth-century Spain, or Marxist-Leninism bestowed a religious faith on the Soviet Union. An attack on a hegemonic creed becomes an assault on the foundations of a regime, or what the Germans more properly characterize as the *Herrschaftsordnung*, the prevalent structure of command and authority in a particular society.

Another explanation for the heated rhetoric is that it's exactly what the media engage in when they're trying to draw attention to themselves. And the more explicitly partisan the "news source" is, the more intense its invective. In the United States, Republican news commentators insist that Barack Obama is a socialist, and even a Marxist, although there is no evidence that the incumbent president holds traditional socialist positions. He certainly has not attempted to nationalize the means of production, which has been a hallmark of socialist programs since the nineteenth century. At most Obama has pushed along a mixed economy, an arrangement accepted by his party and its Republican opposition, in the direction of more government control. Yet explaining what has occurred in this fashion would not have the effect of exciting voters and galvanizing donors into providing campaign contributions. Exaggeration is in the nature of political journalism, particularly where there is an advocacy angle.

But more may be at work here. The European "Far Right" calls into question an existing order of reality and its value structure. Having recently heard on FOX News the young neoconservative Ben Shapiro declare that because of his bigotry Vladimir Putin no longer belonged to the "West,"[20] I had to chuckle that anyone would limit membership in the "West" to those who applaud the gay movement. Until recently the Western world, including the United States, viewed nonheterosexual behavior at least as negatively as the Russian president does. But that would not have been the young Shapiro's experience. In his mind, being "conservative" means being for gay and feminist self-expression or for whatever forms of that self-expression could help his Republican sponsors win electoral victories. Another contributor to *National Review*, Jillian Kay Melchior, has extended the new "conservative" social agenda even further. According to this commentator, the United States has abandoned our Ukrainian allies to Russian expansionists and thereby turned a "cold shoulder" to such presumed Western values as "transgendered rights."[21]

My book *The Strange Death of Marxism* defines as the dominant ideology of Western societies a fusion of cultural Marxism and consumer capitalism.[22] No

major Western political party still advocates such socialist schemes as national-
izing industries or creating a "workers' state." At the same time, no "right center" party challenges any longer the changes that have been introduced in recent
decades regarding women's rights, gay marriage, and expanded expressive freedoms. Any attempt to restrict immigration here or in Europe immediately evokes
outrage from both the media and such advocates of big business interests as the US
Chamber of Commerce.[23] Bearers of this "intolerant" position, it is now believed,
must be narrow-minded, be prejudiced, and as activist judges are insisting, wish
to act unconstitutionally.

The Left and the respectable Right, or what substitutes for a Right, may now
have accepted this expanded notion of tolerance, and therefore the "conservative"
side in the United States restricts its main debating points to Obamacare, excess
spending, and readily usable scandals that can be tied to the other party, more
specifically, Hillary Clinton.[24] The opposition is either convinced of the rightness
of the other side's cultural values or else has decided that it's not worth opposing
what all progressive people are now supposed to believe. Unlike the situation in
France and other European countries, this American political consensus did not
face serious organized opposition until billionaire Donald Trump's seeking the
Republican presidential nomination forced his party to discuss immigration. It
remains to be seen how far Trump can go in dealing with even felonious illegals
in the United States, given the almost monolithic opposition that confronts him
from the media, popular culture, the educational establishment, and most of the
political class. His razor-thin victory in the recent presidential contest should not
be confused with a counterrevolution achieved.

When European parties come along that challenge our consensus, they are
immediately denounced as "anti-Western." Tim rejoices at how far German society has been reconstructed, together with the way Germans exert themselves to
overcome their past. He finds in their reprogrammed country something that
other Western countries would do well to emulate: a postnational society that
embraces multiculturalism and stigmatizes those who resist Tim's path toward
progress. Unfortunately for those of Tim's persuasion, this blueprint may not be
doable everywhere. As someone who remembers a strikingly different West and
revels in true national diversity, I'm delighted that Tim's experiment has hit a snag.

10

The English Constitution Reconsidered

READING WALTER BAGEHOT'S MAGNUM OPUS—which first appeared as a series of essays in *The Fortnightly Review* and was published as a book in 1867—one finds oneself in the presence of a political dinosaur or of someone describing what would soon become one.[1] Commentator Richard Howard Stafford Crossman observed about this work that Bagehot's emphasis on cabinet government as the essential feature of the English polity was falling out of date by the time he was writing.[2] Bagehot was examining "how Cabinet government worked before the extension of the suffrage, before the creation of the party machines, and before the emergence of an independent Civil Service administering a vast, welfare state."[3] It is also incorrect to present Bagehot as a man of the Right. Crossman stresses the overlaps between Bagehot's views of government and those that could be found in the more explicitly democratic J. S. Mill.[4] Both authors considered themselves progressives, and neither had much use for the "dignified" aspects of the traditional constitution associated with the monarchy and House of Lords, except as an emotional prop for the masses.

Russell Kirk was correct when, in *The Conservative Mind*, he noted that Bagehot feared that the rural and village life he had experienced in his native Somerset in Southwest England—where he was born and died—would soon vanish, and "the whole mode and sources of existence will be destroyed and swept away."[5] But contrary to what Kirk suggests, Bagehot never upheld a Tory "party of order" and might have recoiled from Kirk's "conservatism of reflection." The British journalist was a staunch Liberal, a friend of Prime Minister William Gladstone, and a banker who wrote a widely read book about finance and banking, *Lombard Street*.[6] Although Bagehot had no intention of abolishing what he viewed as the ornamental sides of the English constitution, he would have resisted the granting of more power to the "useful" but no longer decisively acting parts of the government.

The monarchy, for example, was useful for its pageantry and the example of middle-class decency set by the royal family. But the kindest thing that Bagehot had to say about this institution was the following: "It introduces irrelevant facts into the business of government, but they are facts which speak to 'men's bosoms' and employ their thoughts."[7] Bagehot had even less complimentary things to say about the monarchy when he was wearing his progressive colors:

> An hereditary king is but an ordinary person, upon an average at best; he is nearly sure to be badly educated for business; he is not very likely to have any taste for business; he is solicited from youth by every temptation to pleasure; he probably passed the whole of his youth in the vicious situation of the heir apparent. . . . [F]or the most part a constitutional king is a damaged common man; not forced to business by necessity as a despot often is, but yet spoiled for business by most of the temptations which spoil a despot.[8]

Although Bagehot sees value in having an "external authority" that could deal with the impasses that arise periodically in parliamentary governments, he would not trust someone "who is nearly sure not to be clever and industrious," namely a monarch, to run the show.[9] He seemed delighted that the monarch's veto power had fallen into such disuse that if the House of Commons condemned Queen Victoria to death, the sovereign would have been required to sign her own death warrant.[10]

Of course such an approving view of monarchical weakness, if uttered today, would hardly cause widespread outrage. Yet 150 years ago—when royal sovereigns and the still unreconstructed House of Lords were thought to be more than ornaments—one would not have expected to hear such views, certainly not in polite circles, and least of all from an alleged member of the English Right. But Bagehot was not speaking as a champion of tradition, save as an advocate of those habits of thinking or fondness for pageantry that had a stabilizing effect on government.

This commentator on English political life also championed the "efficient executive" and "secret republic" that he thought animated the English government of his day. He identified this force of energy with the cabinet and the prime minister, who distributed ministerial responsibilities.[11] It was they who provided the English with "a single sovereign authority," which according to Bagehot gave them an advantage over the citizens of the American republic. Americans were doomed to "having many sovereign authorities" and could only hope "that their multitude may atone for their inferiority."[12] Bagehot regarded the American constitutional system, which rested on a system of checks and balances among the branches of government, to be inferior to how the English parliamentary government had evolved. Unlike the Americans, the English had fused the legislative and executive branches, and—no matter how medieval their political institutions appeared— "the ultimate authority in the English Constitution is a newly elected House of Commons."[13] No matter how the regime might have looked from the outside, a "new House of Commons can despotically and finally resolve" all questions of state, including the "question of making or continuing a war."[14]

Perhaps even more important, out of this body came the cabinets and prime ministers who determined the course of English rule, including England's relations to its colonial empire. Although the prime minister was technically appointed by the monarch, there was little if any latitude exercised by the sovereign in making this determination. The monarch appointed a prime minister under the guidance of the majority party in the House of Commons, an arrangement that perfectly suited Bagehot, who warned against allowing monarchs any more discretionary power.

It would be wrong, however, to imagine that Bagehot did not believe in strong sovereign power. He greatly admired Abraham Lincoln for making the most of a wartime executive in dealing with southern secession. Crossman tells us how grieved he was by Lincoln's assassination because of his reverence for this powerful leader. If he saw the unification of Germany in 1871 as a problem—as did the Earl of Salisbury—it was not because he disapproved of the decisiveness of the Iron Chancellor, Otto von Bismarck. Rather, Bagehot foresaw the dangers to England of a mighty continental competitor and did not wish to see English influence in Europe diminished. If he treated monarchy as a kind of ornament or legal convenience, it was because, as far as this interpreter can understand, he felt neither respect nor affection for it.

The reason, as we have seen, was not that he opposed executive authority per se, any more than did that early champion of the sovereign state Thomas Hobbes, whom the author sometimes quotes. It was rather that Bagehot believed that the "choice of the chief executive should remain in the 'People's House'"[15] and that the prime minister should act as a bearer of the popular will "to carry out within the Constitution desires and conceptions which one branch of the Constitution resists."[16] The obstacle to the executive will, he believed, would come principally from the House of Lords, which retained a veto power. But this "resistance" could be effectively met, if the party in power appointed additional members of its own choosing to the upper house of Parliament, until that body complied with the Commons. Such a measure was threatened by the Liberal government in 1911, when it reduced the veto power that had remained with the Lords.

Despite some comments to the contrary, Bagehot never really argues for a plebiscitary authoritarian government along the lines of French Bonapartism. He was confident that England would continue to be blessed with a fusion of executive and legislative governments lodged in the House of Commons and that this system would be checked by built-in controls. The prime minister, "being the nominee of the party majority is likely to share its feelings," and would depend on continued party support for his administration once he assumed office.[17] Moreover, the House of Commons could dissolve any government if a majority of its members withheld their confidence. Finally, it is the broad middle class that elects Parliament, and this social base even more than the House of Commons and the cabinet, says Bagehot in a later section of his work, served as the true locus of authority.

Fortunately for the United Kingdom, its middle class belonged to a "deferential community," which although not usually well informed about political details, recognized political excellence when it appeared. It was this class that Bagehot thought was the indispensable prerequisite for cabinet government, and he expressed concern that the "highest class" would no longer be able to rule, should England become more democratic:

> In communities where the masses are ignorant but respectful, if you once permit the ignorant class to begin to rule, you may bid farewell to deference forever. Their demagogues will inculcate, their newspapers will recount, that the rule of the existing dynasty (the people) is better than the rule of the fallen dynasty (the aristocracy).[18]

Bagehot varied his opinions in what began as articles for a newspaper, writing about classes and institutions. In some commentaries he vented his ire on monarchs and lords, but elsewhere he rushed to their defense as the protectors of constitutional order and popular morals. Much of this was determined by shifting perspective. Like the historian Thomas Babington Macaulay, Bagehot, who was a self-proclaimed liberal, was writing as a representative of a politically and economically triumphant bourgeoisie. He derided the relics of the political past when he spoke for his ascending class. But he also defended the "theatrical show" of monarch and aristocracy when he contemplated in horror the possible effects of a more advanced democratic government. Unlike J. S. Mill, Bagehot was not an unqualified advocate of extending the suffrage to the lower orders, for all the reasons that we find in the last pages of *The English Constitution*. There Bagehot went into his worst case scenario if the lower class became empowered but lost its deference.

At that point any certainty about how far the United Kingdom had come from "pre-Tudor times" by the 1860s would have to give way to reflection about the utter precariousness of the English constitution:

> A deferential community in which the bulk of the people are ignorant is therefore in a state of what is called in mechanics unstable equilibrium. If the equilibrium is once disturbed, there is no tendency to return to it, but rather to depart from it.[19]

As a further comment, it might be noted that unlike the more progressive protofeminist Mill, Bagehot nurtured little hope of popular uplift through the inculcation of "science" in a system of mass education. Bagehot believed that the perpetuation of public awe toward venerable institutions was what allowed the "best constitution" to go on functioning. Any educational process that drove a wedge between the populace and their objects of awe would cause political and social instability. Bagehot was therefore not a proponent of raising the consciousness of the masses of Englishmen through public education, particularly if the cost would be the weakening of deference for inherited institutions.

The second edition of *The English Constitution*—which came out after the extension of the franchise under Prime Minister Benjamin Disraeli—warned grimly against the possible effects of the new legislation.[20] Although Bagehot believed that there was an "unrepresented class of skilled artisans" to whom one could extend the vote without destabilizing the regime, he lamented that

> the Reform Act of 1867 did not stop at skilled labour; it enfranchised unskilled labour too. And no one will contend that the ordinary working man who has no special skill, and who is only rated because he has a house, can judge much of intellectual matters.[21]

Bagehot blames this act on reckless Tory leaders, who passed it over the heads of their constituents. "On the other side most of the intelligent Liberals were in consternation at the bill"; if they remained silent when it passed, it was because "they would have offended a large section of their constituencies if they had resisted a Tory Bill because it was too democratic."[22] These remarks at the beginning of the second edition, which Bagehot wrote while in declining health, suggests that during his last years he came to question whether all remained right with the English constitution.

The preface to the second edition might well be Bagehot's most truly conservative commentary. There he insisted that there was nothing inherently just or moral about extending the vote, if it would weaken constitutional liberty and the quality of national leadership. Englishmen should not have been congratulating themselves on having a "newly enfranchised class." As Bagehot put it:

> We have not enfranchised a class less needing to be guided by their betters than the old class [of small property owners]; on the contrary, the new class needs it more than the old. The real question is, Will they submit to it, will they defer in the same way to wealth and rank, and to the higher qualities of which these are the rough symbols and the common accompaniments?[23]

As a much younger person, I quoted these lines almost verbatim when the US Congress passed the Voting Rights Act of 1965.[24] Even while acknowledging that the black vote had been deliberately depressed for many decades in violation of the US Constitution, self-styled conservatives need not have rejoiced, which many of them did, that a massive black vote was being mobilized with federal assistance. One effect of that added vote was electoral support for laws and executive acts that reduced traditional restraints on the federal government. The Voting Rights Act also led to measures that increased government surveillance over what has become a greatly restricted liberty of association. Although Bagehot regarded the Reform Act of 1867 as almost unstoppable, he certainly didn't believe that sanctified its passage.[25] Nor did Bagehot equate "justice" with extensions of the franchise, particularly if the effect of the widened suffrage would be a leap into the dark. The Reform Act was something that he knew he and his allies could not hold back, but as an advocate of "rule by the best," he was justified in questioning what he viewed as a falling away from his ideal.

11

Redefining Classes

A S A EUROPEAN HISTORIAN specializing in the nineteenth century, I've never been able to figure out what American journalists and politicians—not to mention academic sociologists—mean when they refer to "classes." This term has two time-tested meanings: either we're talking about social groupings with legally recognized statuses that, until the nineteenth century, enjoyed political rights that other groups did not, or else we mean what Marx understood as "classes," to wit, the socioeconomically dominant forces in a particular time and place, such as the medieval aristocracy or the bourgeoisie that replaced the nobles. Classes are not simply people who fall into a particular, often arbitrarily chosen income bracket or who buy SUVs rather than compact sedans or high-definition televisions, but frown on shopping at Kmart. It is therefore unsettling for a social historian to listen to "economic experts" complaining that the middle class—that is, middle-income families or coinhabitants of a certain suburb—are lacking this or that "middle-class" benefit. "Middle class" used to translate as "bourgeois," which referred to a long-standing social class, not to those who have recently moved up and down the income scale. This bandying about of a onetime historically situated term shows how imprisoned we've become in the last two minutes of our late modernity.

A former colleague of mine who teaches political theory observed that it's now impossible to teach students about Aristotle's conception of the family as a household. The kids get annoyed that an ancient Greek thinker held such a skewed view of family relations. It makes no sense to them, for example, that an aging man was put in charge of other family members. After all, women should be wage earners and make their own decisions about reproductive rights. One young Brazilian exchange student went ballistic when the instructor failed to scold Aristotle for not discussing same-sex marriage. "Isn't this about family togetherness?" asked the student, bewildered.

This present-mindedness applies, admittedly in a less dramatic way, to those who bring up "class" in analyzing current social trends. And it shows up in Charles

Murray's otherwise informative, best-selling book of social commentary, *Coming Apart*.[1] Hailed by the celebrated British historian Niall Ferguson as a defense of traditional family values, the work calls for a return to "the republic's original foundations of family, vocation, community, and faith."[2] Presumably those folks whom Murray points to as worthy of emulation are the high achievers. They are awash in college degrees and IKEA accessories and reside in Murray's not so fictitious Boston suburb of Belmont. These well-healed model residents are placed in sharp contrast to the less well-educated, often unemployed white population of Fishtown, a place that is located near Philadelphia and that warehouses failed white Americans.

According to Murray, the white working force has been declining economically and morally since the second half of the last century, and loads of statistics are marshaled to drive home this point.[3] Among this sizable white population, one now sees the effects of chronic unemployment, low educational performance, and dysfunctional family life. In Belmont, by contrast, the residents are doing fabulously well, producing multidigit double incomes and sending their 1.2 kiddies, or whatever the current reproductive rate is for yuppies, to tony schools. Unfortunately these Belmont residents and their yuppie groupies do nothing for their disadvantaged cousins in Slumtown. They engage in "condescending nonjudgmentalism" instead of presenting themselves as social models for those who need their wondrous example.

Despite my respect for Murray's research and occasionally bold arguments, I find nothing in his book that resembles a traditional bourgeoisie among Belmont's residents. His paradigmatic Americans are mostly super test-takers, who, according to Murray, are endowed with high IQs. They marry people who are culturally and professionally like themselves. Strong gender roles—which were characteristic of traditional classes—hardly exist among Belmonters. While both parents are out amassing wealth, their progeny are being raised by hired help. Wealth-gatherers have relatively low divorce rates, but that may be partly owing to the mathematical fact that divorce is an expensive, time-consuming, commercial transaction for those in a certain income bracket. But this apparent monogamy does not prove that Belmonters are leading vibrant family lives and brimming with "faith and community."[4]

Murray's protagonists do not come by their radical social views entirely by accident. If they don't feel that they belong to a bourgeois, white Christian society, the reason may be that they don't. They are disproportionately Jewish agnostics, Chinese atheists, and whatever other category may fit Murray's circle of friends. Urban high achievers often see themselves as outsiders in terms of the Western past, rather than as people assuming a mantle of leadership bequeathed by nineteenth-century White Anglo-Saxon Protestant Brahmins. Murray's successful

earners include Hollywood moviemakers and those in same-sex marriages, a con-
jugal situation that the author explains in a *Wall Street Journal* interview is "not a
big deal."[5] Murray may be confusing the capacity to earn lots of money with traditional bourgeois values, although the two are not entirely the same. His wealth-
accumulators do not represent a resurrected bourgeoisie, nor are they likely to
bring to fruition the vision of America's founders of a country of yeoman farmers
and sober Christian merchants. The fact that so many "conservatives" are swayed
by Murray's linkage may indicate how little they can recall of any society other
than their own.

12

Did Mussolini Have a Pope?

I N *MUSSOLINI AND THE POPE* DAVID I. KERTZER pursues a deeply
engaged approach to historical questions that is now in academic and journalistic favor.[1] If we accept the axiom that no antifascist enthusiasm goes
unrewarded, then it is understandable why Kertzer, a history professor at Brown
University, received a Pulitzer Prize for his latest book and the additional honor
of seeing his work lavishly praised in *the New York Review of Books*.[2] According to
a report available online, Kertzer's study of the dealings between the Italian *Duce*
and Pope Pius XI convulsed the Italian government. This bombshell caused the
Italian Senate to hold a special session, at which the author lectured his audience
on the Italian-Catholic past.[3] Fame and fortune can still be extracted from the
politics of guilt, and even from misplaced or exaggerated guilt.

In an earlier, equally acclaimed book, Kertzer focused on papal anti-Semitism
down through the ages and maintained that anti-Jewish attitudes among church
dignitaries paved the way for Nazi atrocities.[4] Kertzer tells us that Jews, as well as
other non-Catholics, suffered disabilities living in the Papal States as late as the
nineteenth century. One might likewise note that Jews and other non-Anglicans
suffered disabilities in England during the same time period. But is difficult to
imagine that this situation would have resulted in mass extermination in the
twentieth century for groups that had been previously discriminated against.
Clearly other factors were far more decisive in producing this catastrophe.

No informed person would deny that the Catholic Church was intolerant
throughout much of its history and went after those engaging in religious error,
and that in earlier ages churchmen spoke out intemperately against Jews. One can
also easily demonstrate that over the centuries Protestants have generally been
more tolerant of Jews than the Catholic Church. But the focus here is not on these
comparative attitudes as they played out in past centuries. Rather, we are looking at whether inherited anti-Jewish prejudices made Catholic authorities anti-
Semitic in a way that shaped political actions in the interwar period.

Here one may accuse Kertzer of being overly deterministic in the way he approaches his subject. For example, he excoriates the Jesuit Pietro Tacchi Venturi, who negotiated with Mussolini on behalf of the papacy when the fascist leader was about to enact anti-Jewish laws in 1938.[5] According to Kertzer, Father Venturi was delighted with Mussolini's intention, because Il Duce was carrying out a Jesuit "dream" of removing "noxious Jewish influences" from Christian society.[6] But there are other ways to explain the negotiations with Mussolini, who was then moving into Hitler's orbit. First, Mussolini's Jesuit negotiator was trying to moderate an accomplished fact. He was working to limit the disabilities that were about to be placed on Italian Jews, so they were relatively light in comparison to what had been inflicted on their brothers and sisters in Germany.[7] Father Venturi may have been trying, however ineptly, to make the best of a bad situation. Second, he hoped to persuade the fascist government to lay off Catholic youth organizations, which they were trying to take over. The fascists were already engaging in this practice after taking power, although they stopped for a few years after concluding the Lateran Pacts.

In return for this favor, Venturi indicated that the papacy would not protest the anti-Jewish laws that Mussolini was about to impose. Perhaps the papacy should have openly protested those laws, yet it is difficult to see how the church could have deterred Mussolini from his disastrous course in 1938. Least of all need we assume that Catholic anti-Semitism was at work in order to explain what Kertzer thinks was the most wicked thing done by the church in fascist Italy. Father Venturi was making what he understood to be a practical agreement. Furthermore, as Kertzer points out, the "irascible" and disgusted Pope Pius XI became furious when informed of its contents. Whatever may have been the pope's inherited attitude toward Jews, he emphatically opposed the anti-Semitism of the Third Reich and became livid with rage over Mussolini's attempt to imitate it.[8]

Kertzer does recognize that at least some of the ideological cement that the pope invoked in trying to build a relationship with Mussolini was the appeal to a shared struggle against Protestantism. The fascist struggle against Protestantism, rather than anti-Semitism, was the common interest that Italian fascists stressed in seeking the friendship of the church after 1929. This unifying link between Catholicism and the fascist movement was designated *Romanitas*: the participation in a shared heritage of hierarchy and authority going back to the ancient Romans. Protestantism embodied the counterprinciple, against which the papacy and the Italian government were urged to stand firm. Indeed, the fascists saw this confrontation as taking place on an international level and pitting Roman authority against corrosive Protestant individualism and the capitalist profit motive characteristic of Northern European societies.[9]

In *Il fascismo e l'Oriente,* Renzo de Felice documents to what extent Italian fascist efforts to gain influence in Asia were dictated by Mussolini's rivalry with the English. Whether in Egypt, Iraq, Palestine, or India, the fascist leader saw himself as competing with the English government and English people as he built bridges to Arabs, Zionists, Indians, and Turks.[10] Mussolini's well-documented outreach to Zionist leaders in 1933 and 1934 and during the early months of 1935, according to de Felice, was intended, "besides gaining for Il Duce sympathy in Europe and America as the protector of the Jews," to "intensify tensions in Palestine and to create further difficulties for England in one of the most sensitive points of its empire."[11]

Another historian of Italian-Zionist relations in fascist Italy, S. I. Minerbi, places Mussolini's onetime warm relations with Zionists, and especially with the right-wing Jewish nationalist Zev Jabotinsky, in the context of his effort to "replace Great Britain in Palestine, while uprooting (the English-governed) mandate status of the region."[12] Mussolini pursued this policy in defiance of his foreign office in the Palazzo Chigi, which urged a more balanced approach to the conflict between the Arabs and Jewish Zionists. And he took this path owing to his fixed view of England as a geopolitical enemy in the eastern Mediterranean as well as a continuing cultural adversary.

In an anthology dealing with the problems of creating a unitary Italian identity, an editor of the Milanese daily *Corriere della Sera,* Ernesto Galli della Loggia, emphasizes two factors that have unified Italians down through the centuries: their Latin and Catholic legacies, or *retaggi.*[13] Despite the persistent invasions and occupations of the Italian peninsula and Sicily and despite the paucity of arable land for agriculture (Italian industrialization developed late and up until after World War II sporadically), all Italians could take pride in their Roman and Roman Catholic antecedents. From the late nineteenth century on, there arose among Italian elites a passion to recapture the glory of the Roman past, including the domination of the Mediterranean and the creation of an overseas empire bordering that sea. Mussolini spoke about the Mediterranean as *Mare Nostro,* and the nationalist poet Gabriel D'Annunzio hailed a mobilized Italy standing *prora al vento,* that is, bow toward the wind. The sedulous attempt made by the fascists to fuse a Latin national identity with the Roman Catholic loyalties had nothing to do with hating Jews. Their declared enemies in 1929 were the plutocratic Protestant nations, which fascist publicists were then denouncing almost nonstop.

Catholic clergy throughout Europe opposed the Nazis, and more than a few spoke out against Hitler's racial anti-Semitism. In Germany Catholic leaders were far more willing than the state-controlled Evangelical Church to scold the Nazis. Up until March 1933, when they caved in under misdirection from the Holy See, the Catholic Center Party in Germany remained a bulwark of resistance to the Third Reich and even ran Jews as candidates in electoral districts in Berlin. Even the very progressivist *Der Spiegel*, which is hardly known for its fondness for either German nationalism or clericalism, has stated that Catholic voters were far less receptive than Protestant ones to Nazi Party candidates.[14] Only 17 percent of the support that went to Nazi candidates before March 1933—in what was then a controlled election—came from German Catholics. The attempts at demonstrating some special Catholic affinity for the Nazi Party are less than convincing. Recent attacks on Pope Pius XII as "Hitler's pope" are so far removed from any truth that one flinches to read such overstatements. Pope Pius XII saved Italian Jews during the Nazi occupation of Italy and—as Rabbi David G. Dalin points out in a widely publicized defense that reads very much like the expression of gratitude that came after the war from Israeli political leader Golda Meier—the pope helped Jews whom he managed to save in difficult circumstances.[15]

The decision of Dutch Catholic bishops to speak out against Nazi anti-Semitism brought as retribution the deportation of Jewish converts to Catholicism together with other hapless Dutch Jews. In Poland during the Nazi occupation, Catholic priests who denounced Nazis were thrown into concentration camps or summarily killed. The same happened in Germany to clerical opponents of the regime. It would be untrue to say that no Catholic clergy anywhere collaborated with the Nazis. Unfortunately, there were priests in Croatia, Slovakia, and elsewhere who did. That said, there is no specifically Catholic pattern of such behavior. Devout Catholics, much as Calvinists in France and Hungary, Lutherans in Denmark, and Orthodox in Bulgaria, behaved honorably and in some cases heroically in the face of the Nazis' tyranny.

In any case, the fact that the Catholic Church had discriminated against Jews in the past did not make it especially receptive to Nazi race doctrines or the idea of Aryan supremacy. Kertzer admits that the papacy generally, and Pope Pius XI in particular, rejected racial anti-Semitism. Indeed the pope famously emphasized in an interview with a Belgian newspaper in 1938, "that spiritually we are all Semites."[16] A concordat that the church reached with the Nazi state in 1933, and which was prepared by Cardinal Eugenio Pacelli, the Germanophone future Pope Pius XII, broke down as soon as it became apparent that Hitler would not tolerate independent religious organizations. This led to the papal encyclical drafted in German (also by Pacelli), *Mit brennender Sorge,* in March 1937, which underlined the heightened conflict between Rome and Berlin. By then the papacy had given up on the possibility of any cooperation with the Nazi order. Because of his association with Hitler, moreover, as Kertzer points out, Mussolini was "losing his luster" in Catholic circles and among Catholic clergy throughout the West.[17]

Note that most of the attacks on Pope Pius XII as a Nazi sympathizer condemn him for his supposed nonaction. Harder to show, even minimally, is that this pope, or his predecessor Pius XI, displayed any sympathy for the Nazis. In a balanced though critical treatment, *Pius XII and the Holocaust,* José M. Sanchez[18] demonstrates the often conflicting roles in which the pope considered himself caught, trying to balance the interests of the institution he was chosen to lead with a moral obligation to speak out against a colossal evil. Although Sanchez does not go as far as Dalin in praising his subject's example of leadership, he does depict him as a thoroughly decent clergyman laboring with immense responsibility.

The fact that Pius XII was concerned at the end of the war with a Communist takeover in Italy and France and the presence of Stalin's armies in Central Europe did not reveal any evil intent. The pope's attitudes were perfectly justified and certainly did not prove that he was rooting for the Third Reich. I tried to make this self-evident point as forcefully as possible in the *British Spectator*[19] in response to John Cornwell's imputations of Nazi sympathies to Pius in *Hitler's Pope.*[20] Although Kertzer professes to be neutral in his reference to Cornwell's book, he frets that little attention has been paid to Cardinal Eugenio Pacelli's role in Italy in the years before the war. Quite plainly Kertzer believes that Cardinal Pacelli encouraged "collaboration" with the Italian fascist regime well into the 1930s.[21] Omitted from this implied reproach are the following details. Up until the late 1930s Mussolini's government did not discriminate against Jews. Indeed, from 1934 until 1936, when Mussolini switched sides and helped form the Axis, *Il Duce* was outspokenly anti-Nazi; offered asylum to German Jews; and provided training space for the Revisionist Zionists, who deeply admired the Italian fascists.[22]

Contrary to the "advance praise" lavished on the dust cover, Kertzer's book does not stray far from conventional accounts of the events in question. Although "the staggering evidence" that the Vatican put at the author's disposal is thought to have turned his book into an eye-opener, one can dispute whether these added facts change our historical picture in any significant way. Much of what occupies the book is already old hat: for example, that Italian Jesuits over the centuries deplored Jewish influences in Christian society, that Mussolini—despite having a Jewish mistress and biographer and despite his willingness to promote Jews to high places in his regime—uttered anti-Jewish comments before the late 1930s, and that in 1938 he arbitrarily stripped Jews of professional positions and membership in the Fascist Party.

Starting in the fall of 1943, the Italian Social Republic—over which Mussolini was made the largely powerless titular head and which was closely overseen by Nazi Germany—rounded up Jews in its shrinking area of control. Thereafter the Schutzstaffel (SS) and its Italian collaborators shot Jews or helped deport them to camps, where some of the detainees were killed and others died of ill treatment.

All these things can be easily proved, with or without access to special documents stored in the Vatican. But if Kertzer had left his brief at this, no one who counted in academic and journalistic circles would be hailing his accomplishment. As so often is the case with "best sellers" in history, success comes from the interpretive twist given to plain facts rather than from the facts themselves.

Kertzer has achieved international fame by playing up the horrifying character of "fascism" and its connection to Roman Catholicism, which before the Second Vatican Council discriminated against the Jews as a people. But these revelations about the church's record of prejudice and the willingness of the fascist government to end the Italian state's conflict with the religious institution of its population are nothing new. Kertzer also brings up something else that is widely known and which my recently published book on fascism examines in depth, namely that there was a symbolic and organizational connection between Latin fascism and the Catholic matrix out of which the fascist founding fathers came.[23] Of course this family resemblance need not reflect negatively on the Catholic Church. Movements borrow from existing organizational and social models in trying to mobilize followers. The fact that Marxists appeal to a vision of the end times that has roots in the Old Testament prophets and in the primitive church does not prove that the Bible is responsible for Marxist-Leninism. It demonstrates that modern ideologies draw upon religious sources in defining their identities.

Kertzer seems to be insisting that we regard fascist Italy from the moment Mussolini came to power as an especially evil regime. He is perceptibly irritated, and shows it throughout his work, with those who had truck with the fascist devil. Later American cardinal Francis Spellman, who in 1929 was working in the Vatican, is depicted even as a young man as the reactionary figure his critics on the Catholic Left have delighted in hating. Monsignor Spellman committed the indiscretion of writing to his mother from Rome expressing satisfaction that the Italian state and the papacy had come to a jurisdictional agreement.[24] But Kertzer makes room for many others in his rogues' gallery of "undemocratic" churchmen. Cardinal Pietro Gasparri—the papal secretary of state who negotiated the Lateran agreements in 1929 and who signed them on behalf of the papacy—is made to look like a contemptible wheeler-dealer. To its discredit, the institution for which Gasparri worked "had no special fondness for democracy" and was merely concerned with "whether Mussolini could be trusted to honor his promise to restore the Church's influence in Italy."[25]

It is difficult to grasp why the papacy's decision to deal with the existing Italian government in 1929, rather than the one that Kertzer would have preferred, was a moral outrage. Fairness requires us to recognize that the Italian state and the church were at war during the ramshackle, corrupt *partitocrazia* that Mussolini replaced in 1922. Kertzer's Italian "democracy" had been unable to quell the violence and civil unrest that gripped Italy after World War I. One may point this out even while acknowledging the opportunistic role played by the fascist *squadristi*, who went from being antibourgeois revolutionaries to a self-proclaimed force of order. And although fascist brawlers engaged in street fights with revolutionary socialists, they were not the only side creating violence.

Allow me to raise the question of why the fascist state from its inception was so wicked that the papacy should never have made an agreement with its representatives. Among the evil states of the last hundred years, Mussolini's government seems relatively benign, certainly until the late 1930s. Except for a few assassinations, mostly outside Italy, it did not kill its critics. Furthermore, except for its intermittent hectoring of church organizations, it left the economy and civil society largely free, and it was quite tolerant of the Jews up until the late 1930s. Until Mussolini's disastrous decision to make a pact with Nazi Germany, the fascist government enjoyed the effusive approval of Prime Minister Winston Churchill, President Franklin Delano Roosevelt and his brain trusters, the *New Republic* magazine, and a multitude of Jewish organizations. The virtues ascribed to this regime were mostly exaggerated, but so is its present demonization, which may reflect the current political climate.

In comparison with Third World dictatorships that the papacy now recognizes or negotiates with, Italy in 1929 was an oasis of religious freedom. This raises another question: Is Kertzer similarly outraged that the papacy now makes overtures to Saudi Arabia, the People's Republic of China, and a host of African kleptocracies? What about Communist Cuba, a brutally anticlerical government, to which Pope Francis is reaching out? Are these negotiating partners any better than Mussolini's government was in 1929? To be provocative, I couldn't imagine Mussolini requiring Catholic or Protestant clergy to desist from criticizing same-sex marriage lest they become subject to criminal prosecution. This now happens with increasing frequency in "liberal democracies" like Canada.

13

Heidegger and Strauss: A Comparative Study

RICHARD L. VELKLEY, Celia Scott Weatherhead Professor of Philosophy at Tulane University and the author of two previous books, one on Rousseau and the other on the moral foundations of Kantian philosophy, has brought out another challenging study, *Heidegger, Strauss, and the Premises of Philosophy*.[1] Velkley's subtitle, "On Original Forgetting," is intended to call to mind Plato's view that the entrapment of the soul in the body causes forgetfulness. (Plato speaks of the "plain of forgetfulness [perdion lēthēs]" and the "river of non-caring [potamos Amelētos]" in Book Ten of the *Republic*, where Socrates, through the Myth of Er, recounts the soul's journey toward Earth.)[2] The human person must devote his life to contemplation as an act of retrieving those eternal truths that had been lost with birth. Learning as conceived by Plato was a prolonged act of recalling (*anamnēsis*) what the soul would again be aware of once distanced from its earthly prison.

"Original forgetting" also calls to mind the concept popularized by the German philosopher Martin Heidegger, who viewed his intellectual task as "uncovering" the truth of being. This "uncovering" or "unconcealment," according to Heidegger, required systematic inquiry. The failure to know or even begin to explore our identity betrayed the persistence of "*Seinsvergessenheit*," a forgetting that the philosopher should seek to undo. Overcoming this forgetting could only be undertaken by working through and then moving beyond ready-to-hand superficialities as we struggled toward self-understanding. Unlike Plato, Heidegger believed that self-discovery entailed a dimension of time. *Zeitlichkeit* or *Historizität* (time- or history-centeredness) provided the context in which *Seiende*, those who had still not probed beneath the surface of their existence, could uncover their specific being (Dasein).[3] This inquiry was ultimately framed by our mortality. There was no transcendence in Heidegger's thought in either the Platonic or biblical sense; what gave our lives meaning and direction was experiencing a life situation (*Mit-in-der-Welt-sein*) while inescapably moving toward our end (*Sein zum Tod*).[4]

This being-toward-death, according to Heidegger, does not simply mean that we are moving physically toward death. It teaches that we can organize our lives and their attendant projects on the understanding that we are destined to disappear from the world. This represents the final point in the ascent of the individual through engagement with his temporally situated being, going from superficial encounters (*Zu-und Vorhandensein* or the apophantic) through various acts of attending to things or to others (*Sorge* or *Besorgung*) and from there to a life project that ends in death. In Heidegger's view there is no dualism between consciousness and the surrounding world. "Being in the world" is a necessary step in the work of defining our Dasein.

In a remarkable (and, in my opinion, problematic) fashion, Velkley has paired Heidegger with the German Jewish commentator on political texts Leo Strauss. Strauss was acquainted with Heidegger's work while still in interwar Germany and openly expressed admiration for his outstanding philosophical achievement. After attending Heidegger's lectures at the University of Freiburg in 1922, Strauss visited Franz Rosenzweig and told this Jewish theologian that "Max Weber is an orphan child" "compared to Heidegger."[5] Both Strauss and his companion, the Plato scholar and mathematician Jacob Klein, marveled at Heidegger's "Destruktion of the tradition. He intended to uproot Greek philosophy, especially Aristotle, but this presupposed the laying bare of its roots as it was in itself and not as it had come to appear in light of the tradition and of modern philosophy."[6]

Velkley discusses at length the famous disputation between Heidegger and the neo-Kantian philosopher (and Strauss's dissertation director at the University of Hamburg) Ernst Cassirer in Davos, Switzerland, in 1929.[7] The difference between these two formidable minds centered on their interpretations of Kant's *Critique of Pure Reason,* a subject on which both disputants were then writing studies. Cassirer, in line with other neo-Kantians, interpreted Kant's work as both providing a theory of the natural sciences and establishing a "realm of freedom" through the positing of a universal moral law. Heidegger vigorously challenged these contentions (he was then at work on his tractate *Kant and the Problem of Metaphysics)* and tried to give Kant's *Critique* an existential twist. What Kant was doing, Heidegger insisted, was linking the moral law to the "project" that each of us must undertake in order to grasp our distinctive Dasein.

For those who read the lectures of the two disputants, it should be clear that Cassirer had the stronger argument about Kant's intention in his first *Critique.* Cassirer's examination of Kant's theory of transcendental deduction, which elaborates on the relation between sensory data and the structure of human consciousness, was superbly done. Although Heidegger may have been the greater original philosopher, he was clearly not the more convincing interpreter of Kant. But the most revealing statement about the debate was made by Strauss, who was present in Davos and whose relevant comments were published after World War II: this debate "revealed the emptiness of this remarkable representative of established academic philosophy to anyone who had eyes to see."[8]

Let us allow for the fact that Strauss profoundly disliked his fellow German Jew Cassirer, who refused to direct his *Habilitationsschrift,* the completion of which would have permitted Strauss to obtain a professorial rank. Let us also grant that Heidegger was a deeper thinker than Cassirer and was laying out his ontological premises in an original interpretation of Kant's *Critique.* What must still be asked is how Cassirer's meticulous reading of Kant's work as presented in Davos "revealed emptiness." Cassirer was one of the foremost Kant scholars of his age, and "productive imagination," which Cassirer found foreshadowed in Kant, was a subject that he understood in depth. This concept had been fleshed out in Cassirer's three-volume work on symbolic logic, published in the 1920s, and was at least incipiently present in the volume that accompanied the complete edition of Kant's work produced by the Bruno Cassirer Publishing House in 1918.[9] Strauss's judgment suggests not only his irritation with Cassirer but, even more significantly, his deep veneration for Heidegger.

Velkley is therefore correct to point out that Strauss's connection to Heidegger should be seen as an enduring aspect of his life and thought. This was the case even if there is no indication that Heidegger was aware of Strauss at the time that Strauss was complimenting his brilliance. A connection between the two was there, even if Strauss after his exile from Nazi Germany railed against the influence of German thought and transmitted this attitude to his disciples. Strauss continued to extol Heidegger as a brilliant philosopher into the postwar years, even if these comments made little impression on his students, who usually take a markedly negative view of Nietzsche and Heidegger and of German thought in general.

Velkley explains that Heidegger and Strauss were both dealing with the "aporia of being" and in a continuing way with Plato's image of the Cave in *The Republic.*[10] They both understood that the masses of mankind were not disposed to reflect on the nature of being and could only glimpse philosophical truth (Platonic *epistē-mai*) through myths or vague opinions (*doxai*). In Heidegger's thought the truth problem becomes even more complicated; there we encounter "the radicality of freedom that has no ground in human nature" and "which can appear, or disappear only at the whim of history or fate."

Furthermore, "the promise of freedom will appear most forcefully at those moments when ordinary destruction, with its ontic or merely 'natural' concerns, is most threatened with destruction. In this way, nihilism, as the complete immersion in beings, can destroy itself when its negative force is turned against the beings, thus compelling human life to be free for the openness of Being."[11] Velkley seems to be saying that both havoc and nihilism were regarded by Heidegger as useful for ontological self-exploration. Although this may be Velkley's reading, it is entirely possible to study Heidegger's most famous and most widely distributed work, *Sein und Zeit,* and come to different conclusions. Perhaps not coincidentally, Velkley makes negative judgments about Heidegger that also prevail among Strauss's disciples.[12]

He then goes on to depict Strauss as someone who admired but recoiled from the implications of Heidegger's ontology. Strauss adopted this sense of distance even while learning from Heidegger. Both embraced the insight that Plato's philosophy opened the door to basic ontological questions. Note, however, that the merit in the Platonic discourse for both men was mostly its *eristikē,* the mode of discourse that shapes and pervades the dialogues. Plato's dialogues and myths were thought by both of Velkley's subjects to yield not so much definitive answers as a sense of what philosophy is about. For Heidegger and Strauss as well as Plato, "the aporia of Being" remained both an obstacle and a challenge in philosophy, from its classical form on. This aporia drove humans' inquiry but never furnished conclusive answers to our first-order questions. Strauss was also fascinated by Heidegger's reconstruction of Aristotle's ontology. No longer would this field of inquiry focus on the unity of being emanating from a Supreme Being; instead it would examine a multiplicity of *Seiende* trying to come to terms with their distinctive Dasein.

If I read Velkley right, he is suggesting (while also intermittently denying) that Strauss examined Heidegger's premises but then moved on to a higher moral plane, thereby escaping the nihilistic and relativistic implications of Heideggerian existentialism. In his concluding pages Velkley praises Strauss for understanding "that the appeal to History has the effect of concealing the skeptical and aporetic nature of philosophy as the critique of custom and law. This is the real meaning of Strauss's claim that Heidegger's thought has no room for political philosophy."[13]

Velkley also quotes Strauss to the effect that there are answers to how politics should be practiced, and this may oblige us to combat those who hold other positions. "The biggest event of 1933 would rather seem to have proved, if such a proof was necessary, that man cannot abandon the question of the good society and that he cannot free himself from the responsibility for answering it by deferring to History or to any other power different from his own reason."[14] Velkley notes approvingly that, presumably unlike Heidegger, Strauss never "regarded only philosophers as having a right to appeal to reason."[15] Allow me to express my skepticism on this last point. Do Strauss and his acolytes really "appeal to reason" when they intersperse their "political philosophy" with civics lessons and value instruction? Although these lessons may (or may not) be helpful, they are not, as far as this reader can determine, pure exercises in philosophical reasoning or inquiry.

The big elephant in the room to which Velkley refers several times is Heidegger's displays of Nazi sympathy in 1933 and occasionally thereafter. A subject that need not concern us here, it may nonetheless be behind Velkley's effort to prepare an informative study on Heidegger while dragging in someone of a very different stripe as a foil. But there are certain inherent problems with this approach. Whereas Heidegger, despite his disastrous foray into politics, was a seminal philosopher in a traditional area of philosophical investigation, Strauss wrote learned commentaries on political texts. Whereas Heidegger in *Sein und Zeit* approached "conscience" in the context of the self-consciousness of Dasein, Strauss, particularly in his later period, moralized about politics while reproaching "political scientists" for their value neutrality. Strauss's most widely read work, *Natural Right and History,* which came out of his Walgreen Lectures delivered at the University of Chicago in 1949, includes a vigorous defense of what he considered to be the best regime of the modern era. Strauss extols American democracy while laying bare what he saw as the evils of historicism, positivism, and relativism.[16]

Although one can learn from Strauss's commentaries, especially those of his early German period, in the present work he is reduced to a kind of papier-mâché hero. Velkley would do well to read my book *Leo Strauss and the Conservative Movement in America,* which challenges the view of Strauss as an ideologically detached philosophical observer.[17] My book also questions the claim made by Strauss and his disciples that political texts and their study are exercises in "philosophy." In Strauss's work after he arrived in America and a fortiori in the works of his disciples, there are sometimes stark political agendas lurking beneath the surface. Let me state that I don't believe that I've spoken the last word on Strauss's commitments. Rather, I cite my writing because I think it would be a good idea if Velkley engaged with counterargument about Strauss, particularly in relation to Heidegger. The superiority of the former, we are made to think, is owing to the fact that he was more open to philosophy, at least as he understood it, and less politically driven. Whether or not those attributions are true, they do not show that Strauss was superior to Heidegger as a philosopher.

Further, Strauss was himself involved, and far longer than Heidegger, in conspicuous political engagements. The intellectual historian Karl Löwith knew both men well and wrote quite critically about his teacher Heidegger as a thinker and political actor.[18] He also recorded Heidegger's pro-Nazi statements but never mistook him for a believing Nazi as opposed to a foolish political adventurer. Löwith also listened patiently to his friend Strauss as he swerved from one political enthusiasm to another, going from being a right-wing Revisionist Zionist and a brief admirer of fascist Italy to a Churchill worshipper and finally a passionate exponent of American liberal internationalism.

Although Heidegger, as Velkley tells us, may have missed the right "lesson of 1933," it is open to question whether Strauss drew the proper one. In any case there is more than one lesson that could be taken from the Nazi catastrophe, depending on one's historical situation and political perspectives. And another point comes to mind here. While neither Strauss nor Velkley may have cared for Heidegger's "meditative" response and withdrawal from politics after his Nazi moment, it is possible to view these gestures as a lesson learned.[19] Velkley's complaint about politicized philosophy should apply to both of his subjects. Why should we chide Heidegger but not Strauss for having "never learned the lesson that all political engagement on behalf of his vision is inherently mistaken?"[20]

A reviewer should not miss these few minor points in a discussion of Velkley's monograph. The interpretation of Plato that is assumed therein is one that Strauss took from Arab philosophy, particularly from Averroes and Avicenna. These medieval authors viewed Plato as a skeptic in terms of his theological references in such dialogues as *Phaedrus, Timaeus,* and *The Republic.* Plato's ideal forms, invocations of the divine, and narratives about the soul were taken by these interpreters and later by Strauss as heuristic devices, that is, as ways of constructing philosophical inquiry. Although a defensible but not obvious hermeneutical perspective, it is nonetheless not the only one through which we can appreciate Plato's invocation of the spiritual.

To illustrate this point: there are elements in the Myth of Er, which comes up at the end of *The Republic,* that we might be justified in regarding as allegorical or heuristic. Whether a dead warrior from Pamphulia was actually returned to life on his funeral pyre, whether there was a celestial spindle designating all the heavenly bodies that the Fates kept revolving in order to maintain cosmic order, and whether Necessity and her three daughters were thought to tower over Socrates's Heaven are all questions we might reasonably raise about Plato's theology. More problematic, however, is to treat the entire account as simply a story that is put into Socrates's mouth about events that he didn't believe take place. It is this tendency among Strauss and his disciples—to find their own theological skepticism present in long-dead thinkers—that may represent the most questionable side of their scholarship.[21]

Velkley cites Jacob Klein as a figure who influenced both Klein's mentor Heidegger and Klein's longtime friend Strauss. Klein was a celebrated polymath who treated the ideal form attached to Platonic numbers and their symbolic reconstruction in mathematics as foundational for medieval Arab algebra. During his career in interwar Germany and later in the United States, Klein attracted a variety of scholars to his productive research. Heidegger and Hans-Georg Gadamer, among many others, were impressed by his tracts—and especially Klein's study of Plato's *Meno* as leading toward a later understanding of numbers (*arithmoi*).[22] Although Strauss was also marked by Klein's work, his efforts to secularize Platonic philosophy arose from other sources. Nor need we assume that Strauss and Klein consistently held the same views despite their friendship of many years. Strauss was personally close to the intellectual historian Löwith (a Protestant of Jewish descent who was driven out of Nazi Germany), yet their writings indicate very different perspectives and interests. Pace Velkley, Carl Schmitt did not call for an "absolute obligation to the state,"[23] but presented the Hobbesian formulation that in return for protection the subject or citizen should be expected to obey the state.

To his credit, Velkley is well schooled in German philosophy and reveals extensive knowledge of Heidegger and Kant in this book as well as in his other writings. His attempts to relate Heidegger's thinking to his understanding of Kant and the German idealist tradition of philosophy show extensive learning in German intellectual history. And it is difficult to argue with Velkley's critical assessment of Heidegger's efforts to create a self-sustaining ontology as a guide to life without traditional metaphysical or theological underpinnings. Although far from original in these strictures, Velkley's formulation of them is worth reading.

His defense of Strauss's concept of "political philosophy" against Aristotle and Heidegger, on the other hand, never proves what it assumes, namely that politics forms a critical aspect of philosophy, as exemplified by the work of Strauss. Having defended elsewhere the Aristotelian distinction between the discussion and practice of politics and philosophy,[24] it might be best to reference my relevant statement and then proceed to other topics. But I would be remiss if I didn't register my dissatisfaction with Velkley's understanding of historicism, which restates Strauss's position without adding anything substantive. Both writers treat the historicist emphasis on temporality as a combination of moral relativism; acquiescence in changing historical circumstances or the mindless worship of "custom and tradition"; and especially in Heidegger's case, frenzied expectation about "one's own time." Unfortunately so much is subsumed here under the same portmanteau category that it is far from clear how all the ascribed characteristics fit together into a single evil.[25]

There are different forms of historicism, some methodological and others characterizing a worldview. The self-described historicist Hans-Georg Gadamer, who was once a student of Heidegger, examined ideas in relation to historic contexts, while understanding the role of one's own historic consciousness in his time-centered approach to texts and thinkers.[26] According to Gadamer, there is no way that one can comprehend a text without taking into account the historical and biographical position of the interpreter and the historical context of the author under consideration. While interpretations should therefore not be treated as objective science, the interpreter's "prejudices" or the attitudes he brings with him may actually enrich his perspective. This methodological historicism involves an act of hermeneutic honesty, and Velkley's own speculations about modernity and postmodernity reveal a historicist bent, whatever else he may choose to call it. And the same is true for the fellow with the white hat in his exposition. Strauss's efforts to correlate the history of political thought to a succession of self-enclosed phases, each of which is characterized by differing cosmological assumptions resting partly on external circumstances, would seem to point back to German historicist concepts. Of course this was precisely the understanding of cultures and societies that Strauss emphatically attacked in other situations.

Examining ideas in relation to their time is the most common form of historicism and does not undermine all truth claims. It does, however, teach us with regard to the political world that, in the words of Carl Schmitt, "historical truths are true only once." Strauss's devotees have a problem with that idea, since they are determined to proclaim a mind-set and political arrangements that are peculiar to their late modern culture as universally applicable. Antihistoricism has all too often been a cover for moral arrogance or pompous parochialism. Another problem arises when we speak of "history as a guide." There are two senses in which this concept can be understood, either as an appeal to the "ancestral," a practice that Velkley and Strauss warn against lest filial pietism close us off to philosophy, or as Heideggerian historicity, which is discussed most fully in the final sections of *Sein und Zeit*. There we are told that if "our Fate constitutes the primal historicity of our being, then history finds its essential weight neither in what is passed nor in the here and now but in the real event of our existence, which emerges out of the future."[27]

Our fate comes out of an act of "resolution" that is pointed toward the future but is also curiously based on an act of repetition. This repetition, however, does not entail any "bringing back of the past," nor is it "an attachment of the present to what is obsolete."[28] Rather, this working out of our projects seeks to "repeat" the existential possibilities that are inherent in our being while requiring us to make a "resolution" for the future. This time-centeredness would seem relevant for the decision making that takes place in individual lives, and it is about individuals that Heidegger is speaking when he declares: "Only real temporality, which is simultaneously finite, makes something like our fate [*so etwas wie Schicksal*], that is our true historicity, possible." For our fate can only be fulfilled "in its time," which necessarily lies in the future.[29] Here we meet historicized time not as a process that embraces entire peoples but as the medium through which individual self-discovery and self-fulfillment is made possible.

Admittedly some of this phraseology is murky, and perhaps unnecessarily so, but Heidegger's linkage of individual destiny, temporality, and historicity does not appear to this reader to be an ominous *démarche*. Heidegger's historicism in *Sein und Zeit* is a call to each individual to locate in his temporality his particular fate and to organize his life accordingly. Despite his predilection for resonant or emotive German phrases about what is fated, the focus of Heidegger's existentialism remains on the individual searching for ontological authenticity. Let me admit that this is not entirely my cup of tea. If asked to choose which form of historicism seemed to me the most satisfying, I would pick Burke's understanding of history and that of other classical conservatives to what is offered in *Sein und Zeit*.[30] Heidegger's notion of historicity ends in self-referential solipsism,[31] even if what leads up to it radiates a conceptual brilliance that is perhaps unmatched by any other twentieth-century philosophical tract.

Velkley's work would have been more cogent if he hadn't tried so doggedly to play off the reckless historicist Heidegger against the honorable democrat Strauss. These comparisons do little to illuminate the thought of either. Finally, one might question Velkley's practice of reading back the themes of the *Rektoratsrede* that Heidegger delivered as a Nazi Party member at Freiburg in 1933 into the last third of Heidegger's *Sein und Zeit*, which deals with *Zeitlichkeit* (temporality). This early classic was published in 1926, while Heidegger's speech in support of Hitler's new order was given in 1933. Although there may be some conceptual nexus between these products of the same mind, one searches in vain through *Sein und Zeit* for evidence of Heidegger's later oration about the German Volk saving the West from the crisis of civilization through the Nazi movement. Velkley's linkage may be even more difficult to demonstrate than the one that is sometimes assumed between *Sein und Zeit* and Heidegger's post–World War II preoccupation with ecology. Although Heidegger's magnum opus devotes many passages to *Besorgen* (caring for objects in the world), it includes no expressions of Nazi sentiment or even German nationalism.[32]

14

Explaining Trump

THIS CHAPTER WAS ORIGINALLY prepared in February and March 2016, when Donald Trump was garnering the primary votes needed to secure the Republican presidential nomination. The remarks that begin with the next paragraph are being retained in the present anthology because they continue to have relevance for our historical situation. Attention is given here to both the strengths and weaknesses of candidate Trump and above all, to the populist following that he attracted in the course of his long, grueling campaign. Essential to understanding this alliance is a recognition of the conflicting tendencies within the quintessentially democratic ideal of equality. What leaders of populist, nationalist movements here and in Europe are coming to grasp may be a self-evident truth: "democratic equality" does not mean the same thing to the white, indigenous working class as it does to a transnational, postbourgeois elite and its multicultural clients. Within modern democracy, or as its devotees refer to this time-bound phenomenon, "liberal democracy," there is a growing conflict between the interests and beliefs of rival claimants to the egalitarian label. From this perspective Trump as a candidate, Marine Le Pen in France, and the heads of the Austrian Freedom Party are hardly "anti-democrats." They are simply trying to restore an older understanding of democracy and even social democracy, as these terms were understood before the rise of our current multicultural elites and their global capitalist interests and notions of universal citizenship.[1]

The revolt spearheaded by Donald Trump is against what he denounces as the "establishment." That revolt targets intertwining elites that are considered to be concealing their privileged position in what they insist is the best of all possible democracies. This rebellion is advancing simultaneously on both the social-cultural Left and the populist Right. But there is a difference between the two sides in terms of their specific characteristics. Whereas a hero of the millennials and academic class, Senator Bernie Sanders, fully reflects a now prevalent Left, combining support for gays, feminists, and embattled racial minorities with radical redistributionist policies, Trump and the populist Right, for which he has become a mouthpiece, are harder to classify.

A comment that *Washington Post* columnist Peggy Noonan picked up from a Trump fan in March 2016 indicates the degree of resentment against established power that permeates Trump's candidacy. The supporter whom Noonan quotes harbors "no illusions about various aspects of his character," but was backing Trump because it's time for "a junkyard dog."[2] Although Noonan, who previously endorsed Obama and establishment Republicans in presidential races, does not share the view she presents, she nonetheless acknowledges that the speaker has a right to be disturbed: "we [have] a low information elite," and the public has discovered that it's easier to change elites than it is for elites to change the public. As someone who has long distrusted the very elites Noonan has served over the years, I would have been happier had the junkyard dog arrived much earlier. And I would have been even more delighted if this canine had spoken in whole sentences and sounded knowledgeable in TV debates instead of repeating ad infinitum the phrase, "Make America great again."

This is not to deny Trump's success in making himself newsworthy. This real estate mogul has been dominating news in the United States and internationally ever since he announced his candidacy for the Republican presidential nomination in June 2015. Trump is known to be a deeply divisive figure, who in a two-way race with his likely Democratic opponent, Hillary Clinton, would lose the distaff vote by about 17 percent. He has also emerged as the major domestic villain of the establishment Republican-neoconservative press. In fact no one has rattled our political-journalistic establishment as often as "the Donald," as this billionaire real estate mogul has referred to himself and is referred to by his fans. From his speeches about sending back our 11 million plus illegal immigrants (instead of amnestying them) to their homelands, mostly south of our border, to his persistent announcement, "I'm not politically correct," "the Donald" is everything that our establishment is not. He revels in needling the Left, takes no prisoners, and projects a macho image that reminds one of Putin (with whom he shares a mutual admiration society).

There's already been very loud talk from such establishmentarians as George Will and Bill Kristol and throughout the GOP media empire (paid for mostly by Rupert Murdoch) that it may be necessary to create a new Republican Party that would reflect the "moderate" views of the party past and of such glaringly unsuccessful presidential nominees as Mitt Romney and John McCain. The establishment favorites, Jeb Bush and Marco Rubio, did not do well against Trump, and both ended up dropping out, after Rubio had lost ignominiously against Trump in his home state of Florida. The state Republican committees have been busily working against an eventual Trump victory by changing rules for voting in their primaries. Since Trump enjoys backing that reaches beyond his technical party affiliation, state committees want to allow only registered party members to vote for the Republican nominee.

Discussion is also under way among party operatives about how to block the Donald's nomination at the convention in Cleveland this summer if he falls short of the necessary 1,237 delegates. This is still a possibility at the end of March 2016, when Trump has reached the 739 delegate mark (while Cruz, his nearest rival, stands at 465). Although Cruz would have to win almost 80 percent of the remaining delegates to reach the magic number, Trump has to start breaking the 50 percent barrier in order to get there. But this is not something that Trump seems able to do, even with open primaries, since his pluralities rarely go above 40 percent. In a brokered convention, a majority of the delegates (who would be bound only for the first ballot) conceivably could be enticed into supporting someone more to the liking of the party leadership, but not necessarily Cruz, whom many in the establishment dislike almost as much as Trump. But the price that in all likelihood the manipulators would have to pay would be a walkout by Trump and his stalwart followers.

This, however, would not be the worst outcome for many of Trump's opponents in the GOP. One can easily imagine that establishment donors, and more surreptitiously, neoconservative pundits, would cut a deal with the Democratic presidential candidate Hillary Clinton, whom they find more congenial than Trump. The establishment GOP holds flexible social views, like those of a left-leaning Tory David Cameron in England. They seek to court gays and feminists, and they lean leftward on all immigration-related issues, except on allowing especially dangerous-looking Muslims to enter the country. Finally, they call for getting tough with "the Russian thug" and for standing up "for human rights" throughout the world by "projecting American strength." An effusive endorsement of the Israeli Right is de rigueur among establishment Republicans. And this has less to do with courting Jewish voters (who vote overwhelmingly Left) than it does with the Republican Party's donor base. Establishment Republican think tanks and politicians like Marco Rubio are awash in funds from wealthy Zionists, like the Las Vegas casino owners Sheldon Adelson and Steve Wynn. Needless to say, Boeing, Haliburton, and other producers of military hardware have not stinted in their support of the GOP establishment.

It is not that Hillary would feel especially beholden to neoconservative deal makers if they helped get her elected. But their positions generally mesh well, if we discount the posturing that establishment Republican candidates engage in when they're trying to appeal to the Evangelical vote. In all probability, it would make no difference to most of this establishment which party they linked up with, providing their foreign policy concerns and need for sinecures were met.[3] Even the Obama administration has not been totally impenetrable to neoconservative aspirations, and one of their leading publicists, Robert Kagan, has seen his wife Victoria Nuland rise to high position as a foreign policy adviser in the Obama administration. Trump, by contrast, scares the bejesus out of the neoconservatives, as one immediately discovers from reading such organs of theirs as the *Wall Street Journal*, *National Review*, and *Weekly Standard*.

The reason for this has far less to do with Trump's actual positions, which are often nebulous, than with the difficulty that the neoconservatives and the GOP establishment would have in managing him as a candidate or as president. Trump is different from that easily influenced fellow who occupied the White House before Obama, and whom his advisers talked into launching a "preventive war" against Iraq. Trump cannot be scripted. He pays for his campaign out of his considerable fortune and makes fun of his opponents "for belonging to other people." He also sounds insufficiently belligerent about "leading from the front," a favorite slogan of Rubio and Jeb. Although Trump has promised to "wipe out ISIS," and although his pro-Jewish sentiments cannot be questioned (his daughter is married to an Orthodox Jew), he speaks about "negotiating" with rather than confronting Putin. The Republican establishment candidates want nothing less than a showdown with the Russian government, which they tell their constituents is an extension of the Soviet tyranny or else a repressive nationalist regime that persecutes homosexuals.

The last reason that the Republican establishment and the neoconservatives are resisting Trump is the one they most often give: "He's not a real conservative." This charge does have some semblance of credibility, since Trump as late as 2008 was a Hillary Clinton supporter and until recently fit in easily with GOP establishment donors. His politics were very much the same as those of the Australian media baron Rupert Murdoch, who has subsidized most of the leading neoconservative PR organs (including the *Jerusalem Post*). Like Murdoch, who has turned against Trump as a political nuisance, the Donald used to be liberal on most social issues, including immigration, as well as friendly toward Israel. His movement toward the Right has been a recent occurrence, and when Trump tells his Evangelical audiences about his conversion from being pro- to anti-abortion or his rediscovery of his Presbyterian identity, one is justified in questioning his sincerity.

But those who accuse him of political hypocrisy while claiming to be on the Right, like Jonah Goldberg at *National Review*, have happily acclaimed the legalization of gay marriage and still endorse amnesty for illegals. Moreover, the Christian traditionalist in the Republican presidential race, Ted Cruz (and Mike Huckabee while he was still running), has not been exactly a favorite of those accusing Trump of being a faux conservative. Although Cruz has been within striking distance of Trump, the neoconservatives and establishment Republicans have also gone after him. He's been denounced as a religious extremist (Cruz has openly opposed gay marriage) along with failing to keep faith with a neoconservative foreign policy, as defined by, among others, neoconservative journalist Max Boot. A WSJ star editorialist, Boot is offended that Cruz "attacks democracy promotion" and does not share his vision of bringing the present model of American democracy to the rest of humanity.[4]

The media establishment has pulled out much of the same denunciatory ammunition against Trump that it once deployed against Buchanan when that populist presidential candidate tried to scramble the ideological cards. Although Trump has behaved churlishly, Buchanan was treated just as badly by the media and political establishment even when he practiced exemplary courtesy. Of course those who are attacking Trump are correct to view him as a disruptive force, from the perspective of their interests.

Someone who hardly supports him, Jim Tankersley, explains in the *Washington Post*: "Donald Trump is winning" precisely because "he can speak to the anxieties that are animating so many of the [Republican] party's core voters."[5] The frequently heard complaint against him in the establishment Republican press, namely that he appeals to the uneducated without college diplomas, can be understood in a different way. Those afflicted with stagnating or declining incomes have no interest in competing with cheap foreign labor and feel particularly impacted by crimes associated with illegals. As one of his reluctant admirers points out in the *Post*: "He's a huckster. He's a loudmouth New Yorker. People don't like people like that." But on the positive side, continued the speaker from Rappahannock County, Virginia, "He just seems like the guy who can take on the people who Trump supporters think have been screwing with them for so long."

David Frum, in the *Atlantic*, perceptively observes that the emotion of college students when they mounted the Occupy Wall Street demonstrations pales beside the feelings being released by Trump's candidacy. Among Republican voters and many independents who have rallied to Trump, there is "a rebellion against the power of organized money."[6] Those who were Tea Party rebels are angry that the GOP establishment treated them like mindless foot soldiers, while others who cheer on Trump are reacting against the arrogance of wealth. Although a self-admitted billionaire, Trump depicts himself as someone who can see through the tricks of other members of the affluent class, and he proclaims his readiness to punish corporate executives who move their operations outside the country, to the detriment of American workers. A social war, notes Frum, has erupted in the Republican Party, and it may split that party apart. "The dividing line that used to be the most crucial of them all, class, has become a division within the parties, not between them." Moreover, those who are coming over to Trump "aren't necessarily superconservative. They don't often think in ideological terms at all. But they do feel strongly that life in this country used to be better for people like themselves, and they want the old country back."

The Trump supporters, who may be on the verge of destroying the Republican Party as we know it, bear a striking resemblance to the National Front in France. Both are identified with the populist Right and have been incessantly denounced as fascist or Nazi-like by the media-political establishment. Both groups are shuffling the political cards by incorporating working-class programs into anti-immigration parties that, as Frum remarks about Trump's followers, "want their country back." Finally, each party can claim about 40 percent of the electorate but may have problems capturing any more. The rest of their countries' voters stand with the Left or with a socially left-leaning, globalist corporate establishment.

The accusations of "fascism" that are brought against both populist movements are the kind of boilerplate that one might expect from those in power who are trying to remove a pesky opposition. The charge of being "fascist" has become so widespread among establishmentarians that it now means nothing more than that so-and-so offends. As far as I know, neither Marine Le Pen nor Donald Trump has called for a corporate economy in which everything would be in the state and nothing outside of it. Comparisons drawn between Trump's opposition to allowing Muslim migrants to enter the United States (for the time being) and the refusal of Western countries to accept refugees from Nazism are totally misleading. Many of the migrants beating on our gates came from Turkey and other countries where they were already residing because they were trying to reach First World societies. (Let's thank that ultimate antifascist blockhead Angela Merkel for sending out the invite.) There is also the fact that refugees from Nazism did not pose the danger of terrorism that is demonstrably present in the wandering Muslim droves.

That said, there are critical differences between the National Front and Trump's following. Unlike Trump and his grassroots support, the National Front is a well-organized party with periodically updated platforms (the latest of which was framed and circulated in 2014). Again unlike Trump, Marine Le Pen speaks in whole sentences and is highly articulate in responding to her critics. She does not shoot from the hip, like the Donald or Marine's father Jean-Marie. Equally important, unlike Trump, the National Front could conceivably form a government in the multiparty system that exists in France. If the Front could build an alliance with French splinter parties or peel off members of Sarkozy's UMP (recently renamed Les Républicains), it would be in a position to head its own government. When Trump began his populist campaign, it was hard to imagine that he would place himself in such a position. Then I had the impression that he would not capture the Republican presidential nomination but would wreck what needed wrecking. If Trump's rude break-in at the Republican country club would result in the election of Hillary Clinton as president, I certainly wouldn't weep.

I'd take solace in Bismarck's inspired aphorism: "There is a Providence that protects idiots, drunkards, children and the United States of America." ("*Es gibt eine Vorsehung, die beschützt Idioten, Betrunkene, Kinder und die Vereinigten Staaten von Amerika*.")[7]

Viewing the American political scene in late March 2016, it appears that Trump has still not gone away as the worst nightmare of the GOP establishment and the neocon camarilla. Although still no shoe-in for the Republican presidential nomination, Trump has already moved halfway toward gaining the 1,236 delegates needed to achieve his goal. It is still possible that Cruz and Ohio governor John Kasich, who continue to oppose him, may succeed in discomfiting Trump, whose popularity index in their party has never gone above 40 percent. And both the Republican and Democratic establishment presses are happily assisting the "Stop Trump" candidates, who each and every day pound Trump for real and fictitious failings (his change of ideological colors in an opportunistic manner illustrates a credible line of attack; his being a fascist in the tradition of Mussolini or an anti-Semite like David Duke exemplifies a ritualistic smear that is now pulled out against any politician who goes off the ranch in what is perceived to be a right-wing direction).

Among the most intriguing ambiguities in this electoral contest is the charge that Trump is subverting "conservatism" by running against establishment Republican candidates. This complaint reveals hypocrisy of a magnitude rarely encountered in human affairs. This is illustrated by David Brooks, the resident "conservative" columnist at the *New York Times,* genuflecting before the most recent failed Republican presidential candidate, Mitt Romney, for denouncing Trump as a threat to "conservatism."[8] Brooks's charge and his defense of Romney as the rightful, true conservative enemy of Trump are ludicrous in more than one way. First, Brooks has been a gushing admirer of President Obama,[9] and his claim to speak for the Right outside the editorial room of the *New York Times* is at the very least suspect. Second, Romney fawned shamelessly over Trump while running for president in 2012, and there is little in his recent declamations that is not contradicted by his obsequiousness when he was courting Trump as a backer.

In a particularly biting commentary, Richard Goodwin of the *New York Post* stresses Romney's chutzpah in assaulting the current presidential front-runner. This, according to Goodwin, is coming from someone who in 2012 ran one of the most lackluster presidential campaigns in recent history.[10] Although there is much that is flawed about Trump, it is ridiculous to imagine the Republicans could win the presidency with a "failed retread" who is trying to remain part of the political scene. There is nothing that qualifies Romney to be a spokesman for any Right, except for large corporations. He ran his presidential campaign from the center and moved gingerly toward the center Left on social issues after he gained the nomination, lest he be viewed as too extreme.

Despite his empty attributions, Brooks does cause us to reflect on the question: "What is conservatism?" As readers of my work and those who know my personal history would understand, this question has engaged me for decades, and the crusade against Trump has underscored once again the vacuous PR quality of the term in question. Why does Trump's willingness to negotiate with President Putin, rather than engage him in a military confrontation, or to broker a peace between the Israelis and Palestinians, prove that he is not a "conservative?" That term has become so intertwined with Republican talking points or with efforts to give doctrinal gravity to certain party interests that it has lost any meaning outside of two recognizable groups: media figures trying to differentiate the two parties in elections and GOP loyalists and party workers seeking to give their partisan attachments some deeper metaphysical significance. Of all the charges leveled against Trump, the accusation that he is destroying "conservatism" may be among the most ridiculous. Actually he is challenging the hegemony of party bosses and exposing the decorative wrapping in which GOP elites have packaged their interests.

A very unfriendly but also perceptive observer of Trump, Jonathan Chait, notes in New York[11] what should be obvious but is not frequently mentioned. Trump is viewed as a wrecker by the Republican establishment and their neoconservative talking heads because he has dared to reverse certain priorities: "The Republican Party has for decades been organized around a stable hierarchy of priorities, the highest of which is to reduce taxes for the wealthiest Americans, i.e. 'job creators,' and loosen regulation of business. As long as their party is anchored by its economic consensus, conservatives tolerate wide disagreement on social issues." Trump "proposes to invert the party hierarchy, prioritizing its right-wing social resentments while tolerating ambiguity on economics. And his popularity suggests that many average Republicans aren't maniacally obsessed with shrinking the size of government." Although one can challenge a number of Chait's assumptions—for example, that reducing taxes for the wealthiest is the highest GOP priority (as opposed, for example, to being aggressively liberal internationalist in foreign affairs), that Republican politicians are "maniacally obsessed with shrinking government," and that Republicans have made absolutely no efforts to attract minority voters—his presentation of the "threat" to the GOP establishment represented by Trump and his constituency is correct. Trump's enemies in the party have noticed his inversion of the "party hierarchy" when he elevates social concerns that are found on the Right above the economic interests of the party's donor class.

Finally, it should be pointed out that the Trump candidacy has underscored the problem of legitimacy in a society and polity that claim to be "democratic." In American democracy, equality has become the highest value in terms of what politicians and political journalists invoke. This association is nothing new in the history of political thought. It goes at least as far back as Aristotle's *Politics*, and the justification now given for the exercise of power by those who exercise it is that someone or other must give direction to our society, so that we can continue to move toward greater "equity," "fairness," or whatever other synonym is now made to stand for equality.

Although other values may have purchase in modern democracy, such as freedom, social cohesion, and individual excellence, equality has a moral worth that exceeds that of other competing values. Note that this observation is not being extended backward to the founding of the American Republic or attributed to the authors of America's original constitutional design. It is being applied to the way the United States and other Western-style "liberal democracies" have developed during the last hundred years or so, which is in the direction of embracing democratic equality as their highest political ideal. And this judgment is not gainsaid to whatever degree this ideal is not met. Political ideals are never perfectly realized in practice, and the fact that masses of people are mobilized for the purpose of achieving greater equality would suggest the staying power of equality as an ideal.

Even "democratic" freedom exists as an instrumental good that in a democracy is usually subordinated to equality. French political theorist Bertrand de Jouvenel argues in his classic *On Power* that equality progressively swallows up freedom in modern democracy, taking what had once been an aristocratic privilege and making it available to every individual through the state. Unlike medieval and early modern conceptions of "libertas," which were vested in classes and corporations, the now regnant notions of freedom are bound up with a managerial state that guarantees an "equal right" to be free.

This leads to the vicious cycle that Jouvenel sums up in his oft-quoted aphorism: "Conceived as the foundation of liberty, modern democracy paves the way for tyranny. Born for the purpose of standing as a bulwark against Power, it ends by providing Power with the finest soil it has ever had in which to spread itself over the social field."[12] In democracy economic privilege may continue to exist but is typically justified as leading to an increase in equality. For example, by allowing the poor to have more educational and vocational choices, Republicans assure us, we can close the socioeconomic gap. What benefits those in higher economic brackets, such as lowering marginal tax rates, will presumably open up more jobs to those who are at the bottom of the socioeconomic heap and thereby lessen inequality. Like all measures intended to reduce taxes, this policy is defended on egalitarian grounds.

Contrary to the view of a majority of public sector employees, racial minorities, feminists, and Democratic politicians, the demand for equality is by no means a strictly leftist thing. That demand is equally prevalent on the populist Right, which, as fate would have it, is now being energized. Why should we imagine that the gay activist in San Francisco demanding further rights for his group or the millennialist supporter of Bernie Sanders calling for more government-provided college tuition has the corner on egalitarian politics? Why can't the blue-collar Evangelical in Alabama, who correctly sees his group as despised by present leftist elites while his economic prospects continue to fall, have an equally valid claim to democratic equality? Why is the latter being ignored when he observes that foreign labor forces are being imported to drive down his wages and that entire sectors of the economy have been sent to countries with low production costs? What deeply offends such claimants to equal treatment are elites who despise their moral and cultural beliefs while adding to their economic misery. Indeed, Third World immigration seems designed to promote the interests of these already hated elites, by replacing a native workforce with cheap labor (some of it illegal) and by creating the kind of cultural chaos in which the beliefs of those who are being marginalized will be diluted in an America they no longer recognize.

Carl Schmitt underlined as a problem of modern constitutional governments appealing to popular sovereignty an excessive dependence on legality.[13] Such governments have to legitimate themselves by pointing to their legal foundation and to their use of fixed procedures in reaching decisions. But at times it becomes apparent that those who are stressing legality also possess the power and resources that allow them to determine what is legal for others. Thus it becomes clear that these elites are not simply the instruments of a fixed legal order but those who decide how others will live. The question then becomes whether these elites can legitimate their continued rule as bearers of something other than impersonal legality. Can they rule as representatives of the democratic will, that is, by advancing what is understood to be equality? An elite in a democracy that is not seen as committed to this goal puts itself in a precarious situation.

Now those elites who identify with certain egalitarian interests, namely those of the social Left, can still make headway with the help of aggrieved minorities and general media and academic approval. Hillary Clinton can still conceivably win the presidency. Despite her personal baggage, her coalition remains cohesive and mobilized. Meanwhile, the spokespersons for the other claimants to equality, the ones who are classified as trailer-park trash and snake handlers, are encountering heavy weather. Their claimants to equality are despised by the media and educational elites, and *National Review* editor Kevin Williamson has recently pounced on the white working class as the denizens of a fever swamp roiled by unjustified social resentments.[14] This spurned demographic is rallying to Trump because neither the social Left nor the spokespersons for the GOP donor base wish to recognize its interests or democratic sensibilities.[15] This demographic returns the favor by denying both the legality and legitimacy of those who scorn it.

The following comments were added on November 24, 2016.

Those who viewed the Trump movement as a right-wing phenomenon may have been correct, however hysterically or opportunistically they made this observation. A politically effective Right in the United States will not likely come out of self-described cultural conservatives lavishing praise on the shining lights of the postwar conservative movement. Nor should one expect such a Right to emerge from Republican think tanks that are committed to liberal internationalism as a foreign policy and to the support of global capitalist donors. A Right that can push back with power against the Left must be able to harness the grievances of those who have been excluded by the ruling class and who offer a counter-ideology adapted to the present hour. Such a hypothetical or evolving Right might be expected to invoke a historical community and/or organic national ties against the advocates of globalization, fluid human identities, and human rights rhetoric. French political thinker Arnaud Imatz views this pattern of thinking as coming out of a "non-conformist Right" in his own country, going back to nationalist revolutionaries in the interwar years, then progressing through the partisans of Charles de Gaulle defending French national sovereignty against American and Soviet imperialism, and finding more recent expression in breakaway French socialists who have rediscovered their loyalty to a historic French nation and a European identity.[16]

Imatz notes (as I do in *The Strange Death of Marxism*) that

> the post-Marxist Left in France, even in its most radical form, does not oppose globalization. It claims to want to extend its economic benefits to the totality of the human race. It seeks to disseminate human rights all over the planet. This Left never call into question the global dogma of the interdependence of peoples and cultures and [like its American model] wishes to turn its land into a great melting pot, thereby ending any traditional association with a French nation. Far from disturbing what American elites call "democratic capitalism," the post-Marxist Left plays the role of the useful idiot that it had once mocked in French defenders of the American connection.[17]

Imatz sees a single, unitary culture (*la culture unique*) taking the place of inherited European national cultures, and he maintains that economically, politically, and culturally France and the rest of Western Europe have fallen under the influence of something specifically American, and in its Atlanticist and "democratic capitalist" forms, nation devouring.

Curiously, what is condemned as an imported American ideology has generated a revolt in its homeland. The populist movement that has been centered on Donald Trump reflects most of the same forces that are associated with nonconformist thinkers and communitarian revolt in France. Moreover, the reaction exhibited by representatives of our elites, whether Democrats, establishment Republicans, or neoconservative journalists, dovetails with those diatribes heard in Europe. Barack Obama's comments in 2008 about "people who cling to their guns and religion"[18] or Hillary Clinton's mockery of a "basket of deplorables,"[19] that is, those swarms of bigots who have rallied to Donald Trump, recall the attacks launched on the National Front's constituency in France. And this need not surprise us. An establishment that battles for a liberal internationalist American foreign policy, governmentally negotiated free trade agreements, and a globalist understanding of nationhood is reacting with concern to those who challenge its hegemony. Whatever one may think of these elites, they are justified in viewing those who are reacting against them as a danger of the first magnitude.

Let's also not think that if Trump turns out to be something less than what his followers (like my working-class neighbors in Central Pennsylvania) were hoping for, it would mark the end of their revolt against distant elites with antitraditional values and alien economic interests. We may be witnessing what is only the beginning of a populist insurgency from a transformed, energized Right. Unlike the American conservative movement, this populist Right does not genuflect before the gods of capitalism. In fact, it is not this Right but the social Left that is warming to a globalist economy run by a multinational capitalist class. It is the multicultural Left in the new political constellation that can make its peace with the immigration politics and "human rights" internationalism of, say, the *Wall Street Journal* or *Commentary*.

The real lines of division between Right and Left are between those who wish to preserve inherited communities and their sources of authority and those who wish to "reform" or abolish these arrangements. In the modern democratic world, one no longer encounters the entire package of an earlier Right, let alone that of classical conservatism, as outlined in an earlier chapter. One no longer finds a viable ideology that combines a defense of particularity and organic relationships with a positive assessment of hierarchy. But the populist Right offers as much of an older Right as the present permits. It is among other things a response to the globalist Left and more specifically, to the custodians of "political correctness," who view with increasing exasperation an unwanted populist insurgency. Spokesmen for the current populist Right would answer the question "What is the principle of society?" less eloquently but no differently than a character in Benjamin Disraeli's Tory democratic novel of 1845, *Sybil*. Disraeli's mouthpiece in this controversial social novel "prefers association to gregariousness" and would never mistake "density of population" or mere human "contiguity" for a rooted community.[20]

Furthermore, when neoconservative apologists gild the lily for something called "democratic capitalism," they no more than the populist Right have in mind returning to a pre-welfare-state America. "Democratic capitalists," as establishment Republicans and neoconservatives sometimes call themselves,[21] accept most existing entitlement programs and are cautious about scaling back an expanding public administration. But they differ from the populist Right in this respect: they welcome a globalist economy, with all its disruptions, even if it causes unemployment and dislocation for lots of American workers. From the perspective of these optimists, things will work out for those who suffer deprivation in the short run. But for those who are uprooted from long-settled homes in the American Rust Belt and forced to become nomads in search of work, the world looks different. Trump, by addressing the demands of this constituency, has not moved the Republican Party to the left. He is appealing to a socially conservative and preponderantly white segment of the population that the present ruling class and its media surrogates have not been especially interested in.

Afterword

I T WAS THE SUMMER OF 1950, and my parents had packed me off to an overnight camp in the Catskill Mountains that was adjacent to a body of water surrounded by hemlocks, called Sackett Lake. On the other side of the lake stood a resort, The Laurels, where the affluent parents of some of our campers went to do whatever grown-ups did at such places. Presumably they were there to dine, dance, and enjoy the well-groomed golf course and evenly lined tennis courts. But being in such surroundings was not my destiny that summer. I was not at camp to revel in sumptuous pleasures. My parents sent me there because I was neither sociable nor physically dexterous, and they may have hoped that once out of their sight I would acquire characteristics that I never manifested at home.

Unfortunately I didn't undergo the desired maturation during my exile. I also didn't relish being away from my home in Bridgeport, Connecticut, even though I hadn't been exactly overwhelmed with friends while there. Each time my parents came to visit me at camp—which could only be accomplished by driving three and a half hours mostly westward and by crossing the Hudson River at Beacon with a ferry because no bridge had been built there yet—I would greet them with tears. I also demanded that they take me home immediately in the Pontiac they came with. They would not oblige until camp was over at the end of August.

While at Camp Winston, which is what my place of confinement was named, I spent lots of time trying to master the various sports that were made available to us. Although I took up swimming decades later as an exercise, as a preadolescent in 1950 I had zero interest in this activity. For one thing, the lake water stayed cold most of the summer. To make matters worse, my head would go under each time I endeavored to do something called "the dead man's float," which we learned was the preliminary step to learning the Australian crawl. Since I didn't care much for this first step, I had no reason to believe that what followed would be any more pleasant.

The one camp activity that I truly enjoyed was arts and crafts. That was due to the person in charge, a kindly, middle-aged Jewish lady who belonged to something with the word "socialist" in it and who let us do pretty much what we wanted. Clay and wood abounded in the arts and crafts cabin, and as long as we seemed to be using them, our instructor assumed we were being creative. In this cabin, one could also pick up the latest news on campus, which often had to do with the families of the campers. One piece of news that still sticks in my mind concerned Jorge, a contemporary of mine in an adjacent bunk who spoke with a Spanish accent. During the summer Jorge was informed that his father, who headed some unidentified South American country, had been removed from a key political position. Years later I figured out that this dignitary had been over-thrown in a coup in a country in which such upheavals transpired with remark-able regularity. I trust that Jorge's father suffered no worse fate than being ejected from his role as *jefe* for a day. The other camper who suffered anxious moments that summer was a red-haired, freckled fellow, who spent part of the summer in our bunk. His father had been born in Russia, and he agonized over a political figure named "McCarthy," who had begun to rise to prominence in the United States. The only "McCarthy" I was then aware of was a ventriloquist dummy, and even then I doubted that this was the figure who had upset the father of the kid with the red hair.

I later discovered that the father was a New York financier without any sus-picious political connections. But since the United States was then embroiled in conflict with Stalin's Russia, and since the junior senator from Wisconsin was denouncing Russian agents, Mr. Morgan, which was the name of the worried father, thought that he might be targeted. As far as I know, this never happened, and unlike me, the red-haired camper was sent back to Camp Winston the fol-lowing year, at the astronomically high cost of nearly $1,000. This price took into account the purchase of the required camp uniforms, which could only be obtained at a badly cluttered store located somewhere in Lower Manhattan. Not incidentally, the store where the purchases had to be made was owned by the brother of the owner of the camp.

One event that I still remember fondly from my summer at Camp Winston was a visit by the former middleweight champion of the world, Jake LaMotta. This later boxing legend was training across the lake for his forthcoming bout with Sugar Ray Robinson. Although the scheduled bout would not take place until the following February in Madison Square Garden, Jake was making an unac-customed effort to train properly. He had already fought Robinson, who was a more gifted boxer, five times and prevailed only once. Jake's strengths were his grit and iron jaw, but it was questionable whether these qualities would suffice to overcome the pugilistic skill of Jake's opponent, who pound for pound may have been the greatest middleweight of all times. Whereas *Ring Magazine* rates Jake fifty-second among the eighty greatest boxers of the last eighty years, Robinson invariably places near the top in such listings. Since our first meeting, I have had a warm spot for LaMotta, although Robinson remains the boxer I admire more than anyone else in his sport.

Many years later I saw Robert De Niro playing LaMotta in *Raging Bull*, which was one of the two nicknames the boxer employed, the other being the "Bronx Bull." There was a seamy side to LaMotta's life, which is now continuing into its ninety-third year, and his stormy temper and his equally stormy multiple mar-riages belong to that narrative. LaMotta kept his career going much longer than he should have and took a beating in the fight with Robinson for which he was preparing at the time of our meeting. That fight had to be stopped in the thirteenth round, lest LaMotta suffer long-lasting injuries from the pounding. This match has been characterized as the second "St. Valentine's Day Massacre." The first of the two massacres famously took place in Chicago, Illinois, on February 14, 1929, and entailed the shooting of rival gangsters by the henchmen of Al Capone.

What I remember most about LaMotta's visit in August 1950 was that he play-boxed with me and then called me in a jovial manner "champ." That gesture revealed his nicer side and made an awkward eight-year-old feel better about himself. Years later I could not imagine that the LaMotta whom I watched committing mayhem against his family in the De Niro movie was the person who came to Camp Winston and play-boxed with me. As someone who had trouble hanging up his gloves, LaMotta continued to box as a light heavyweight with waning success until 1957. Once out of this sport, he plied other trades, such as selling real estate in Florida and playing minor roles in movies.

But Jake found a cause in 1990 that has occupied his time and energy ever since. He became closely associated with the International Boxing Hall of Fame, which was set up in Canastota, New York, about twenty miles east of Syracuse. On the outskirts of this scenic village—about a stone's throw from the New York Thruway and within sight of the restaurant-motel owned by former boxing great and Jake's contemporary, Tony Graziano—stands the boxing museum that Jake helped establish and visits periodically. He is also a regular at annual events, including a gala dinner held by the museum and its sponsors, which was scheduled in 2015 for mid-June.

The museum is not at all accidentally near the spot where another famous middleweight, Carmen Basilio, had grown up, on an onion farm in dire circumstances amid multiple siblings. Basilio, who also lived into his nineties and who bestowed his name on the civic arena in Syracuse, joined his fellow former middleweights (of Italian American origin) in raising money for the museum. Like Jake, Basilio fought Robinson, albeit with more success, wresting the middleweight crown from the aging champion in 1957—in one of the most exciting fights in boxing history. He then lost his crown the following year after a shattering blow to his eye.

As fate would have it, I planned to be near the museum in June, since my wife was attending a family reunion in nearby DeWitt. Since I wasn't eager to listen to the childhood memories of my wife's family, I chose to do something more to my liking while in Upstate New York. I signed up for the Boxing Hall of Fame dinner on June 13, 2015, which would be held at the Oncenter in downtown Syracuse, and went to the festivities specifically to renew my relations with Jake.

Although I had doubts that my boyhood hero would remember me, I would recognize him from the advertisements for the event. Jake would be a guest of honor at the dinner, and it would be hard not to identify him sitting at the table reserved for retired "modern boxers." By the curious definition established by the commission that approves entries into the International Boxing Hall of Fame, "modern boxers" are the ones who have retired since the 1940s. The "old-timers" are no longer in this world unless they've managed to live into their hundreds.

I can't say this reunion brought me emotional satisfaction. Jake was in far less vigorous condition than I had hoped. Any time I tried to elicit a response to some clumsily posed question, his wife jumped in to shield him from his obtrusive admirer. Before long our abbreviated exchange was rendered even shorter by security people urging me to return to my table so that Jake could finish his meal, although from what I could see, there was no evidence that he was in a hurry to do so. After such strenuous urging, I gave up my efforts to engage him in conversation and turned to some of the other honored guests, who seemed less guarded and more open to conversation.

The most personable of that year's inductees to the International Boxing Hall of Fame was the gigantic Riddick Bowe, who towered over most of the other attendees. Bowe—who stands six feet five and has a formidable eighty-one-inch reach—defeated heavyweight champion Evander Holyfield in an unforgettably dramatic bout in November 1992. *Ring Magazine* proclaimed that frenetic contest the "fight of the year," and Bowe held onto his title until he retired in 1996. Neither this physically imposing figure nor the other former fighters whom I met at the banquet—including Mickey Ward, Ray Mercer, and Ray "Boom Boom" Mancini—indulged in what boxers call "trash talk." All of them expressed gratitude to the fans who had made their lucrative careers possible.

Some may wonder why I have chosen to end this anthology, which is otherwise filled with bookish material, by describing my relationship to a nonagenarian former boxer and others in his perilous trade. In a strange way that I have rarely thought about, my life has been enriched by my interest in boxers, going back to the primal experiences of meeting Jake and later watching Gillette's *Friday Night Fights* with my father on our antediluvian TV set with a ten-inch screen. I can't say that I was ever much of a boxer myself. Moreover, the only connection that I have to the sport is through my father, who once punched out someone who was breaking into our house at night. My passion for boxing matches irritated a longtime friend, who recently passed. This friend and colleague lived for the Republican Party and was annoyed that I cared more about boxing than the candidates who ran for president. I even dared to express this unsettling view to my students, when I contrasted the courage of pugilists to the slithering cowardice of career politicians. I did make an exception, however, for such relentlessly principled figures as Pat Buchanan and Ralph Nader.

I also expressed pleasure to my colleagues that the nephew of the boxer Hector Comacho, who recently died in a car crash, chose to take one of my classes. Although the young man was a better-than-average student, we discussed boxing rather than political theory once class was over. When my friend asked sarcastically what I had in common with boxers, I responded that it was about as much as I had in common with politicians. Let me admit, however, that the question was valid, even if it had been asked to irk me. I have little in common with most boxers.

That said, I remain impressed by their raw physical courage. War heroes have never elicited from me the same excited response, perhaps because soldiers typically act in organized groups rather than as individuals driven back on personal resources. Besides, war stories I have heard entail actions that were taken outside my range of vision. I can watch boxing matches while they're going on. The gutsiness of those who participate in them brings to mind how Heidegger translated Plato's phrase *megala panta episphalē* as *Alles Grosse steht im Sturme* (all great things stand up in the storm). Heidegger's rendering in German is far more dramatic than the original Greek phrasing. Having pointed this out, let me say in closing that I have no reason to believe that Heidegger was watching a boxing match when he urged us to remain steadfast in a crisis.

Notes

Notes to Foreword

1. Paul E. Gottfried, *Encounters: My Life with Nixon, Marcuse, and Other Friends and Teachers* (Wilmington, DE: ISI Books, 2009).

2. Arthur Schopenhauer, *Parerga and Paralipomena: Small Philosophical Writings (Parerga und Paralipomena: Kleine philosophische Schriften)* (Berlin: Verlag, 1851).

3. Arthur Schopenhauer, *Parerga and Paralipomena: Small Philosophical Writings (Parerga und Paralipomena; kleine philosophische Schriften)*, ed. Arthur Hübscher. (Wiesbaden, Hesse, West Germany: E. Brockhaus, 1966), 157–59.

4. Gottfried, *Encounters*, 45–62.

5. Alistair Horne, *The Fall of Paris: The Siege and Commune, 1870–71* (New York: St. Martin's Press, 1966), 37.

6. Ibid.

7. "Gauck Called Persecution of the Armenians Genocide (Gauck Nennt Verfolgung der Armenier Völkermord)." *Süddeutsche Zeitung*, April 27, 2015, politics (Politik) sec., http://www.sueddeutsche.de/politik/gedenkgottesdienst-im-berliner-dom-gauck-nennt-verfolgung-der-armenier-voelkermord-1.2448888.

8. Severin Weiland, "Memorial Service: Gauck Speaks Clearly of the Armenian Genocide (Gedenk-Gottesdienst: Gauck Spricht Klar Von Völkermord an Den Armeniern)." *Der Spiegel*, April 23, 2015, politics (Politik) sec., http://www.spiegel.de/politik/deutschland/armenier-joachim-gauck-spricht-klar-von-voelkermord-a-1030261.html.

9. A work that laboriously challenges all received assumptions about the Armenian massacres, including the alleged German involvement, is Sean McMeekin, *The Russian Origins of the First World War* (Cambridge, MA: Harvard University Press, 2011), esp. 141–47, 242–43.

10. Eric Foner, *Reconstruction: An Unfinished Revolution* (New York: HarperCollins, 2002).

11. Paul Gottfried, "Eric Foner Taken to Task in Pat Buchanan's Conservative Magazine," *History News Network*, May 4, 2009.

12. Robert Zaller, *The Parliament of 1621: A Study in Constitutional Crisis* (Berkeley: University of California Press, 1971).

13. Robert L. Paquette, "The Unemancipated Country: Eugene Genovese's Discovery of the Old South," *Academic Questions* 27, no. 2 (2014): 204–12.

14. Richard H. Reeb and Felicia Chernesky, "Letter to the editor," *Academic Questions: A Publication of the National Association of Scholars*, July 23, 2014, 256–58.

Notes to Chapter 1

1. Paul E. Gottfried, *Encounters: My Life with Nixon, Marcuse, and Other Friends and Teachers* (Wilmington, DE: ISI Books, 2009).

2. Martin Heidegger, "*Hölderlin's Hymn: The Ister*" ("*Hölderlins Hymne: Der Ister*"). (Lecture presented at the University of Freiburg, Freiburg im Breisgau, Baden-Württemberg, Germany, 1942).

3. Martin Heidegger, *Hölderlins Hymne "Der Ister", Gesamtausgabe* (Frankfurt am Main: Vittorio Klostermann Verlag, 1996), vol. 55.

4. Friedrich Hölderlin, *Works, Letters, and Documents (Werke, Briefe, Dokumente)* (Munich, Germany: Wincker Verlag, 1963), 195–96.

Notes to Chapter 2

1. Caspar von Schrenk-Notzing, *Lexikon Des Konservatismus* (Graz, Austria: Leopold Stocker Verlag, 1996), 397–98.

2. Philip Rieff and Elisabeth Quinn, *The Triumph of the Therapeutic: Uses of Faith After Freud* (Wilmington, DE: ISI Books, 2006).

3. Robert A. Nisbet, *The Sociological Tradition* (New York: Basic Books, 1966).

4. Robert A. Nisbet, *The Social Philosophers: Community and Conflict in Western Thought* (New York: Thomas Y. Crowell Co., 1973).

5. Robert A. Nisbet, *The Present Age: Progress and Anarchy in Modern America* (New York: Harper & Row, 1988).

6. Ibid., 133–34.

7. Ibid.

8. Robert A. Nisbet, *Twilight of Authority* (Indianapolis, IN: Liberty Fund, 2000).

9. Nisbet, *Present Age*, 63.

10. Ibid., 74.

11. Brad Lowell Stone, *Robert Nisbet, Communitarian Traditionalist* (Wilmington, DE: ISI Books, 2000), 88–91.

12. Nisbet, *Present Age*.

13. Ibid., 74–75.

14. Robert A. Nisbet, *Prejudices: A Philosophical Dictionary* (Cambridge, MA: Harvard University Press, 1982), 59–61.

15. Nisbet, *Sociological Tradition*.

16. Robert A. Nisbet, *The Making of Modern Society* (New York: New York University Press, 1986).

17. Robert A. Nisbet and Robert G. Perrin, *The Social Bond*, 2nd ed. (New York: Alfred Knopf, 1977).

18. Nisbet, *Social Philosophers*.

19. Alexis de Tocqueville, and Gerald E. Bevan, *Democracy in America* (London: Penguin Books, 2003).

20. Robert A. Nisbet, *The Quest for Community: A Study in the Ethics of Order and Freedom*, 8th ed. (San Francisco, CA: ICS Press, 1990).

21. Stone, *Robert Nisbet*, 2–9.

22. Paul Gottfried, *Sociology as an Art Form* (New Brunswick, NJ: Transaction Publishers, 2002).

23. George H. Nash, *The Conservative Intellectual Movement in America since 1945*, 2nd ed. (Wilmington, DE: ISI Books, 1996).

24. Nisbet, *Quest for Community*.

25. Russell Kirk, *The Conservative Mind: From Burke to Eliot*, 7th ed. (Chicago: Regnery Books, 1986).

26. Willmoore Kendall, *Contra Mundum* (New Rochelle, NY: Arlington House, 1971), 45–46.

27. Frank S. Meyer, *In Defense of Freedom: A Conservative Credo* (Chicago: Henry Regnery Co., 1962), 129–41.

28. Robert A. Nisbet, *The Degradation of Academic Dogma: The University in America 1945–1970* (New York: Basic Books, 1971).

29. Russell Kirk, *Decadence and Renewal in the Higher Learning: An Episodic History of American University and College since 1953* (South Bend, IN: Gateway Editions, 1978).

30. Henry Adams, *The Degradation of the Democratic Dogma* (New York: Macmillan, 1920).

31. W. Wesley McDonald, *Russell Kirk and the Age of Ideology* (Columbia: University of Missouri Press, 2006), 19–21.

32. Ibid.

33. Kirk, *Conservative Mind*, 457–501.

34. Ibid.

35. Kirk, "The Idea of Conservatism," in Kirk, *Conservative Mind*.

36. Kirk, *Conservative Mind*, 253–374.

37. Ibid., 8.

38. Fossey John Cobb Hearnshaw, *Conservatism in England: An Analytical, Historical, and Political Survey*, 2nd ed. (New York: H. Fertig, 1968).

39. Kirk, *Conservative Mind*.

40. Edmund Burke, *Reflections on the Revolution in France, and on the Proceedings in Certain Societies in London Relative to that Event: In a Letter Intended to Have Been Sent to a Gentleman in Paris* (London: James Dodsley in Pall-Mall, 1790).

41. Kirk, *Conservative Mind*, 9.

42. Ibid., 205.

43. Ibid., 7.

44. Ibid.

45. Robert A. Nisbet, *The Social Group in French Thought* (New York: Arno Press, 1980).

46. Robert A. Nisbet, "The French Revolution and the Rise of Sociology in France," *American Journal of Sociology* 49, no. 2 (1943): 156–164.

47. Robert A. Nisbet, "Conservatism and Sociology," *American Journal of Sociology* 58, no. 2 (1952): 156–64.

48. Nisbet, *Sociological Tradition*.

49. Nisbet, *Social Philosophers*.

50. Ibid., 417.

51. Ibid., 417–18.

52. Nisbet, *Making of Modern Society*.

53. Ibid., 198.

54. Nisbet, *Quest for Community*.

55. Robert A. Nisbet, "Image of Community," in Nisbet, *Quest for Community*, 21.

56. Nash, *Conservative Intellectual Movement in America*, 279–81.

57. McDonald, *Russell Kirk and the Age of Ideology*, 204–5.

58. Paul E. Gottfried, *Encounters: My Life with Nixon, Marcuse and Other Friends and Teachers* (Wilmington, DE: ISI Books, 2009), 165–70.

59. Ibid., 197–204.

60. Russell Kirk, *The Intelligent Woman's Guide to Conservatism* (New York: Devin-Adair Co., 1957).

61. Russell Kirk, *A Program for Conservatives* (Chicago: Henry Regnery Co., 1962).

62. Nisbet, *Quest for Community*.

63. Ibid.

64. Ibid., 249.

65. Ibid., 250.

66. Ibid.

67. Ibid., 250–251.

68. Ibid.

69. Paul Gottfried, *After Liberalism: Mass Democracy in the Managerial State* (Princeton, NJ: Princeton University Press, 1999).

70. Robert A. Nisbet, *The Sociology of Emile Durkheim* (New York: Oxford University Press, 1974).

71. Émile Durkheim, *The Division of Labor in Society (De la Division du Travail Social)* (Paris: Presses Universitaires de France, 1893).

72. Nisbet, *Sociology of Emile Durkheim*, 16.

73. Émile Durkheim, *The Rules of Sociological Method (Les Règles de la Méthode Sociologique)* (Paris: Félix Alcan, 1895).

74. Nisbet, *Sociology of Emile Durkheim*, 17.

75. Émile Durkheim and Joseph Ward Swain, *The Elementary Forms of the Religious Life (Les Formes Élémentaires de la Vie Religieuse)* (London: George Allen & Unwin, Ltd., 1912).

76. Nisbet, *Sociology of Emile Durkheim*, 37.

77. Nisbet, *Sociological Tradition*.

78. Nisbet, *Sociology of Emile Durkheim*, 27–28.

79. Ibid., 272.

80. Ibid., 269.

81. Ibid., 272–77.

82. Nisbet, *Twilight of Authority* (Indianapolis: Liberty Fund, 2000).

83. Ibid.

84. Nisbet, *Sociology of Emile Durkheim*, 272.

85. Émile Durkheim, *Suicide (Le Suicide: Étude de Sociologie)* (Paris: Presses Universitaires de France, 1895).

86. Nisbet, *Quest for Community*.

87. Robert A. Nisbet and Robert G. Perrin, *The Social Bond*, 2nd ed. (New York: Alfred Knopf, 1977).

88. Robert A. Nisbet, *Conservatism: Dream and Reality* (Minneapolis: University of Minnesota Press, 1986).

89. Gary North, "Robert Nisbet on Conservatism," LewRockwell.com, April 1, 2005.

90. Ibid.

91. Robert A. Nisbet, *The Present Age: Progress and Anarchy in Modern America* (New York: Harper & Row, 1988).

92. Nisbet, *Conservatism: Dream and Reality*.

93. North, "Robert Nisbet on Conservatism."

94. Gottfried, *Encounters*, 197–98.

95. Nisbet, *Sociological Tradition*.

Notes to Chapter 3

1. Leo Strauss, *Liberalism, Ancient and Modern* (New York: Basic Books, 1968).

2. Ibid.

3. Ibid.

4. Arnold Gehlen, *Moral and Hypermoral: A Pluralist Ethic (Moral und Hypermoral: Eine Pluralistische Ethik)* (Königstein im Taunus, Hesse, Germany: Athenäum Verlag, 1969).

5. Ibid.

6. Karl Marx and Friedrich Engels, *The Communist Manifesto (Manifest Der Kommunistischen Partei)* (London: Workers' Educational Association, 1848).

7. Karl Marx, *Capital: Critique of the Political Economy (Das Kapital, Kritik Der Politischen Ökonomie)* (Hamburg, Germany: Verlag Von Otto Meisner, 1867).

8. Linda C. Raeder, *John Stuart Mill and the Religion of Humanity* (Columbia: University of Missouri Press, 2002).

9. Maurice Cowling, *Mill and Liberalism*, 2nd ed. (Cambridge, UK: Cambridge University Press, 1990).

10. Raeder, *John Stuart Mill and the Religion of Humanity*.

11. Ibid.

12. David C. Stove, *Darwinian Fairytales: Selfish Genes, Errors of Heredity, and Other Fables of Evolution* (New York: Encounter Books, 2006).

13. Ibid.

14. Romans 13, *The New American Bible* (Iowa Falls: World Bible Publishers, 1986).

15. Ibid.

16. Christopher Dawson, *Gods of Revolution* (Washington, DC: CUA, 2015); and Mircea Eliade, *Mythes, rêves et mystères* (Paris: Gallimard, 1972), 21.

17. Karl Mannheim, *Ideology and Utopia (Ideologie and Utopie)* (Bonn, North Rhine-Westphalia, Germany: F. Cohen, 1929).

18. Karl Mannheim, *The Conservative Thought: Sociological Contributions to Becoming the Political-Historical Thinking in Germany (Das Konservative Denken: Soziologische Beiträge zum Werden des Politisch-Historischen Denkens in Deutschland)* (Tübingen, Baden-Württemberg, Germany: Mohr Siebeck Verlag, 1927).

19. Richard Mervin Weaver, *Visions of Order: The Cultural Crisis of Our Time* (Baton Rouge: Louisiana State University Press, 1964).

20. Marx, *Capital.*

21. Israel Shamir, "The French Spring." *Counterpunch*, April 17, 2013, http://www.counterpunch .org/2013/04/17/the-french-spring/.

22. Ibid.

23. Mencius Moldbug, "Unqualified Reservations: Reactionary Enlightenment," *Blogspot*, April 18, 2016, https://unqualified-reservations.blogspot.com/.

24. An explosive new book on Merkel's career that I recommend strongly to German readers is *Das Erste Leben der Angela M.* by Ralf Georg Reuth and Günther Lachmann (2013).

25. A particularly ludicrous example of such a warning has come from the Sydney Antifascist Action group in Australia, which has been going after a "paleoconservative" website, the Australian Traditionalist Forum, for posting dangerous hate speech. The website under attack features commentaries on Kirk and other dead cultural conservatives and has occasionally criticized gay marriage. This website operates hand to mouth and is anything but inflammatory. Indeed, it would hardly be noticed if the antifascists had not decided to target it. https://antifascistactionsydney.wordpress.com/category /sydney-traditionalist-forum/8.

26. Samuel T. Francis, *Beautiful Losers: Essays on the Failure of American Conservatism* (Columbia: University of Missouri Press, 1994).

27. Ibid.

28. Friedrich Nietzsche, *Thoughts Out of the Season (Unzeitgemäße Betrachtungen)* (Munich: Goldman Verlag, 1964), 73.

29. Martin Heidegger, *Time and Being (Sein und Zeit)* (Tubingen, Germany: Max Niemeyer Verlag, 1993), 382–86.

30. A book that examines the shifting meanings of "Right" and "Lleft" since the eighteenth century is Arnaud Imatz's encyclopedic study *Droite/gauche: Pour sortir de l'équivoque* (Paris: Pierre-Guillaume de Roux, 20016). Imatz demonstrates not only that Left and Right sometimes change places (*chassé-croisé*) with regard to certain positions but also the persistence of a particular kind of Right that is designated as "nonconformist." Despite his reservations about the permanence of ideological polarities, his study more or less shows (62–71), that there are "essentialist" ideological poles that persist in the face of changing historical situations.

Notes to Chapter 4

1. Jonathan Steinberg, *Bismarck: A Life*. (New York: Oxford University Press, 2011), 480.

2. Ibid., 478.

3. Ibid.

4. Ibid., 481.

5. Ibid.

6. Otto Pflanze, *Bismarck and the Development of Germany* (Princeton, NJ: Princeton University Press, 1971).

7. A. J. P. Taylor, *Bismarck: The Man and the Statesman* (London: Hamish Hamilton, 1955).

8. Christian Graf von Krockow, *Otto von Bismarck* (Stuttgart, Baden-Württemberg, Germany: Deutsche Verlagsanstalt, 1997).

9. Christoph Nonn, *Bismarck: A Prussian and His Century (Bismarck: Ein Preusse und sein Jahrhundert)* (Munich: C. H. Beck, 2015).

10. Carsten Kretschmann, "Otto Von Bismarck: Helmsman and Wave Rider (Otto Von Bismarck: Steuermann Und Wellenreiter)," *Frankfurter Allgemeine Zeitung*, July 4, 2015, politics (Politik) sec., http://www.faz.net/aktuell/politik/politische-buecher/otto-von-bismarck-steuermann -und-wellenreiter-13514093.html.

11. Hans Christof Kraus, *Bismarck: Size, Limits, and Achievements (Bismarck: Grösse, Grenzen, Leistungen)* (Stuttgart, Baden-Württemberg, Germany: Klett Cotta, 2015).

12. Ibid.

13. Ibid., 264–307.

14. Ibid.

15. Ibid., 244–47.

16. Ibid., 130–49.

17. Ibid.

18. Steinberg, *Bismarck: A Life*.

19. A. J. P. Taylor, *The Course of German History: A Survey of the Development of German History Since 1815* (London: Routledge Classics, 2001).

20. William M. McGovern, *From Luther to Hitler: The History of Nazi-Fascist Political Philosophy* (New York: Houghton Mifflin, 1941).

21. Fritz Fischer, *Hitler Was Not An Accident (Hitler war kein Betriebsunfall)* (Munich: C. H. Beck, 1998).

22. Fritz Fischer, *Germany's War Aims* (New York: Norton, 1967).

23. Gunter Spraul, *The Fischer Complex (Der Fischer-Komplex)* (Halle/Saale, Saxony-Anhalt, Germany: Projekte-Verlag, 2011).

24. Jürgen Habermas, "The Public Use of History (Vom öffentlichen Gebrauch der Historie)," in *Historical Dispute: The Documentation of the Controversy About the Uniqueness of the Nazi Extermination of the Jews (Historikerstreit: Die Dokumentation der Kontroversen um die Einzigkeit der nationalsozialistischen Judenvernichtung)* (Munich: R. Piper, 1987).

25. Harry Elmer Barnes, *The Genesis of the World War* (New York: Knopf, 1929).

26. Harry Elmer Barnes, *In Quest of Truth: Debunking the War Guilt Myth* (Chicago: National Historical Society, 1928).

27. Harry Elmer Barnes, *Perpetual War for Perpetual Peace: A Critical Examination of Foreign Policy of Franklin Delano Roosevelt and Its Aftermath* (Westport, CT: Greenwood Press, 1969).

28. Barnes, *In Quest of Truth*, 230.

29. Ibid.

30. Barnes, *Perpetual War for Perpetual Peace*. For a devastating, carefully written, and abundantly documented assessment of Churchill's role in unleashing international strife before and during 1914, see Ralph Raico's "Rethinking Churchill," in *The Costs of War*, 2nd ed. (New Brunswick, NJ: Transaction Publishers, 1998).

31. Sean McMeekin, *The Russian Origins of the First World War* (Cambridge, MA: Belknap Press, 2011).

32. Richard J. Evans, "The Road to Slaughter: Richard Evans Reviews Sean McMeekin's *The Russian Origins of the First World War*," *New Republic*, December 5, 2011. For its insights on the war economy of the beleaguered Central Powers, see Alexander Watson's *Ring of Steel: Germany and Austria in World War One* (New York: Basic Books, 2014).

33. McMeekin, *Russian Origins of the First World War*.

34. Ibid.

35. Terence Zuber, *Inventing the Schlieffen Plan: German War Planning, 1871–1914* (New York: Oxford University Press, 2002).

36. Gerhard Ritter, *The Schlieffen Plan: Critique of a Myth*, trans. Andrew Wilson and Eve Wilson (London: Oswald Wolff, 1958).

37. Andreas Bracher, *Battle for the Russian Culture (Kampf um den russischen Kulturkeim)* (Basel, Switzerland: Perseus Press, 2015).

38. Ritter, *Schlieffen Plan: Critique of a Myth.*

39. Edward Grey, *Twenty Five Years, 1892–1916* (London: Frederick A. Stokes, 1925), 2:11.

40. Ibid., 1:321.

41. Ibid.

42. Ibid., 2:22. Perhaps the most balanced, up-to-date study—and one that is exhaustive—of the origins of the war is Christopher Clark's *The Sleepwalkers: How Europe Went to War in 1914* (New York: Harpers, 2013).

43. Johann Sebastian Bach, *St. Matthew Passion (Passio Domini nostri J.C. secundum Evangelistam Matthæum)*, BVW 244 (Leipzig, Electorate of Saxony, Holy Roman Empire: J. S. Bach, 1727).

44. Rainer Zitelmann, *Hitler: Self-Image of a Revolutionary (Hitler: Selbstverständnis eines Revolutionärs)* (New York: St. Martin's Press, 1987), 414–65.

45. Hannah Arendt, *The Origins of Totalitarianism*, 3rd ed. (New York: Harcourt, Brace, and Jovanovich, 1973), 305–91.

46. Henry Ashby Turner Jr., *Hitler's Thirty Days to Power* (New York: Basic Books, 1996).

47. Ibid., 165.

48. Ibid.

49. Ibid., 166.

50. Ibid.

51. Ibid.

52. Ibid.

53. Herbert Butterfield, *The Whig Interpretation of History* (New York: W. W. Norton, 1965).

54. Victor Davis Hanson, *The Western Way of War: Infantry Battle in Classical Greece*, 2nd ed. (Berkeley: University of California Press, 2009).

55. Donald Kagan, *On the Origins of War and the Preservation of Peace* (New York: Doubleday, 1995), 81–89.

56. Victor Davis Hanson, "Lessons of World War I," *National Review Online*, February 14, 2014, http://www.nationalreview.com/article/371300/lessons-world-war-i-victor-davis-hanson.

57. Victor Davis Hanson, *Hoplites: The Classical Greek Battle Experience* (London: Routledge, 1993).

58. Victor Davis Hanson, "Lessons of World War I," in *Victor Davis Hanson's Private Papers*, February 18, 2014, http://victorhanson.com/wordpress/?p=7019.

59. Butterfield, *Whig Interpretation of History.*

60. Ibid., 77–78.

61. Ibid., 78.

62. William M. McGovern, *From Luther to Hitler.*

63. On the extent to which the British war party acted without parliamentary oversight in making far-reaching alliances and declaring war, see Helmut Roewer, *Unterwegs zur Weltherrschaft: Warum England den Ersten Weltkrieg auslöste und Amerika ihn gewann* (Zurich: Scidinge Hall, 2016), 39–102. While Roewer attaches major responsibility for the war to certain British cabinet members, and to the military officers and journalists allied with them, he views most of the British cabinet, the deceived members of Parliament, and above all, the British people as free of blame. This stands in glaring contrast to the advocates of the Fischer-thesis, who not only blame the Central Powers exclusively for World War One but also extend blame to almost the entire German people for the catastrophe.

64. Walter Karp, *The Politics of War: The Story of Two Wars Which Altered Forever the Political Life of the American Republic, 1890–1920* (Mt. Kisco, NY: Moyer Belt Ltd., 2003).

65. Hans Hans Fenske, *The Beginning of the End of Old Europe: The Allied Refusal of Peace Talks (Der Anfang vom Ende des alten Europa: Die alliierte Verweigerung von Friedensgesprächen, 1914–1919)* (Munich: Olzog, 2013).

66. Roy P. Basler, ed., "Abraham Lincoln to Horace Greeley, 22 August 1862," in *The Collected Works of Abraham Lincoln* (New Brunswick, NJ: Rutgers University Press, 1953).

67. Butterfield, *Whig Interpretation of History*.

68. Turner, *Hitler's Thirty Days to Power*.

69. Ibid.

70. Dumas Malone, *Jefferson and His Times* (Charlottesville: University of Virginia Press, 2005).

71. Polybius, *Historiae* (Stuttgart: Teubner Verlag, 1962), bk. 1.

72. F. W. Walbank, *Polybius* (Los Angeles: University of California Press, 1990), 130–56.

73. Polybius, *Historiae*, bk. 6.

74. Ibid., bk. 1, 3.4–5.

75. Ibid., bk. 1, 3.5.

76. Ibid., bk. 1, 3.5–6.

77. Ibid., bk. 1, 4.1–3.

78. Ibid., bk. 1, 4.

79. Ibid., bk. 1, 3–4.

80. Ibid., bk. 1, 63.7–9.

81. Ibid., bk. 1, 4.4.

82. Ibid., bk. 1.

83. Jonah Goldberg, *Liberal Fascism* (New York: Doubleday, 2008).

84. "*The New York Times* Non-Fiction Best Sellers of 2008," *New York Times*, last modified July 8, 2015, https://en.wikipedia.org/wiki/The_New_York_Times_Non-Fiction_Best_Sellers_of_2008.

85. Ashley Killough, "Ted Cruz: Democratic Party Home to 'Liberal Fascism' against Christians," *CNN Politics*, April 26, 2015, http://www.cnn.com/2015/04/26/politics/ted-cruz-liberal-fascism-iowa-speech/index.html.

Notes to Chapter 5

1. Abraham Lincoln, *Gettysburg Address* (Gettysburg, PA, 1863).

2. *Wikipedia*, s.v. "Liberal Democracy," https://en.wikipedia.org/wiki/Liberal_democracy.

3. Paul Gottfried, *After Liberalism: Mass Democracy in the Managerial State* (Princeton, NJ: Princeton University Press, 1999).

4. *Webster's Unabridged Dictionary*, 2nd ed. (New York: Random House Reference, 2014).

5. Ibid.

6. Renzo de Felice, *Breve Storia del Fascismo* (Milan: Mondadori, 2000), 86.

7. Tony Judt, "What Is Living and What Is Dead in Social Democracy?," *New York Review of Books*, December 17, 2009, http://www.nybooks.com/articles/2009/12/17/what-is-living-and-what-is-dead-in-social-democrac/; an earlier reference to "liberal democracy" in the same source is in a book review written by Alan Ryan in May 2001 (http://www.nybooks.com/articles/2001/05/17/live-and-let-live/). For an impassioned hymn to "liberal democracy" as the hope of the human future, see Isaiah Berlin's "A Message to the 21st Century," *New York Review of Books*, October 23, 2014, http://www.nybooks.com/articles/2014/10/23/message-21st-century/.

8. John Adams, *A Defence of the Constitutions of Government of the United States of America* (Boston: Edmund Freeman, 1788).

9. Ibid.

10. Ibid.

11. John Adams, "Letter to John Taylor of Caroline, Virginia" (Quincy, MA, 1814), in ibid.

12. Allan David Bloom, *The Closing of the American Mind: How Higher Education Has Failed Democracy and Impoverished the Souls of Today's Students* (New York: Simon and Schuster, 1987).

13. Paul Gottfried, *Leo Strauss and the Conservative Movement in America* (New York: Cambridge University Press, 2014), 106–14.

14. James W. Ceaser, *Liberal Democracy and Political Science* (Baltimore, MD: Johns Hopkins University Press, 1990).

15. Ibid., 19.

16. Ibid., 16.

17. Ibid., 143.

18. Ibid., 170.

19. Ibid., 23.

20. Ibid.

21. Ibid., 20.

22. Ibid., 22.

23. Ibid.

24. Ibid., 24.

25. Paul Gottfried, *Leo Strauss and the Conservative Movement in America: A Critical Appraisal* (Cambridge, UK: Cambridge University Press, 2012).

26. Ibid.

27. Ceasar, *Liberal Democracy and Political Science*, 173–74.

28. George W. Carey, *The Federalist: Design for a Constitutional Republic* (Urbana: University of Illinois Press, 1989).

29. Ibid.

30. Ibid.

31. John Fonte, *Sovereignty or Submission: Will Americans Rule Themselves or Be Ruled By Others?* (New York: Encounter Books, 2011).

32. Keith Preston, *Attack the System: A New Anarchist Perspective for the 21st Century* (London: Black House Publishing, Ltd., 2013).

33. Ibid.

34. Ibid.

35. Ibid.

36. Ibid.

37. Ibid.

38. Ibid.

39. Ibid.

40. Ibid.

41. Jeff Guo, "The Two Reasons It Really Is Harder to Get a Job Than It Used to Be," *Washington Post,* October 28, 2015, https://www.washingtonpost.com/news/wonk/wp/2016/10/28/why-it-really-is-harder-to-get-a-job-than-it-used-to-be/.

42. See the assessment of Samuel T. Francis in John B. Judis, "The Return of the Middle American Radical," *National Journal,* October 5, 2015, and his posthumously published mammoth manuscript on managerialism, *Leviathan and Its Enemies* (Arlington, VA: Washington Summit Publishers, 2016), 1–97. A particularly insightful study of the growth of administrative power through military preparation is Murray Rothbard's "War Collectivism in World War One," in *A New History of Leviathan,* ed. Murray Rothbard and Ronald Radosh (New York: E. P. Dutton, 1976), 66–110. A work that deals with Rothbard, Francis, and other right-leaning critics of the modern state is George Hawley's *Right-Wing Critics of American Conservatism* (Lawrence: University Press of Kansas, 2016), esp. 128–206.

43. Gottfried, *After Liberalism.*

44. Preston, *Attack the System.*

Notes to Chapter 6

1. Woodrow Wilson, *The State: Elements of Historical and Practical Politics* (New York: D.C. Heath & Co., 1889).

2. Ibid., 3–8.

3. Ibid.

4. Ibid.

5. Wilson, *The State*.

6. Ibid.

7. Wilson, "Earliest Forms of Government."

8. Henry Sumner Maine, "Chapter V," in *Ancient Law: Its Connection to the Early History of Society, and Its Relation to Modern Ideas* (London: John Murray, 1861).

9. Wilson, *The State*.

10. Thomas Hobbes, *Leviathan; or, The Matter, Forme [sic] and Power of a Common Wealth Ecclesiasticall [sic] or Civil* (Thomas Hobbes, 1651).

11. Michael Oakeshott, *Hobbes on Civil Association*. (Berkeley: University of California Press, 1975).

12. Hobbes, *Leviathan*.

13. Michael Oakeshott, "Introduction to *Leviathan*," in *Hobbes on Civil Association*.

14. Carl Schmitt, *The Leviathan in the State Theory of Thomas Hobbes (Der Leviathan in der Staatslehre des Thomas Hobbes)* (Hamburg, Germany: Hanseatische Verlagsanstalt, 1938).

15. Carl Schmitt, *The Customs/Division of the Earth in the International Political Law of the Europe (Der Nomos Der Erde Im Völkerrecht Des Jus Publicum Europaeum)* (Köln, North Rhine-Westphalia, West Germany: Greven, 1950).

16. Ibid. French legal historian Michel Villey has explored at great length the recent origin of natural and (derivatively human) right thinking in the West. He distinguishes it antiseptically from both classical concepts of "right" and medieval scholastic treatments, in *Le droit et les droits de l'homme* (Paris: Presses Universitaires de France, 1998). See also *La formation de la pensée juridique moderne,* ed. Michel Villey, Stéphane Rials, and Eric Desmons (Paris: Presses Universitaires de France, 1968).

17. Martin Van Creveld, *The Rise and Decline of the State* (New York and Cambridge, UK: Cambridge University Press, 1999), 394–408.

18. Ibid., 408–14.

19. Ibid., 415–21.

20. Wolfgang Reinhard, *History of State Power: A Comparative Constitutional History of Europe from Its Beginnings to the Present Day (Geschichte Der Staatsgewalt: Eine Vergleichende Verfassungsgeschichte Europas Von den Anfängen bis zur Gegenwart)* (Munich: Beck, 1999).

21. Ibid.

22. Ibid.

23. See Thomas Molnar, *Authority and Its Enemies* (New Brunswick, NJ: Transaction, 1995); "Une théorie des rapports internationaux: Est-elle formulable?," *Revue européens des sciences internationals et Cahiers Vilfredo Pareto* 19 (1981): 225–26; and Paul Gottfried, "The Historical and Communal Roots of Legal Rights and the Erosion of the State," in *Rethinking Rights: Historical, Political and Philosophical Perspectives* (Columbia: University of Missouri Press, 2009), 153–76.

24. Alexis de Tocqueville, *The Old Regime and the French Revolution (L'Ancien Régime et la Révolution)* (Paris: Michel Lévy Frères, 1856).

25. Ibid.

26. Alexis de Tocqueville and Gerald E. Bevan, *Democracy in America* (London: Penguin Books, 2003).

Notes to Chapter 7

1. Yuval Levin, *The Great Debate: Edmund Burke and Thomas Paine and the Birth of Right and Left* (New York: Basic Books, 2014).

2. Domenico Fisichella, *Democracy against Reality: The Political Thought of Charles Maurras (La Democrazia Contro la Realtà: Il Pensiero Politico di Charles Maurras)* (Rome, Italy: Carocci, 2014).

3. Stéphane Giocanti, *Maurras: Chaos and Order (Maurras: Le Chaos et L'Ordre)* (Paris: Flammarion, 2006).

4. Levin, *Great Debate*, 85.

5. Ibid., 86.

6. Ibid.

7. Edmund Burke, *Reflections on the Revolution in France, and on the Proceedings in Certain Societies in London Relative to That Event: In a Letter Intended to Have Been Sent to a Gentleman in Paris* (London: James Dodsley in Pall-Mall, 1790).

8. Peggy Noonan, "Review of *The Great Debate: Edmund Burke, Thomas Paine, and the Birth of Right and Left*," Amazon.com, 2014.

9. Levin, *Great Debate*.

10. Aristotle and Terence Irwin, *Nicomachean Ethics* (Indianapolis, IN: Hackett Publishing Co., 1985).

11. Frank S. Meyer, *In Defense of Freedom: A Conservative Credo* (Chicago: H. Regnery Co., 1962).

12. Ibid., 61.

13. Burke, *Reflections on the Revolution in France*, 48.

14. Numa Denis Fustel de Coulanges, *The Ancient City: A Study on the Cult, Law, and Institutions of Greece and Rome (La Cité Antique: Étude sur le Culte, le Droit, les Institutions de la Grèce et de Rome)* (Paris: Durand, 1864).

15. Fisichella, *Democracy against Reality*.

16. Jean-Jacques Rousseau, *Du contrat social (Of the Social Contract)* (Paris: Flammarion, 1966), 70 and 76.

Notes to Chapter 8

1. Herbert Butterfield, *The Whig Interpretation of History* (New York: W. W. Norton, 1965).

2. Ibid.

3. Herbert Butterfield, *The Englishman and His History* (London: Bentley House, 1931).

4. Sir Edward Coke. *Institutes of the Lawes of England* (London: Edward Coke, 1628–1644).

5. United Kingdom, Parliament, House of Commons, "The Petition Exhibited to His Majestie [*sic*] by the Lordes [*sic*] Spirituall [*sic*] and Temporall [*sic*] and Commons in this present Parliament assembled concerning divers Rightes [*sic*] and Liberties of the Subjectes: [*sic*] with the Kinges [*sic*] Majesties Royall [*sic*] Aunswere [*sic*] thereunto in full Parliament." 3 Car 1 c 1,1627.

6. Herbert Butterfield, "Conclusion to *The Englishman and His History*" (London: Bentley House, 1931).

7. Butterfield, *Englishman and His History*.

8. Butterfield, *Whig Interpretation of History*.

9. Butterfield, *Englishman and His History*.

10. Ibid.

11. Ibid.

12. Ibid.

13. Ibid.

14. Ibid.

15. Ibid.

16. Butterfield, *Whig Interpretation of History*.

17. Ibid.

18. Ibid.

19. Ibid.

20. Herbert Butterfield, *Christian Diplomacy and War* (London: Epworth Press, 1953).

21. Ibid.

22. Ibid.

23. John Lukacs, *Historical Consciousness; or, The Remembered Past*, rev. ed. (New York: Schocken Books, 1985).

24. Theodor Mommsen, *Römische Geschichte: Die Begründung der Militärmonarchie*, vol. 5 (Altenmünster: Jazybee Verlag Jürgen Beck), esp. 261–494.

25. Numa Denis Fustel de Coulanges, *La Cité Antique* (Paris: Hachette, 1866).

26. Francis Parkman, *France and England in North America*, 2 vols. (Cambridge, MA: DaCapo Press, 2001).

27. Butterfield, *Whig Interpretation of History*.

28. Ibid.

29. Georg Wilhelm Friedrich Hegel, *The Phenomenology of Spirit (Phänomenologie des Geistes)* (Bamberg and Würzburg, Bavaria, Germany: Joseph Anton Goebhardt, 1807).

Notes to Chapter 9

1. Seth Lipsky, "A Chance for an Ally: Conservative Rising in Britain," *New York Post*, May 29, 2014, opinion sec.

2. Peter Hitchens, "Letter from London: UKIP'S Tremor, Here's Hoping It Turns into an Earthquake," *American Spectator*, May 27, 2014, opinion sec.

3. Gabriele Parussini, "National Front's Marine Le Pen of France Leads Anti-EU Drive," *Wall Street Journal*, May 23, 2014, Europe sec.; and Roger Cohen, "The Banality of Anger," *New York Times*, May 26, 2014, opinion sec.

4. The Editors (von Redaktion), "Why Is There No Right-Wing Party? (Warum Gibt Es Keine Rechte Partei?)," *Die Freie Welt*, March 20, 2013, politics (Politik) sec.

5. Paul Gottfried, "Viktor Orban and the National Question in Hungary." *The Unz Review: An Alternative Media Selection* (blog), February 14, 2012, http://www.unz.com/pgottfried/viktor-orban -and-the-national-question-in-hungary/.

6. Many right-wing European nationalists are wary of an American empire and often support tariffs to protect their national workforces.

7. Tim Stanley, "European Fascism Has Returned? It Never Went Away and It Probably Never Will," *Daily Telegraph*, May 28, 2014, world sec.

8. Ibid.

9. Ibid.

10. Association for Diplomatic Studies and Training, "The Long Arm of History—Kurt Waldheim Banned for His Nazi Past," n.d., http://adst.org/2015/06/the-long-arm-of-history-kurt -waldheim-banned-for-his-nazi-past/.

11. Florian Thomas Rulitz, *The Tragedy of Bleiburg and Viktring: Guerrilla Violence in Carinthia on the Example of the Anti-Communist Refugees in May 1945 (Die Tragödie von Bleiburg und Viktring: Partisanengewalt in Kärnten am Beispiel Der Antikommunistischen Flüchtlinge im Mai 1945)* (Klagenfurt am Wörthersee, Carinthia, Austria: Hermagoras, 2011).

12. Kenneth R. Langford, "An Analysis of Left and Right Wing Terrorism in Italy" (master's thesis, Defense of Intelligence College, 1985). Although Langford's study only goes up to 1985, it would have been difficult for Italian National Revolutionaries and other neofascist groups to catch up to the thousands of acts of terrorism committed by the Red Brigades in the intervening years.

13. T. Dugdale-Pointon, "The Red Brigade Terrorist Group," 19 November 19, 2007, http:// www.historyofwar.org/articles/weapons_red_brigades.html.

14. "A Nasty Party: The Centre-Right Frets over the Rise of the Far Right," *The Economist*, June 18, 2009, Europe sec.

15. Marton Dunai, "Anti-Semitism Taboo under Threat in Hungary," *Reuters*, May 21, 2014, http://www.reuters.com/article/us-hungary-antisemitism-idUSKBN0E10E420140521.

16. Marton Dunai, "Hungary's Fidesz Wins European Poll, Jobbik Stalls," *Reuters*, May 25, 2014, world sec.

17. Stanley, "European Fascism Has Returned?"

18. Ibid.

19. Ibid.

20. Ben Shapiro, "5 Reasons Putin Thinks He Can Outplay Obama," *Breitbart*, March 3, 2014, national security sec.

21. Jillian Kay Melchior, "Cold Shoulder," *New York Post,* October 9, 2015, 27.

22. Paul Gottfried, *The Strange Death of Marxism: The European Left in the New Millennium* (Columbia: University of Missouri Press, 2005).

23. Tony Lee, "Chamber of Commerce: Conservatives the 'Problem' in Amnesty Battle," *Breitbart*, January 26, 2014, big government sec.

24. Tim Stanley, "The 'Neo-Fascist' Dark Enlightenment Is More Sad Than Scary," *Daily Telegraph*, January 22, 2014, U.S. politics sec.

Notes to Chapter 10

1. Walter Bagehot, *The English Constitution* (London: Chapman and Hall, 1867).

2. Richard Howard Stafford Crossman, *The Myths of the Cabinet Government* (Cambridge, MA: Harvard University Press, 1972).

3. Bagehot, *English Constitution*.

4. Crossman, *Myths of the Cabinet Government*.

5. Russell Kirk, *The Conservative Mind: From Burke to Eliot*, 7th ed. (Chicago: Regnery Books, Inc., 1986).

6. Walter Bagehot, *Lombard Street: A Description of the Money Market* (London: H. S. King & Co., 1873).

7. Bagehot, *English Constitution*.

8. Ibid., 160.

9. Ibid.

10. Ibid.

11. Ibid.

12. Ibid., 154.

13. Ibid.

14. Ibid.

15. Ibid., 98.

16. Ibid.

17. Ibid., 157–58.

18. Ibid., 33.

19. Ibid.

20. Walter Bagehot, *The English Constitution*, 2nd ed. (London: H. S. King, 1872).

21. Ibid., 198.

22. Ibid.

23. Ibid.

24. Voting Rights Act of 1965, Pub. L. No. 89–110, 79 Stat. 437 (1965).

25. Representation of the People Act 1867, 30 & 31 Vict. c. 102.

Notes to Chapter 11

1. Charles A. Murray, *Coming Apart: The State of White America, 1960–2010* (New York: Crown Forum, 2012).

2. Ibid.

3. Ibid.

4. Ibid.

5. Demetria Gallegos, "Charles Murray Answers Questions on America's Growing Class Divide," *Wall Street Journal*, February 4, 2012, review sec.

Notes to Chapter 12

1. David I. Kertzer, *Mussolini and the Pope: The Secret History of Pius XI and the Rise of Fascism in Europe* (New York: Random House, 2014).

2. Alexander Stille, "The Pope Who Tried," *New York Review of Books*, April 23, 2015, http://www.nybooks.com/articles/2015/04/23/pope-who-tried.

3. Kertzer, *Mussolini and the Pope*.

4. David I. Kertzer, *The Popes Against The Jews: The Vatican's Role in the Rise of Modern Anti-Semitism* (New York: Knopf, 2001).

5. Kertzer, *Mussolini and the Pope*, 308–13.

6. Ibid., 308.

7. Ibid.

8. Ibid., 191–93.

9. James Strachey Barnes, *The Universal Aspects of Fascism* (London: Williams and Norgate, 1929).

10. Renzo deFelice, *Il fascismo e l'Oriente (Bologna: Mulino, 1988)*, esp. 5–40, 187–241.

11. Ibid., 149.

12. S. I. Minerbi, "Gli ultimi due incontri Weizmann-Mussolini (1933–1934)," *Storia Contemporanea* (September 1974): 476.

13. Ernesto Galli della Loggia, *The Italian Identity (L'identità italiana)* (Bologna, Emilia-Romagna, Italy: il Mulino, 1998), 31–57.

14. Florian Altenhöner, "The Way to Dictatorship: The Cross at the Nazis," *Der Spiegel*, January 29, 2008, http://www.spiegel.de/spiegel/spiegelspecialgeschichte/d-55573698.html.

15. David G. Dalin, *The Myth of Hitler's Pope: How Pius XII Rescued Jews from the Nazis* (Washington, DC: Regnery, 2005).

16. Kertzer, *Mussolini and the Pope*.

17. Ibid., 258.

18. José M. Sanchez, *Pius XII and the Holocaust: Understanding the Controversy* (Washington, DC: Catholic University of America Press, 2002).

19. Paul Gottfried, "The Church and the Holocaust," *Spectator*, February 16, 2002, http://archive.spectator.co.uk/article/16th-february-2002/16/the-church-and-the-holocaust.

20. John Cornwell, *Hitler's Pope: The Secret History of Pius XII* (New York: Viking, 1999).

21. Kertzer, *Mussolini and the Pope*, 403.

22. Ibid.

23. Paul E. Gottfried, *Fascism: Career of a Concept* (DeKalb: Northern Illinois University Press, 2015).

24. Kertzer, *Mussolini and the Pope*, 106.

25. Ibid., 149.

Notes to Chapter 13

1. Richard L. Velkley, *Heidegger, Strauss, and the Premises of Philosophy: On Original Forgetting* (Chicago: University of Chicago Press, 2011).

2. Plato, *Politeia*, Oxford Classical Texts (Oxford: Oxford University Press, 1965), X.621 a–d. In the Myth of Er, told by a warrior resurrected from the dead, there is a depiction of the soul bearing the lot (laxos) it has chosen for its future reincarnation and then drinking water that causes it to forget everything it had previously experienced (panton epilanthanesthai). Together with the preceding narrative about mother Necessity and her daughters, the three Fates, from whence the soul receives its

new lot and then has that destiny confirmed, it is possible to find foreshadowed certain Heideggerian concepts, such as Being toward Death.

3. See particularly *Sein und Zeit*, 7th ed. (Tübingen: Max Niemeyer Verlag, 1993), particularly the famous third chapter on *Zeitlichkeit*, 301–431. This treatment of temporality in relation to Being is so freighted with Heidegger's invented terminology that interpreters can spend a lifetime trying to unravel its meanings.

4. Ibid., 255–69.

5. Quoted in *The Rebirth of Classical Rationalism: An Introduction to the Thought of Leo Strauss*, ed. Thomas L. Pangle (Chicago: University of Chicago Press, 1989), 28.

6. Ibid.

7. For an accessible treatment of the debate, which seeks to be evenhanded, see Peter E. Gordon, *Continental Divide: Heidegger, Cassirer, Davos* (Cambridge, UK: Harvard University Press, 2012).

8. Quoted in *The Rebirth of Classical Rationalism: An Introduction to the Thought of Leo Strauss*, ed. Thomas L. Pangle (Chicago: University of Chicago Press, 1989), 28.

9. See Ernst Cassirer, *The Philosophy of Symbolic Forms*, 3 vols., trans. Ralph Manheim (New Haven, CT: Yale University Press, 1965); *Immanuel Kants Werke, vol. XI*, ed. Ernst Cassirer (Berlin: Bruno Cassirer Verlag, 1918), esp. 147–231.

10. Velkley, *Heidegger, Strauss, and the Premises of Philosophy*, 75 and 76.

11. Ibid., 94.

12. See, for example, Michael Gelven's *A Commentary on Heidegger's Being and Time*, rev. ed. (DeKalb: Northern Illinois University Press, 1989); Hubert L. Dreyfus, *Being-in-the World* (Cambridge, MA: MIT Press, 1991); Charles Guignon, *Heidegger and the Problem of Knowledge* (Indianapolis, IN: Hackett, 1983); David E. Cooper, *Existentialism: A Reconstruction* (Chicago: University of Chicago Press, 1990); and Stanley Rosen, *The Question of Being: The Reversal of Heidegger* (South Bend, IN: St. Augustine's Press, 2002). Although a recognizably Straussian approach to interpreting Heidegger, Rosen's book is heavily documented and aims at being dispassionate.

13. Velkley, *Heidegger, Strauss, and the Premises of Philosophy*, 161.

14. Ibid.

15. Ibid.

16. See Leo Strauss, *Natural Right and History* (Chicago: University of Chicago Press, 1953), 5–8, 26–27, 320–23.

17. Paul Gottfried, *Leo Strauss and the Conservative Movement in America* (New York City: Cambridge University Press, 2012).

18. Karl Löwith, *Heidegger: Denker in dürftiger Zeit* (Frankfurt am Main: Fischer Verlag, 1953).

19. Velkley, *Heidegger, Strauss, and the Premises of Philosophy*, 117.

20. Ibid., 84.

21. See Gottfried, *Leo Strauss and the Conservative Movement in America*, 83–95.

22. See Jakob Klein, *A Commentary on Plato's Meno* (Chapel Hill: University of North Carolina Press, 1965).

23. Velkley, *Heidegger, Strauss, and the Premises of Philosophy*, 67.

24. See Gottfried, *Leo Strauss and the Conservative Movement in America*, 131–41.

25. Velkley, *Heidegger, Strauss, and the Premises of Philosophy*, 121–30.

26. The paradigmatic statement of Gadamer's historically conscious hermeneutic is *Wahrheit und Methode: Grundzüge einer philosophischen Hermeneutik* (Tübingen, West Germany: J. C. B. Mohr, 1972).

27. *Sein und Zeit*, 386.

28. Ibid., 385.

29. Ibid.

30. A work that finds a radically conservative subtext running throughout *Sein und Zeit* is Alexander Dugin's *Martin Heidegger: The Philosophy of a New Beginning*, trans. Nina Kouprianova, preface Paul Gottfried (Arlington, VA: Washington Summit Publishers, 2014). It goes without saying that Dugin is looking for a philosophical defense for his organic Russian nationalism.

31. Two critiques of Heideggerian ontology that focus on its asocial aspect, the first of which is explicitly Marxist, are Herbert Marcuse, "Beiträge zu einem Historischen Materialismus," *Philosophische Hefte,* special issue on *Sein und Zeit (1928):* 45–68; and Panajotis Kondylis, *Die Neuzeitliche Metaphysikkritik* (Stuttgart: Klett Cotta Verlag, 1990), 367–68, 449–51.

32. See Michael E. Zimmerman, "The Heidegger-Deep Ecology Relationship," *Environmental Ethics* 15 (Fall 1993): 195–224. In an otherwise informative study, the author feels mysteriously obliged to "re-evaluate" Heidegger's passionate support for environmentalism in view of his one-time membership in the Nazi Party. Heidegger's enthusiastic adhesion to the party in 1933, followed by a chilling of his relationship to it, has long been a matter of record. It is also foolish to abandon what seemed compelling arguments by Heidegger for one's own position because of a political path that he took in 1933, but which he later described as "the greatest stupidity of my life." Should one feel similarly compelled to repudiate Prokofiev's musical achievements because of the composer's occasional kowtowing to Stalin? Would one be required to question whether the earth revolved around the sun, if one heard this scientific fact coming from someone with questionable personal associations?

Notes to Chapter 14

1. This distinction is made with admirable precision by the French geographer and social commentator Christophe Guilluy in the French publication *Point* (http://www.lepoint.fr/chroniques /christophe-guilluy-nous-allons-vers-une-periode-de-tensions-et-de-paranoia-identitaire-21-09 -2016-2070040_2.php).

2. Peggy Noonan, "The Republican Party Is Shattering," *The Wall Street Journal,* March 3, 2016, http://www.peggynoonan.com/the-republican-party-is-shattering/.

3. One particularly extreme example of neoconservative hostility toward Trump is an essay published in *Foreign Policy* by Max Boot two days before the election: "Why This Lifetime Republican Is with Her" (http://www.maxboot.net/articles/258-this-lifetime-gop-voter-is-with-her.html). Apart from his support for an aggressive "pro-democracy" foreign policy and his advocacy of government-negotiated free trade agreements, there is no evidence that Boot has any rightist identity.

4. Max Boot, "Ted Cruz: The Anti-Reagan," *Commentary,* December 14, 2015, www .commentarymagazine.com/politics-ideas/ted-cruz-anti-ronald-reagan.

5. Jim Tankersley, Scott Clement, and Peyton Craighill, "Why Donald Trump Is Winning," *Washington Post,* August 5, 2015, https://www.washingtonpost.com/news/wonk/wp/2015/08/05/why -donald-trump-is-winning.

6. David Frum, "The Great Republican Revolt," *The Atlantic,* January/February 2016, http:// www.theatlantic.com/magazine/archive/2016/01/the-great-republican-revolt/419118/

7. Paul Gottfried, "Republican Terror and Anger," *The Unz Review: An Alternative Media Selection,* December 29, 2015, *http://www.unz.com/pgottfried/terror-and-anger/.*

8. David Brooks, "Donald Trump, the Great Betrayer," *New York Times,* March 4, 2016, http:// www.nytimes.com/2016/03/04/opinion/donald-trump-the-great-betrayer.html?_r=0.

9. David Brooks, "I Miss Barack Obama," *New York Times,* February 9, 2016, http://www .nytimes.com/2016/02/09/opinion/i-miss-barack-obama.html.

10. Michael Goodwin, "Romney Is Too Much a Coward to Say What's Really on His Mind," *New York Post,* March 3, 2016, http://nypost.com/2016/03/03/romney-is-too-much-of-coward-to -really-say-whats-on-his-mind/.

11. Jonathan Chait, "Why, Exactly Is Trump Driving Conservatives So Crazy?," *New York,* March 7–20, 2016, 22.

12. Bertrand de Jouvenel, *On Power,* trans. J. F. Huntington (New York: Viking, 1949), 268.

13. Carl Schmitt, *Legalität und Legitimität,* 2nd ed. (Berlin: Duncker und Humblot, 1968), 9–11, 31.

14. Kevin D. Williamson, "The Buchanan Boys: The Trump Voters Aren't a New Phenomenon," *National Review*, February 4, 2016, http://www.nationalreview.com/article/430769/donald-trump-pat-buchanan.

15. Scott Greer, "National Review Writer: Working-Class Communities 'Deserve to Die,'" March 12, 2016, http://dailycaller.com/2016/03/12/national-review-writer-working-class-communities-deserve-to-die.

16. Arnaud Imatz, *Droite/gauche: pour sortir de l'équivoque* (Paris: Pierre-Guillaume de Roux, 2016), 117–83.

17. Ibid., 272; and Paul Gottfried, *The Strange Death of Marxism: The European Left in the New Millennium* (Columbia: University of Missouri Press, 2005).

18. Ed Pilkington, "Obama Angers Midwest Voters with Guns and Religion Remark," *The Guardian*, April 14, 2008, https://www.theguardian.com/world/2008/apr/14/barackobama.uselections2008.

19. Abby Philip, "Clinton: Half of Trump's Supporters Fit in 'Basket of Deplorables,'" Washington Post, September 9, 2016, https://www.washingtonpost.com/news/post-politics/wp/2016/09/09/clinton-half-of-trumps-supporters-fit-in-basket-of-deplorables/.

20. Benjamin Disraeli, *Sybil or The Two Nations*. (New York: Oxford University Press, 1998), 65.

21. See the seminal work on this subject by Michael Novak, *The Spirit of Democratic Capitalism* (New York: Simon and Schuster, 1982).

Index